Naval Leadership and Management, 1650–1950

Naval Leadership and Management, 1650–1950

Essays in Honour of Michael Duffy

Edited by
Helen Doe and Richard Harding

THE BOYDELL PRESS

© Contributors 2012

All Rights Reserved. Except as permitted under current legislation
no part of this work may be photocopied, stored in a retrieval system,
published, performed in public, adapted, broadcast,
transmitted, recorded or reproduced in any form or by any means,
without the prior permission of the copyright owner

First published 2012
The Boydell Press, Woodbridge

ISBN 978 1 84383 695 7

The Boydell Press is an imprint of Boydell & Brewer Ltd
PO Box 9, Woodbridge, Suffolk IP12 3DF, UK
and of Boydell & Brewer Inc.
668 Mount Hope Ave, Rochester, NY 14620, USA
website: www.boydellandbrewer.com

A catalogue record for this book is available
from the British Library

The publisher has no responsibility for the continued existence or accuracy
of URLs for external or third-party internet websites referred to in this book,
and does not guarantee that any content on such websites is,
or will remain, accurate or appropriate.

Papers used by Boydell & Brewer Ltd are natural, recyclable products
made from wood grown in sustainable forests

Printed in Great Britain by
CPI Group (UK) Ltd, Croydon, CR0 4YY

Contents

List of Tables — vii
List of Editors and Contributors — ix
Acknowledgements — xiii
List of Abbreviations — xiv

Michael Duffy: An Appreciation — 1
   Roger Knight

Introduction — 11
   Richard Harding

Leadership: The Place of the Hero

1. Admiral Rainier's Management Challenges, 1794–1805 — 29
   Peter Ward

2. Neglect or Treason: Leadership Failure in the Mid-Eighteenth-Century Royal Navy — 43
   Richard Harding

Leadership and Organisational Frictions: Contested Territories

3. Who has Command? The Royal Artillerymen aboard Royal Navy Warships in the French Revolutionary and Napoleonic Wars — 61
   Gareth Cole

4. 'The Marine Officer is a Raw Lad and therefore Troublesome': Royal Naval Officers and the Officers of the Marines, 1755–1797 — 77
   Britt Zerbe

Management Capability and the Exercise of Naval Power

5. High Exertions and Difficult Cases: The Work of the Transport Agent at Portsmouth and Southampton, 1795–1797 — 95
   Roger Morriss

6. Forgotten or Ignored, the Officers at Invergordon: 'We are doing this for you as well you know' — 109
   Mike Farquharson-Roberts

7. 'To Excite the Whole Company to Courage and Bravery': 123
   The Incentivisation of British Privateering Crews, 1702–1815
   DAVID J. STARKEY

The Evolution of Management Training in the Royal Navy, 1800–1950

8. New Kinds of Discipline: The Royal Navy in the Second Half 143
   of the Nineteenth Century
   OLIVER WALTON

9. Towards a Hierarchy of Management: The Victorian and 157
   Edwardian Navy, 1860–1918
   MARY JONES

10. Leadership Training for Midshipmen, c.1919–1939 173
    ELINOR ROMANS

Select Bibliography 193

Index 203

List of Tables

Table 3.1 List of bomb vessels, their tenders and their stations, 4 August 1800   67

Table 6.1 Ranks and numbers of officers to be made redundant   114

Table 7.1 Licensed vessels by war and region, 1702–1815   126

Editors and Contributors

Editors

Professor Richard Harding, University of Westminster
Richard Harding is both a naval historian and Professor of Organisational History at the University of Westminster where he is Head of Department of Leadership and Development. He is currently chairman of the Society for Nautical Research and a past editor of its journal, the *Mariner's Mirror*. He is the author of *Amphibious Warfare in the Eighteenth Century* (1991) and *Seapower and Naval Warfare, 1650–1830* (1999). He has written numerous articles and edited books on naval subjects.

Dr Helen Doe, University of Exeter
Helen Doe is a maritime historian with a previous international career in industry. She worked at a senior level for a multinational company and was involved in both leadership and management development training. She gained her Ph.D. from the University of Exeter in 2007 and is a Fellow of the Centre for Maritime Historical Studies at Exeter. She has published articles in the *Mariner's Mirror*, *The International Journal of Maritime History*, *The Journal for Maritime Research* and *Economic History Review*. Her book, *Enterprising Women in Shipping in the Nineteenth Century*, was published by Boydell Press in 2009. She is a Council Member of the Navy Records Society and a Fellow of the Royal Historical Society.

Contributors

Dr Gareth Cole, University of Exeter
Gareth Cole graduated with a Ph.D. from the University of Exeter in July 2008 having written a thesis entitled 'The Office of Ordnance and the Arming of the Fleet in the French Revolutionary and Napoleonic Wars, 1793–1815'. This was completed under the supervision of Dr Michael Duffy who had also supervised his MA dissertation. Gareth is currently working for Library Services at the University of Exeter as a data curation officer. His book, *Arming the Royal Navy, 1793–1815*, was published in January 2012.

Mike Farquharson-Roberts, University of Exeter
Mike Farquharson-Roberts graduated from medical school MB BS in 1971 and proceeded FRCS(Eng) and then joined the Royal Navy, becoming a

consultant orthopaedic surgeon in 1983. He attended the Royal College of Defence Studies in 2001, gaining an MA in international studies. Leaving clinical medicine, he filled a variety of medical administrative posts in the Armed Forces, retiring in 2007. He is currently a Ph.D. student at the University of Exeter.

Dr Mary Jones
Mary Jones gained her BA in History as a mature student at the University of Reading. She then taught for some years before studying for her MA ('Captain Clayton and the Australia Station, 1885–1888) and a Ph.D. ('The Making of the Royal Naval Officer Corps, 1860–1914') at the University of Exeter, under the good auspices of Michael Duffy. She has written for the *Mariner's Mirror*, the Navy Records Society and the Tasmanian Historical Association. She has edited the letters of Admiral John Marx (1852–1939), published in *A Naval Life* (Persona Press, 2007), and is currently editing the letters of Lt-Cdr Ralph Clayton (1882–1916).

Professor Roger Knight, University of Greenwich
Roger Knight spent most of his career in the National Maritime Museum, leaving as Deputy Director in 2000. Since then he has been Professor of Naval History at the Greenwich Maritime Institute, University of Greenwich. He has written numerous books and articles on eighteenth-century naval history. In July 2005 he published *The Pursuit of Victory: The Life and Achievement of Horatio Nelson*. He has led a Leverhulme-funded project into naval victualling, resulting in the publication (with Martin Wilcox) of *Sustaining the Fleet, 1793–1815: War, the British Navy and the Contractor State* (2010). He is also writing a bigger book on the British government in the Napoleonic Wars, to be published in time for the bicentenary of Waterloo.

Dr Roger Morriss, University of Exeter
Roger Morriss wrote his Ph.D. thesis on Britain's royal dockyards during the French Revolutionary and Napoleonic Wars, which was revised and published as a book in 1983. He has written a biography of Sir George Cockburn (1772–1853), compiled a guide to British Naval Papers in North America, completed a Navy Records Society volume (begun by Richard Saxby) on the Channel Fleet and the blockade of Brest, 1793–1801, and written about changes in naval administration, 1760–1850. Roger began his career as a teacher, worked at the National Maritime Museum between 1979 and 1995, and since then he has taught maritime and naval history at the University of Exeter, and courses at the Universities of Bristol and Greenwich. He has been General Editor of the Navy Records Society since 2000 and is on the council of the Hakluyt Society.

Elinor Romans, University of Exeter

Elinor Romans is a third-year Ph.D. student at the University of Exeter. She is studying the recruitment and training of Royal Navy officers in the inter-war period but is generally interested in twentieth-century naval history.

Dr David J. Starkey, University of Hull

David J. Starkey graduated from the University of Leeds with a degree in Economic History. He gained his MA and Ph.D. at the University of Exeter. He was then appointed Research Fellow in the Maritime History of Devon project at the University of Exeter, an appointment that was followed by two further research fellowships in maritime history at Exeter. In 1994, Dr Starkey joined the History Department at Hull when he became the holder of the first permanent lectureship to be dedicated to maritime historical studies in the UK university sector. He is now the Director of the Maritime Historical Studies Centre, University of Hull. He has published extensively including his significant book, *British Privateering Enterprise in the Eighteenth Century* (University of Exeter Press, 1990).

Dr Oliver Walton, Kingston University

Oliver Walton is post-doctoral research fellow at the University of Duisburg, Essen. He gained his BA at the University of Exeter followed by a MA in Maritime History and a Ph.D. on the Social history of the Royal Navy c.1856–1900. In 2000 he was the winner of the Julian Corbett Prize. He has been a researcher for the Prince Albert Society, a Visiting Professor at the Economics University, Prague, and *Gastprofessor* at the Universität Bayreuth. His publications include 'Royal Naval Engineers and the Creation of the Steam Navy', *Historical Research* (2004) and 'The Journal of Louis Parsons' in M. Duffy (ed.), *Naval Miscellany* Vol.VI (Naval Records Society, 2003).

Dr Peter Ward, University of Exeter

Peter Ward retired in 1997 after a career in international personnel management, consisting of employment with NV Philips, Hewlett Packard Corp., and 3Com Corp., in the UK, Europe, the US, and Hong Kong. He has a BA (Hons.) in Modern History from the University of Liverpool (1968), an MSc in Personnel Management (University of Bradford, 1975) and in 2003 he gained his MA in Naval History from the University of Exeter. He has recently been awarded a Ph.D. for his thesis on Admiral Rainier.

Dr Britt Zerbe, University of Exeter

Britt Zerbe was awarded a BA in History from the University of New Mexico in the United States, following which he moved to Kameoka, Japan, and spent two years teaching. Upon leaving Japan he travelled to the UK to continue his studies at the University of Exeter's Centre for Maritime Historical Studies, where he was later awarded a MA and Ph.D. His doctoral thesis focussed on the development of the British Marine Corps' doctrine and identity from 1755 to 1802. He is currently engaged in writing articles on a variety of issues centred around the British Marine Corps of the eighteenth century, as well as preparing his thesis for publication.

Acknowledgements

This work would not have been possible without the enthusiasm of the authors and their willingness to respond cheerfully to the editors' queries and requests. We are grateful to those all who attended the conference at the University of Exeter in September 2009, whose criticisms and comments stimulated the idea of this book. We are also grateful to Peter Sowden of Boydell and Brewer who has been constantly supportive and whose advice was essential to bring this project to a successful conclusion.

Finally with this book we thank Michael Duffy whose friendship and support we have valued over many years.

The Editors

Abbreviations

AWO	Admiralty Weekly Orders
BL	British Library
MO	Monthly Orders
NMM	National Maritime Museum
TNA	The National Archives

Michael Duffy: An Appreciation

Roger Knight

It is not easy to write an appreciation of a moving target, which perhaps best describes Michael Duffy at his retirement in the autumn of 2009. He has not found it easy to leave a busy teaching job after forty years. At the time of writing, he still has five Ph.D. students working on their theses, to add to the remarkable total of twenty who have already been through his hands over twenty-seven years. The growing list of books which his students have generated now stands at nine, and more than a dozen substantial articles. It is typical of Michael that he takes more pleasure in their success than from his own very long list of publications, which can be seen after this preface. The list of works by Michael Duffy and his students' publications will have many additions in the coming years.

It all started at Oxford, where Michael was taught by Piers Mackesy and then supervised by P. G. M. Dickson, and his early research for his D.Phil. was on British diplomacy during the French Revolutionary War. He was appointed to the post of Assistant Lecturer at the University of Exeter in October 1969. He first wrote a study of eighteenth-century satirical prints, and through them he gained a thorough view of the eighteenth-century political world. He went on to edit a series on the subject, selecting six other young scholars, including John Brewer and Paul Langford, every one of whom has gone on to a distinguished career, an early indication of Michael's ability to make a shrewd assessment of his colleagues.[1] He also demonstrated at that time a willingness to take risks and to spread his wings, when he took on the supervision of a thesis on eighteenth-century religion.[2]

What established Michael's career was the publication by Oxford University Press in 1987 of what has proved to be his most influential book. In writing *Soldiers, Sugar and Seapower: The British Expeditions to the West Indies*

---

[1] The English Satirical Print 1600–1832 series, General Editor, Michael Duffy (Chadwyck-Healey, London, 1986), and see the bibliography below.
[2] Robert J. Hole, 'The Role of Religious Arguments in Political Thought in England 1760–1832', Ph.D. 1986. Subsequently published by Cambridge University Press as *Pulpits, Politics and Public Order in England 1760–1832* (Cambridge, 1989).

and the War Against Revolutionary France[3] Michael used political, naval, army and ordnance records in an exemplary study of the workings, and the limitations, of the British government at the beginning of the Great Wars. He reversed the traditional negative thinking on these unpopular and costly expeditions, showing that, in spite of terrible losses to the British army through disease, the capture of the French West Indies islands was a critical part of the eventual defeat of French economic power. Thirty-five years later the book's authority is undiminished. The same strengths can be seen in the work of his first Ph.D. student, Christopher D. Hall. Hall's thesis on Napoleonic War strategy resulted in two books, which arguably have had the most impact of the work of any of Michael's students; *British Strategy in the Napoleonic War* and *Wellington's Navy: Seapower and the Peninsular War*.[4] These wars have been in the centre of Michael's interests for over thirty years. A recent rush of completed theses include the supply of ordnance to the Royal Navy and the expansion of the Hydrographic Office after 1808.[5]

The decade of Michael's maximum effort was the 1990s, when he came to what was then the rather terrifying arena of south-west maritime history, dominated and fought over by Walter Minchington and Basil Greenhill. Both were retired, from Exeter and Greenwich respectively, with enough time on their hands to make life difficult for each other and for all around them. Firstly, Michael saw the opportunity to found the Maritime Historical Studies Centre at Exeter, which he did with Stephen Fisher. They won a Leverhulme grant in 1992 to research change and adaptation in the maritime sector of the British economy since 1880. David Starkey, who had been at Exeter since his undergraduate days, stayed on as Research Fellow, together with Alan Jamieson. Both produced books for the Exeter Maritime Studies series, which now stands at eighteen volumes published since 1990. The two volumes of the *New Maritime History of Devon* in 1992 and 1994 also resulted.[6] Nicholas

---

[3] M. Duffy, *Soldiers, Sugar and Seapower: The British Expeditions to the West Indies and the War Against Revolutionary France* (Oxford, 1987).

[4] Christopher D. Hall, 'Factors Influencing British Strategic Planning and Execution during the Napoleonic War, 1803–15', Ph.D. 1984 (subsequently published by Manchester University Press as *British Strategy in the Napoleonic War 1803–15* (Manchester, 1992, repr. 1999)); Christopher D. Hall, *Wellington's Navy: Seapower and the Peninsular War 1807–1814* (London, 2004).

[5] Gareth Cole, 'The Ordnance Board and the Royal Navy 1790–1815', Ph.D., 2008; Adrian Webb, 'The Expansion of British Naval Hydrographic Administration, 1808–1829', Ph.D., 2010.

[6] Michael Duffy, Stephen Fisher, Basil Greenhill, David Starkey and Joyce Youings, *A New Maritime History of Devon, Vol I: From Early Times to the Late Eighteenth Century* (London, 1992); and *A New Maritime History of Devon, Vol. II: From the Late Eighteenth Century to the Present Day* (London, 1994).

Rodger and Roger Morriss also joined the Centre, providing an impressive critical mass of naval and maritime historians. As the subject became more popular, the teaching load of undergraduates and Masters students became a greater burden, of which Michael, as Director of the Centre from 1991 to 2007, took his full share.

A further boost came with taking the south-west maritime history conferences under the wing of the Centre. These meetings gained a higher profile and organisational improvement such that they are now a cornerstone of the British maritime history calendar: in 2011 the Exeter Maritime History Conference will hold its forty-fifth meeting. Michael's interest in the south-west has also been reflected by his research students. Ian Skinner wrote on the role of the south-west in the Second World War. Michael guided two M.Phil. theses on South Devon coastal communities and a study of East Stonehouse.[7] Perhaps the most 'left field' of all research topics would be Clare Greener's thesis on 'The Professional Gardener in Nineteenth-Century Devon'.[8] However, Michael was again playing to his strengths as gardening and gardening history are also great interests of his.

At this time Michael also took on the editorship of the *Mariner's Mirror*. It is difficult to overestimate the difference he made to this journal, which had fallen on very hard times, with too much Mediterranean archaeology and articles of very doubtful worth, selected by the then editor on unadvised hunches and whims. For some reason, for some periods of time the editorial hand excised all footnotes and references. The nine Duffy years, starting in 1991, steadily improved the standard of articles and reviews, and confidence in the journal returned. At the same time, Michael was writing a very good short study on William Pitt the Younger, which appeared in Longman's 'Profiles in Power' series in 2000.[9] Anyone writing on this subject has always to bear in mind the three great volumes by John Ehrman, the last one of which appeared in 1996. Ehrman was Michael's Ph.D. examiner and knows him well, and had acknowledged Michael's contribution to his second and third volumes.[10] Michael added and developed two themes in journal articles on Pitt's management of the House of Commons and his handling of public opinion. Then in this short book, he told the story of this remarkable prime minister with

---

[7] Geoffrey Doye, 'Communities in Crisis: A Social History of South Devon Coastal Communities, 1815–80' (M.Phil., 2007); Geoffrey Burnard, 'The Development of the Town of East Stonehouse in the Nineteenth Century' (M.Phil., 2008).
[8] Clare Greener, 'The Professional Gardener in Nineteenth-Century Devon', Ph.D., 2010.
[9] Michael Duffy, *The Younger Pitt*, Profiles in Power (London, 2000).
[10] John Ehrman, *The Younger Pitt*, 3 vols. (London, 1969–96).

delightful and telling anecdotes, etching a very sharp, readable and accessible picture of Pitt the man.

But Michael reckons that he got a great deal out of those ten years, particularly from the many subjects and periods on which he had to read articles submitted for *Mariner's Mirror*. Now there was no research student that he would not take on, as can be gauged from the theses completed at this time: current maritime museum philosophy; early Royal Naval hospitals; the Marine Corps between 1755 and 1802; officers in the late Victorian and Edwardian navy; the new navalism of the 1890s; the Chilean naval mutiny of 1931; Anglo-Polish naval relations between the two world wars; the inter-war Fleet Air Arm; amphibious assaults and convoys in the Second World War.[11] Helen Doe's thesis on women in shipping and shipbuilding was published in 2009 as *Enterprising Women and Shipping in the Nineteenth Century*.[12] How Michael managed to fit all this into the working week was and is a mystery – and he was Dean of Arts between 1994 and 1997 and Head of History from 1999 to 2003.

Naval leadership has been a long-held interest, intrinsic to his book on the West Indies amphibious expeditions. It was developed in Tom Wareham's thesis on frigate captains which flourished into two books; *The Star Captains: Frigate Command in the Napoleonic Wars* (2001) and *Frigate Commander* (2004).[13] With Roger Morriss Michael edited essays on the battle of the

---

[11] Robert Hicks, 'The Ideology of Maritime Museums, with Particular Reference to the Interpretation of Early Modern Navigation', Ph.D. 2000; Kathleen Harland, 'The Early Development of Royal Naval Hospitals', Ph.D. 2003; Britt Zerbe, '"That Most Useful Body of Men": The Operational Doctrine and Identity of the British Marine Corps, 1755–-1802', Ph.D. 2011; Mary Jones, 'The Victorian and Edwardian Naval Officer-corps', Ph.D. 2000; Oliver Walton, 'The Social History of the Late Victorian Navy', Ph.D. 2004; Roger Parkinson, 'The Naval Defence Act of 1889 and the Origins of the New Navalism of the 1890s', Ph.D. 2007, published as *The Late Victorian Navy: The Pre-Dreadnought Era and the Origins of the First World War* (Woodbridge, 2008); Carlos Tromben Corbalan, 'The Chilean Naval Mutiny of 1931', Ph.D. 2010; Wanda Troman, 'Anglo-Polish Naval Relations between the Two World Wars', Ph.D. 2000; Philip Weir, 'The Fleet Air Arm between the RAF and the Royal Navy in the Inter-war Period', Ph.D. 2007; Ivor Howcroft, 'The Role of the Royal Navy in the Amphibious Assaults of the Second World War', Ph.D. 2002; Dennis Haslop, 'Learning and implementing lessons of convoy warfare in the Battle of the Atlantic: a comparative study' Ph.D. 2011.

[12] Helen Doe, 'Enterprising Women: Nineteenth-Century Maritime Businesswomen', Ph.D. 2007, published as *Enterprising Women and Shipping in the Nineteenth Century* (Woodbridge, 2009).

[13] Thomas N. R. Wareham, 'The Role of the Frigate Captain in the French Revolutionary and Napoleonic Wars', Ph.D. 1999, subsequently published as *The Star Captains. Frigate Command in the Napoleonic Wars* (Chatham, 2001).

Glorious First of June (2001).[14] In 2009 a fruitful partnership developed with Ruddock Mackay in New Zealand, entirely by e-mail, which resulted in the analysis and comparison of the leadership styles of Hawke and Nelson.[15] Two studies on this long-term theme have been completed in 2011. Peter Ward focused on a completely different type of leader, the skilful management of Peter Rainier in the East Indies in the Napoleonic War, while Byrne McLeod examined the mid-eighteenth-century navy through the eyes of Captain Thomas Burnett.[16]

For the University of Exeter Michael has striven hard for forty years. He has served on every committee, and was always the first in the know when it came to cross-university intelligence. He has also been an important figure on the Councils of the Society for Nautical Research and the Navy Records Society. Quick-witted and cheerful, he has been difficult to resist. Invariably optimistic, determinedly informal, he has worn the laurels of his distinguished career very modestly. If there is a pattern to what he has achieved, it is that he has simplified issues for the sake of others. Several times he has taken an underdeveloped or complex situation and has made it accessible to all: the book on Pitt and his editorship of the *Mariner's Mirror* would be two differing examples of this quality. Through his efforts he has left naval and maritime history more popular and friendly, more defined and more studied, not only at Exeter but through his colleagues and students, much more widely. And we look forward to more from his pen.

Bibliography of Michael Duffy

'"A particular service": The British Government and the Dunkirk Expedition of 1793', *EHR* 91 (1976) 529–554

Editor, *The Military Revolution and the State 1500–1800*, Exeter Studies in History, No.1 (Exeter, 1980), including, 'Introduction: The Military Revolution and the State 1500–1800' and 'The Foundations of British Naval Power' pp. 1–9, 49–85

'"The Noisie, Empty, Fluttring French": English Images of the French, 1689–1815', *History Today* 32 (September 1982) 21–6

---

[14] Michael Duffy and Roger Morriss, eds, *The Glorious First of June: A Naval Battle and its Aftermath* (Exeter, 2001).
[15] Ruddock Mackay and Michael Duffy, *Hawke, Nelson and British Naval Leadership 1747–1805* (Woodbridge, 2009).
[16] Peter Ward, 'Admiral Peter Rainier and the Command of the East Indies Station 1794–1805', Ph.D. 2011; (Anne) Byrne McLeod, 'The Mid-Eighteenth Century Navy from the Perspective of Captain Thomas Burnett and his Peers', Ph.D. 2011.

'British Policy in the War against Revolutionary France' in C. Jones (ed.) *Britain and Revolutionary France: Conflict, Subversion and Propaganda*, Exeter Studies in History, No. 6 (1983) pp. 11–26

'The British Army and the Caribbean Expeditions of the War against Revolutionary France 1797–1801', *Journal of the Society for Army Historical Research* 42 (Summer 1984) pp. 65–73

'First Prize in the Lottery of Life?', *The Listener*, 6 March 1986, 11–12

The Englishman and the Foreigner (London, 1986)

General Editor, 'The English Satirical Print 1600–1832' series (London, 1986):

J. Brewer, *The Common People and Politics 1750–1790s*

H. T. Dickinson, *Caricatures and the Constitution 1760–1832*

M. Duffy, *The Englishman and the Foreigner*

P. Langford, *Walpole and the Robinocracy*

J. Miller, *Religion in the Popular Prints 1600–1832*

J. A. Sharpe, *Crime and the Law in the English Satirical Prints 1600–1832*

P. D. G. Thomas, *The American Revolution*

Soldiers, Sugar and Seapower: The British Expeditions to the West Indies and the War Against Revolutionary France (Oxford University Press, 1987)

'Making the Constitution' in J. Smith (ed.) *The American Revolution: The First Two Hundred Years 1787–1987*, Exeter Studies in History, No.16 (1987), pp. 17–34

'One Revolution Looks at Another'; 'The Revolution in the Colonies'; 'The Brunswick Manifesto'; 'William Pitt and the First Coalition'; 'The Abolition of Slavery', in R. Cobb and C. Jones (eds) *The French Revolution: Voices from a Momentous Epoch, 1789–1795* (Simon and Schuster, 1988), pp. 94–5, 136–7, 151, 177, 213.

'British Diplomacy in the French Wars 1789–1815', in H. T. Dickinson (ed.) *Britain and the French Revolution* (Macmillan, 1989), pp.127–46

'Pitt, Grenville and the Control of British Foreign policy in the 1790s', in J. Black (ed.) *Knights Errant and True Englishmen: British Foreign Policy 1600–1800* (John Donald, 1989), pp. 151–78

'Reflections on the Fall of Napoleon', *History Teaching Review Year Book: The Journal of the Scottish Association of Teachers of History* 3 (1989), 9–16

'The Caribbean Campaigns of the British Army, 1793–1801', in A. J. Guy (ed.) *The Road to Waterloo: The British Army and the Struggle against Revolutionary France and Napoleon, 1793–1815*, The National Army Museum (1990), pp. 23–31

'War, Revolution and the Crisis of the British Empire', in M. Philp (ed.) *The French Revolution and British Popular Politics* (Cambridge University Press, 1991) pp. 118–45

Editor, *The Mariner's Mirror. The Journal of the Society for Nautical Research*, 77 (1991) – 86 (2000)

Editor, *Parameters of British Naval Power 1650–1850*, Exeter Maritime Studies, No. 7 (1992), 149 pp., including: 'Introduction' and 'The Establishment of the Western Squadron as the Linchpin of British Naval Strategy', pp. 1–13, 60–81

'Realism and Tradition in Eighteenth-Century British Foreign Policy', *The Historical Journal* 35 (1992), 227–32

Co-editor, *The New Maritime History of Devon*, Conway Maritime Press, Vol. 1 (1992), Vol. 2 (1994), 272pp., with S. Fisher, B. Greenhill, D. J. Starkey, and J.Youings. (edited work), including 'Editor's Introduction' (with J. Youings); 'Devon and the Naval Strategy of the French Wars 1689–1815', Vol. 1, pp.12–16, 182–91

'War of the Bavarian Succession'; 'Caribbean'; 'Guadeloupe'; 'Holy Alliance'; 'Jamaica'; 'Plantations'; 'Trafalgar', in J. Black and R. Porter (eds) *A Dictionary of Eighteenth Century World History* (Basil Blackwell, Oxford, 1994) pp. 68, 121, 305, 330–1, 367–8, 571, 740–1

'Jervis: St Vincent, 1797', in E. Grove (ed.) *Great Battles of the Royal Navy as Commemorated in the Gunroom of the Royal Naval College, Dartmouth* (Arms and Armour Press, 1994) pp. 105–12

'William Pitt and the Origins of the Loyalist Association Movement of 1792', *The Historical Journal* 39 (1996), 943–62

'The Creation of Plymouth Dockyard and Its Impact on Naval Strategy', in *Guerres maritimes (1688–1713). IVes Journées franco-britanniques d'histoire de la Marine* (Service historique de la Marine, 1996) pp. 245–74

'The Premier Killed by Government', *The Times Higher Education Supplement*, 20 November 1996, p. 24

'Britain as a European Ally 1789–1815', *Diplomacy and Statecraft* 8:3 (1997), 27–47

'The Impact of the French Revolution on British Attitudes to the West Indian Colonies', in D. B. Gaspar and D. P. Geggus (eds) *A Turbulent Time. The French Revolution and the Greater Caribbean* (University of Indiana Press, Bloomington IN, 1997) pp. 78–101

'Pitt and the House of Commons', *History* 83 (1998) 217–24

'British Naval Intelligence and Bonaparte's Egyptian Expedition of 1798', *Mariner's Mirror* 8:43 (1998), 278–90

'Worldwide War and British Expansion 1793–1815' in *The Oxford History of the British Empire* (Oxford, 1998) Vol. II, pp. 184–207

'Coastal Defences and Garrisons, 1480–1914' in R. Kain (ed.) *Historical Atlas of South-West England* (Exeter University Press, 1999), pp. 182–89, 570

'The Man Who Missed the Grain Convoy: Sir George Montagu and the Escape of Vanstabel's Convoy from America in 1794' in *Les marins fran-*

çaise et britannique face aux États-Unis (1776–1865). VII*es* Journées franco-britanniques d'histoire de la Marine (Service historique de la Marine, 1999), pp. 155–67

The Younger Pitt. Profiles in Power (Longman, London, 2000)

'Samuel Hood, First Viscount Hood (1724–1816)' in R. Harding and P. LeFevre (eds) *Precursors of Nelson: British Admirals of the Eighteenth Century* (Chatham Press, London, 2000) pp. 249–77, 413–16

'"Science and Labour". The Naval Contribution to Operations Ashore in the Great Wars with France 1793–1815' in P. Hore (ed.) *Seapower Ashore: 200 Years of Extraordinary Naval Operations* (Chatham Press, London, 2001) pp. 39–52

Co-editor, *The Glorious First of June: A Naval Battle and its Aftermath*, Exeter Maritime Studies (Exeter, 2001), with Roger Morriss, including 'Introduction: the Battle of the Glorious First of June' (with R. Morriss); 'The Man Who Missed the Grain Convoy: Rear Admiral George Montagu and the arrival of Vanstabel's Convoy from America in 1794', pp. 1–11, 101–19

'Contested Empires 1756–1815', in P. Langford (ed.) *Short History of the British Isles 1688–1815* (Oxford, 2002), pp. 213–42

Editor, *The Naval Miscellany*, 6, Navy Records Society 146 (Ashgate, Aldershot, 2003), including 'Preface'; 'Edmund Dummer's "Account of the General Progress and Advancement of His Majesty's New Dock and Yard at Plymouth", December 1694', pp. xi–xiii, 93–147

'Sir Samuel Hood', 'Sir William Hoste', 'Sir Robert Waller Otway', 'Sir Samuel Pym', 'Sir Thomas Staines', 'Sir Richard Strachan', 'James Walker', 'Sir Nesbit Josiah Willoughby', 'Sir James Lucas Yeo', 'Gilbert Elliot, Lord Minto', 'Sir George Duckett' in C. Matthew (ed.) *The New Dictionary of National Biography* (Oxford, 2004)

'La artillería en Trafalgar: adiestramiento, táctica y moral de combate' in A. Guimerá and A Butròn (eds) *Trafalgar y el mundo atlántico* (Marcel Pons Historia, Madrid, 2004) pp. 127–44

'Sir Samuel Hood' in R. Harding and P. LeFevre (eds) *British Admirals of the Napoleonic Wars. The Contemporaries of Nelson* (Chatham Press, London, 2004), pp. 323–45

'The Gunnery at Trafalgar: Training, Tactics or Temperament?' *Journal for Maritime Research* (e-journal, National Maritime Museum, August 2005)

'"All was hushed up". The Hidden Trafalgar', *Mariner's Mirror* 91 (2005) 195–215

Touch and Take: The Battle of Trafalgar 21 October 1805 (The 1805 Club, Shelton, Nottinghamshire, 2005)

'Trafalgar' in J. Black (ed.) *The Seventy Great Battles of All Time* (Thames and Hudson, London, 2005) pp. 183–7

'Trafalgar, Nelson, and the National Memory', *Oxford Dictionary of National*

Biography On-line feature essay, October 2005: http://www.oxforddnb.com/themes/theme.jsp?articlid=92747

'La Flota británica en Trafalgar: victoria y humanidad', in *Ciclo de Conferencias "Trafalgar"*, RAECY Cantabria (Santandar, 2005), pp. 207–14

'The Hidden Trafalgar – Dull Winds or Dull Captains', *Mariner's Mirror* 92 (2006), 226–30

'British Intelligence and the Breakout of the French Atlantic Fleet from Brest in 1799', *Intelligence and National Security* 22 (2007), 601–18

'El embarco de la Armada británica en La Coruña y Vogp en enero de 1809', in A Guimerá Ravina and J. M. Blanco Núñez (eds) *Guerra naval en la Revolución y el Imperio. Bloqueos y operaciones anfibias, 1793–1815* (Madrid, 2008), pp. 367–86

Hawke, Nelson and British Naval Leadership 1747–1805 (Woodbridge, 2009), with Ruddock Mackay

'Festering the Spanish Ulcer. The Royal Navy and the Peninsular War, 1808–1814', in B. A. Elleman and S. C. M. Paine, Naval Power and Expeditionary Warfare. Peripheral Campaigns and New Theatres of Naval Warfare, Cass Series: Naval Policy and History 46 (Routledge, London, 2011), pp. 15–28

Introduction

Richard Harding

For most people naval history is the story of dramatic events. It is the story of powerful technologies in the form of warships, from galleons to nuclear submarines. It is also the story of the courage, determination and perseverance of the people that sailed and fought in these vessels and the grand theatre of battle ranging across seas and oceans that had tremendous consequences for societies ashore. Today, naval history touches the public most obviously in the commemoration of those events, such as the four-hundredth anniversary of the Spanish Armada, 1588, or the bicentenary of the Battle of Trafalgar, 1805. Central to the story is the leader or commander – Drake, Howard, Nelson and Collingwood. The drama is personified as a clash of wills and intellects that is far more familiar and comprehensible to the public than the alien and arcane technicalities of maintaining and fighting a fleet at sea. From this perspective it might be argued that naval leadership is, perhaps, one of the most widely understood aspects of naval history. On the other hand, as the commemoration of great events demonstrates, when historians focus their attention on these campaigns, new interpretations are generated regarding of the quality and practice of contemporary leadership.[1]

However, it is not only the coincidence of anniversaries that prompts historians to investigate naval leadership. Historians are situated in their own historical context. Today, leadership and management are major concerns in modern economies. This has much to do with the changing global economy. Loss of faith in the long-term competitive advantages conferred by particular technological innovations, the potentially unsustainably high capital costs of

---

[1] For example, a rich literature on Nelson and Trafalgar emerged from the bicentenary in 2005. Two collections that reflect upon Nelson's reputation as a leader are; D. Cannadine (ed.), *Admiral Lord Nelson: Context and Legacy* (London, 2005) and G. B. Prida, L. C. Delgardo, V. M. N. Garcia and J .S. Fernández (eds), *Trafalgar: Historia y Memoria de un Mito* (Cadiz, 2008). The biographies of Nelson, some of his officers, and especially the French and Spanish commanders, have produced a far more sophisticated picture of the qualities of these officers and the options open to them than existed before. The forthcoming bicentenary of the British-American War of 1812–1814 is almost certain to bring forth further important reflections on contemporary naval leadership practice.

continuous technological innovation, the new, complex demands of networked organisations and a declining confidence in the quasi-scientific predictability of forecasting or prediction, have made organisations turn more to the energy, discretion and insights of their managers and leaders to build their competitive advantage.[2] Theirs is no easy task as the evolving global economy presents organisations with continual problems of changing scale, scope, resources, function and form. As a result, the early twenty-first century has a large industry of management and leadership development devoted to identifying the issues and assisting people and organisations facing the problems of these changing demands.[3] Naval leaders and managers are not exempt from these pressures as costs, missions, technologies, systems and structures are in a state of continuous flux.

Although the rhetoric about the pace of change and the demands of leadership emerge strongly in contemporary literature from the journalistic to the profoundly academic, neither the problems nor the proposed solutions are new. Economic historians have pointed out that ever since the rise of the large scale industrial enterprise, and with it the disassociation of ownership and close control, the problems of management have existed.[4] Military historians have known that the rise of the mass modern military organisations, particularly in response to the two World Wars in the twentieth century, demanded a sophisticated approach by nations to solving the huge demand for effective commissioned and non-commissioned officers. It was impossible to rely on the traditional social elites to provide either the quantity or quality of leader-

---

[2] For an overview of the different ways of examining an organisation, see C. Demers, *Organizational Change Theories: A Synthesis*, (London, 2007). For the impact of the macroeconomic environment on management and leadership literature, see, E. Abrahamson, 'The Emergence and Prevalence of Employee Management Rhetorics: The Effects of Long Waves, Labor Unions and Turnover, 1875 to 1992', *Academy of Management Journal* 40 (1997), 491–533.

[3] The literature around leadership is huge and expanding every year. A good synopsis of the main theories can be found in P. G. Northouse, *Leadership: Theory and Practice*, 3rd edn, (London, 2010). Leadership is a central theme in political and military history and associated historical biographies, but the history and historiography of leadership theory and practice has yet to be written. In the twentieth century historians' interest in leadership tended to follow the concerns of the day – although at a greater distance and with less intensity than social scientists. For example, in 1974, the experience of the Watergate Scandal and the Vietnam War provided the stimulus for a Library of Congress conference on American leadership in the War of Independence. See, Library of Congress, *Leadership in the American Revolution* (Washington DC, 1974). The relative decline of the British economy provided the basis for historians' reflections on the general quality of industrial leadership. See R. English and M. Kenny (eds), *Rethinking British Decline* (London, 2000)

[4] S. Pollard, *The Genesis of Modern Management: A Study of the Industrial Revolution in Great Britain* (London, 1965).

ship needed to fight vast and intensive campaigns over long periods of time.[5] While the First World War forced societies to expand their officer corps in response to mass continental warfare, and the new science of psychology helped to articulate the needs and provide the tools for selection of leaders, it was the lessons of officer selection and training in the Second World War that fed most forcefully back into the ideology of leadership and management in the second half of the twentieth century.[6] The experience of the Second World War provided the psychological tools of selection that have become so firmly established in modern organisations. The narrative history of that war, in the form of anecdote, case study or metaphor, still provides much of the conceptual architecture for thinking about the demands of leadership, management and strategy.[7] However, it is interesting that naval leadership and

---

[5] T. Travers, 'Command and Leadership Styles in the British Army: The Gallipoli Model', *Journal of Contemporary History* 29 (1994), 403–42. The problems that new organisational requirements posed to the military in the First World War have been a particular focus of research for historians. The 'Lions led by Donkeys' thesis, which dominates popular views of the conduct of the war, provided an acute stimulus to serious research. The interweaving of the practicalities of organisational development in response to the operational needs, with more traditional histories based on the decisions or actions of individual military commanders, has now produced a far more sophisticated and nuanced view of the conduct of leadership and command during this war. Apart from the works of Tim Travers, see also, R. Prior and T. Wilson, *Command on the Western Front: The Military Career of Sir Henry Rawlinson, 1914–1918* (Oxford, 1992); A. Simpson, *The Evolution of Victory: British Battles on the Western Front, 1914–1918* (London, 1995); N. Gardner, *Trial by Fire: Command and the British Expeditionary Force in 1914* (Westport CT, 2003); G. Sheffield and D. Todman (eds), *Command and Control on the Western Front: The British Army's Experience, 1914–18* (Staplehurst, 2004); A. Simpson, *Directing Operations: British Corps Command on the Western Front, 1914–1918* (Staplehurst, 2006).

[6] It is interesting to read the evolving debate on the training of officers for the Royal Navy in the pages of the *Naval Review*. This journal was unofficial, written by serving officers for serving officers, and gives a good flavour of their concerns and lines of thinking. The first explicit reference to psychology appears in 1913. See *The Naval Review*, 1 (1913), 240, 'Psychology'. G. Hayes, 'Science and the Magic Eye: Innovation in the Selection of Canadian Army Officers, 1939–1945', *Armed Forces and Society* 22 (1995/60), 275–95.

[7] The Second World War is the most commonly understood environment of disparate approaches to leadership and sharply distinguished results, which makes this conflict a useful tool for understanding the concept. Cases can be drawn from the conflict and theories superimposed upon it. Whole books have been devoted to this, for example, S. F. Hayward, *Churchill on Leadership: Executive Success in the Face of Adversity* (New York, 1997); A. Roberts, *Churchill and Hitler: Secrets of Leadership* (London, 2003); K. Grint, *Leadership, Management and Command: Rethinking D-Day* (London, 2008). In the crowded and lucrative market for leadership literature more recent and more distant examples are also employed to attract attention. Some relate to specific situations, such as T. Wheeler, *Take Command! Leadership Lessons from the Civil War* (New York, 2000), and S. Jones and J. Gosling, *Nelson's Way: Leadership Lessons from the Great Commander*

management features less prominently in contemporary works on leadership. Although the two World Wars did not produce the huge change in scale or operations that occurred on land, and eventually in the air, it certainly had an impact on the navies, their leadership and management.

The cumulative experience of over a century of large scale industrial enterprise, mass warfare and the continual evolution of academic disciplines including history, provide the basis for what are today some of the key questions about leadership and management. The extent to which leaders are born or made has vexed contemporaries throughout the twentieth century and remains a point of contention as social scientists and evolutionary biologists continue the debate. Similarly, whether leadership depends on an identifiable set of values, skills or capabilities remains contested. Whether leadership is something that lies within the personality and actions of the leader or the minds of the followers still divides scholars. Likewise, whether leadership capability is transferable across contexts or situations, and, if so, how, still has the power to divide opinion. It all adds up to a rich and varied debate across a broad contested territory.

However, what is often overlooked is that these essential questions of leadership and management have a much longer history. As maritime commerce and warfare moved from the local coastal traffic of the Middle Ages to long distance and even oceanic trades, it demanded levels of management and leadership that only became common in most purely land-based activity centuries later. Merchants required confidence in the ability of ships' masters to manage trade, navigation, ship-handling and crew over long periods at great distances with only the most rudimentary communications networks.[8] Similarly, as the state's requirements for naval power increased, so the need for trust in the capability of people from shipwrights and contractors to naval commanders and seamen grew. By the end of the seventeenth century, Spain, France, the United Provinces and England had established economic, political and organisational networks for the creation and sustenance of naval power in European waters and across the Atlantic to the Americas. The states' ways of resolving the problems involved differed and the choices they made had a profound

---

(London, 2005). Others take a wide sweep of illustrative material to reinforce the connections between military leadership and leadership in the civilian world. See, for example, D. J. Rogers, *Waging Business Warfare* (New York, 1987); B. G. James, *Business Wargames* (Tunbridge Wells, 1984); D. Miller, *Commanding Officers* (London, 2001); D. Toms and R. Barrons, *The Business General: Transform Your Business Using the Seven Secrets of Military Success* (London, 2006)

[8] R. Davis, *The Rise of the English Shipping Industry in the Seventeenth and Eighteenth Centuries* (Newton Abbot, 1962), pp. 159–74; P. Mathias, 'Risk, Credit and Kinship in early Modern Enterprise', in J. J. McCusker and K. Morgan (eds), *The Early Modern Atlantic Economy* (Cambridge, 2001), pp. 15–35

influence on how their naval power developed.[9] Traditional patterns of social leadership and accumulated skills were insufficient for the modern navies and the emerging bureaucracy of each state had to address the critical issue of management and leadership of exceptionally large, complex, expensive and technically advanced organisations.

Since the early 1960s there has been a growing recognition of the role that naval administration played in the early stages of bureaucratic development of the modern state in Western Europe. The dominance of the British Royal Navy from the early eighteenth century and the survival of huge quantities of archival material have made the British navy a particularly fruitful area of study. The Royal Navy's long-term success both in the defence of the state and the protection of overseas commerce through to the end of the First World War have given it a particularly important place in the emergence of modern bureaucratic state practice. Although the study of this phenomenon is still fairly new and many issues or aspects of context remain to be explored, there is now almost fifty years of new scholarship on what can be called the 'management' of naval organisations.[10]

This new history of naval management has done much to raise the standard of scholarship and take naval history out of its nineteenth-century preoccupation with battle narratives to inspire young officers and inform statesmen. What has changed less during this period is the study of naval leadership.[11]

---

[9] For an overview of this process, see R. Harding, *Seapower and Naval Warfare, 1650–1830*, (London, 1999).

[10] The literature on British naval administration and management is now substantial. Some of the most significant contributions include, D. Baugh, *British Naval Administration in the Age of Walpole* (Princeton NJ, 1965); R. Morriss, *The Royal Dockyards during the Revolutionary and Napoleonic Wars* (Leicester, 1983); J.M. Haas, *A Management Odyssey: The Royal Dockyards, 1714–1914* (New York, 1994); A. Coats, 'Efficiency in Dockyard Administration 1660–1800: A Reassessment', in N. Tracy (ed.), *The Age of Sail*, vol. 1 (London, 2003), 116–32; R. Morriss, *Naval Power and British Culture: Public Trust and Government Ideology* (Aldershot, 2004); R. Knight and M. Wilcox, *Sustaining the Fleet: War, the British Navy and the Contractor State* (Woodbridge, 2010); R. Morriss, *The Foundations of British Maritime Ascendancy: Resources, Logistics and the State, 1755–1815* (Cambridge, 2011); C. I. Hamilton, *The Making of the Modern Admiralty: British Naval Policy-Making, 1805–1927* (Cambridge, 2011). Studies on other navies are still needed, but an excellent example of this type of work is D. Goodman, *Spanish Naval Power, 1569–1665: Reconstruction and Defeat* (Cambridge, 1997)

[11] The term 'management' is used here to describe the capabilities and systems required to control and order resources towards an organisational objective. It is traditionally distinguished from 'leadership', which is usually associated with the dynamic capabilities of providing the vision, creativity and motivation for people to engage intellectually, physically and emotionally to achieve the organisation's aims. The distinction is contested and has many variations, but it serves for the present purposes.

Internationally, Horatio Nelson remains the iconic naval commander. His commitment to duty, his understanding of his officers, men and ships, as well as those of his enemies, his courage and his ruthless determination to destroy the enemy have become the hallmarks of the ideal aggressive naval commander. For the general reader, successful naval leadership is still seen in essentially heroic, Nelsonic, terms, although studies have now begun to throw more light on how naval leadership worked in the context of a large, complex, globally capable institution.[12] One of the scholars who has done a great deal to develop our understanding of both management and leadership in the Royal Navy is Michael Duffy. Michael Duffy came to naval history from detailed studies of Anglo-Austrian military co-operation in the French Revolutionary War.[13] He brought with him an understanding of the political and diplomatic complexity of leading and managing a campaign of allies. He applied this understanding of inter-organisational co-operation in his fine 1987 study of the British expeditions to the West Indies in the 1790s, *Soldiers, Sugar and Seapower*.[14] His understanding of the managerial and leadership problems that faced the Royal Navy in the wars against France from 1793 to 1815 underpinned his ability to teach and inspire students at the Centre for Maritime Historical Studies at the University of Exeter for the next twenty years.

In September 2009, to mark the occasion of Michael's retirement, a conference, *Officers and Seamen: Management in Naval and Maritime History*, was held at Exeter to celebrate his contribution in this field. It brought together colleagues and students who had been influenced by Michael's work. The papers ranged over a number of crucial elements of naval leadership and management, from command and leadership in battle to the details of naval administration and the training of officers and men. What emerged most strongly from all these papers was that historians had a great deal to offer, not just to naval history, but to the study of leadership and management more broadly. In this respect the conference was not only looking back to recall Michael's contribution, but looked forward to new areas of study within naval history and the manner in which naval historians could contribute to the continuing debate on leadership and management. The essays that are

---

[12] Good examples of this scholarship can be in the following. J. Horsfield, *The Art of Leadership in War: The Royal Navy from the Age of Nelson to the End of World War II* (Westport CT, 1980); J. Sweetman (ed.), *The Great Admirals: Command at Sea, 1587–1945* (Annapolis MD, 1997); J. Hayward, *For God and Glory: Lord Nelson and His Way of War*, (Annapolis MD, 2003); M. A. Palmer, *Command at Sea: Naval Command and Control since the Sixteenth Century* (Cambridge MA, 2005).

[13] M. Duffy, 'British War Policy and the Austrian Alliance, 1793–1801' (unpublished D.Phil. thesis, University of Oxford, 1971).

[14] M. Duffy, *Soldiers, Sugar and Seapower: The British Expeditions to the West Indies and the War Against Revolutionary France* (Oxford, 1987).

brought together in this collection are a selection that illustrates some points of departure to contribute to the evolution of the study naval history and leadership. Four main themes are presented in these essays: the place of the hero in naval leadership; organisational friction in matters of command; the role of management capability in the exercise of naval power; and the evolution of management and training in the Royal Navy.

Leadership: The Place of the Hero

The light that illuminates the idea of naval leadership since the middle of the nineteenth century is overwhelmingly that of Horatio Nelson. The 2005 commemoration of the bicentenary of the Battle of Trafalgar (21 October 1805) provided the opportunity for historians from around the world to discuss and examine a wide range of factors that contributed to the British victory, the public perception of its decisive impact and the contribution of that iconic naval officer. The work that emerged demonstrated the complex issues that have to be considered in order to understand a single victory. The technical, political, social, economic and organisational elements that made up the contesting fleets and their relative capabilities were established in more detail than ever before. Nelson's reputation remained intact – he was a commander of outstanding capability and insight. However, the other factors, both positive and negative, that contributed to the British victory on 21 October are now better understood and a more balanced judgement of the battle is possible. Leaving aside the problems that beset the Franco-Spanish Combined Fleet, they were facing a British Royal Navy that was operationally at a peak of effectiveness. The fighting spirit, which Nelson represented, which was the idealised model for naval officers, was vital, but it was only one element contributing to the superiority of the British fleet over its enemies. The strategic role of the navy was clearly understood at the top of the profession and by the politicians and statesmen who controlled policy. The logistical infrastructure of dockyards, repair facilities and victualling had been developing for over a century and were operating well. The war had been going on since 1793 (with a small interlude between 1802 and 1803), but unlike in the French and Spanish navies, the Royal Navy had not suffered a crippling attrition in personnel. Instead, it benefited from the constant challenge of war in the growing experience and efficiency of both officers and seamen. In short, the navy, of which Nelson's squadron was an important part, was an outstandingly capable organisation – it could ensure it was in the right place, at the right time, with a decisive measure of fighting superiority over its opponents.

To achieve this, the heroes in battle were essential, but more was required. Few commanders were given the opportunity of fighting a large-scale fleet action. This was the ultimate test of an admiral at sea and Nelson excelled.[15] Over the whole eighteenth century, many more commanders had the mundane, but arduous, task of maintaining their squadrons at sea over long periods. Nelson was as expert in this function – overseeing the repair and provisioning of his squadron or organising important intelligence gathering – as he was in battle. These qualities of the squadron commander, which ensured he was in a position to exercise decisive force at the right time, were less glamorous, but no less important. However, Nelson was not alone in possessing these qualities. Peter Ward's study of Admiral Peter Rainier shows how these qualities were important to a commander on a very distant station. Maintaining a squadron of approximately twenty ships on the East India Station for eleven years was a major logistical and diplomatic challenge. Rainier never had to fight the dramatic fleet action which would have made his name, but he quietly negotiated with East India Company officials, local merchant communities and officials to ensure his squadron remained an effective regional force. Such an achievement does not lie in the command of one man, and Rainier's skill was to lead and manage his squadron to ensure that wherever his ships were, they represented and met his values and objectives. It was one of the major achievements of his time in command. As more attention is paid to other squadron commanders, it seems likely that the talent demonstrated at this level of naval leadership and management was quite widespread. If so, an understanding of how naval officers developed their skills in this area of activity needs to be more fully understood.[16]

Naval power rested on an effective infrastructure, blending logistics, professional competence and political support, which in turn demanded high quality leadership and management effectiveness at all levels. The importance of this organisational leadership network is brought out in the essay by Richard Harding. The contrast between the glorious victory at Trafalgar in 1805 and the miserable events of 1744–5, when the Royal Navy failed to stop the Franco-Spanish fleet breaking out of Toulon and Britain itself was threatened with invasion, can hardly be more stark. Whereas contemporaries and historians traditionally found the cause of victory in the personality of Nelson, so they found the cause of failure in the First Lord of the Admiralty, the Earl

---

[15] Nelson as the benchmark of the fighting admiral has recently been developed by Ruddock Mackay and Michael Duffy in their study of Edward Hawke. See, R. Mackay and M. Duffy, *Hawke, Nelson and British Naval Leadership, 1747–1805*, (Woodbridge, 2009). See also, A. Lambert, *Admirals: The Naval Commanders Who Made Britain Great* (London, 2008), particularly pp. 423–5.

[16] See, for example, P. Le Fevre, 'Sir John Borlase Warren,1753–1822', in P. Le Fevre and R. Harding (eds), *British Admirals of the Napoleonic Wars: The Contemporaries of Nelson* (London, 2005), pp. 219–44

of Winchelsea. That Winchelsea was not the equal of Lord Barham (First Lord of the Admiralty in 1805) is not challenged, but that unlike Nelson and Barham, Winchelsea and his senior officers at sea had neither the political nor professional infrastructure to support them. It was only when the political friction between the king and his ministry, led by the Pelham brothers, was resolved in 1746, and the professional leadership of the navy was linked back to the political leadership in the person of Admiral George Anson, that the strategic and operational effectiveness of the navy revived. Further studies of leadership networks may also open the way for rethinking some judgements on the performance of the Royal Navy in other periods.

The study of the period 1744–5 highlights another feature of leadership studies in naval history, that is, their focus on the victor in battle. This is understandable in as much as a great deal of naval history has been written for the education of officers and statesmen and it is the actions of the victors that have dominated attention. The research and publications that were generated by the bicentenary of Trafalgar demonstrated that victory was the consequence of far more than boldness in the face of the enemy. That was an essential but insufficient causal factor.[17] Enough is known of the performance of the French and Spanish navies to be certain that courage was not the preserve of the British fleet. Similarly, the qualities of leadership found in Nelson and other British officers was not a national characteristic, but shared among navies. Leadership from a position of weakness, and even despair, unless crowned by an ultimate complete triumph (rather like Winston Churchill, 1940–1945) has not attracted the attention it deserves. Many organisations, naval and civilian, go through collapses of morale due to a variety of causes. Bringing those organisations back to stability in circumstances which cannot promise a final, indisputable valedictory success is a task undertaken by many leaders. Officers like the Spanish admiral at Trafalgar, Federico Gravina, have only recently received the attention they deserve.[18] These officers performed a vital function in re-establishing stability and improving functionality, but how they worked, what they achieved and their impact relative to other factors remains, for the most part, unknown to history.

---

[17] Michael Duffy has demonstrated that, even at Trafalgar, boldness of the highest level was not essential throughout the entire British squadron to ensure overwhelming victory. See, M. Duffy, '"All was Hushed Up?" The Hidden Trafalgar', *Mariner's Mirror* 91 (2005), 216–40.

[18] A. Guimera, 'Gravina and the Naval Leadership of His Day', *Journal of Maritime Research* 7:1 (2005), 44–69.

Leadership and Organisational Frictions: Contested Territories

On the whole, the issue of command in the Royal Navy has not been a major point of contention.[19] From early laws on authority at sea to the Articles of War and the powerful sustaining heritage of institutional practices, the navy can claim that the clarity of its leadership and command processes have been an important positive feature of its structure. Over the centuries, the undisputed record of operational success strongly reinforces the positive feeling about the quality of command. There have been exceptions to this. The failure of the navy to produce another Trafalgar during the First World War concerned contemporary naval officers and, much later, stimulated an important revisionist study of pre-1914 leadership practice in the Royal Navy.[20] However, in areas where command in the navy inter-acted with other authorities, the issue of organisational frictions was more often present. The matter of command in relation to the civil power in the American colonies was a point of contention throughout the eighteenth century, which, in the case of pressing seamen in the Americas, had, at times, a significant impact on the operational effectiveness of the navy and the views of Americans towards royal power.[21] Throughout the century, command on amphibious operations in conjunction with the army raised questions of command and authority, which, even if generally overstated, caused anxiety, frustration and bad feeling. For the most part, admirals and generals were pragmatic enough to realise that they depended on each other and so long as operational decisions did not impose potentially catastrophic consequences upon them, they were willing to go along with their partner – although they always reserved the right to be critical after the event. Part of the problem of operations with other services was ensuring agreement or a *modus operandi* which did not compromise feelings of proper order. This was clearly at issue when the navy played host to officers and men of the Royal Artillery. This occurred in the manning of bomb vessels, whose mortars were operated by artillerymen, while the ship was crewed and commanded by naval personnel. Gareth Cole's study of this relationship casts important light on how the command and leadership issues

---

[19] 'Command' like leadership and management is a complex and contested term. Here it is used simply to mean the right and ability to have orders obeyed. A useful synopsis of the relations between the three terms can be found in Grint, *Leadership, Management and Command*, 3–18.

[20] A. J. Marder, *From the Dardanelles to Oran: Studies of the Royal Navy in War and Peace, 1915–1940* (Oxford, 1974), pp. 57–61; A. Gordon, *The Rules of the Game: Jutland and British Naval Command* (London, 1996).

[21] R. Pares, 'The Manning of the Navy in the West Indies, 1702–1763', *Transactions of the Royal Historical Society* 19 (1937), 31–60.

developed during the Revolutionary and Napoleonic Wars, and the measures taken to resolve them. Another body that stood slightly apart from the navy was the marines. Although under Admiralty control from 1747, and a standing body since 1755, the marines were both subsumed in the command structure of their ships and had their own command hierarchy. Social and professional factors placed the marine command structure in strict subservience to that of the naval service. Britt Zerbe's analysis of how marine officers pushed forward the military function of the marines and constructed a positive operational image of the corps, to the extent that the 'Royal' prefix was conferred on it in 1802, casts important light on the evolution of a military institution.

Management Capability and the Exercise of Naval Power

It was the re-examination of naval history through the lens of the naval administrator that did so much to re-invigorate the study of naval history in the 1960s and early 1970s. Today, this rich seam of research has not exhausted itself. The vast archival deposits in the National Archives, the National Maritime Museum and elsewhere have many more secrets to disclose and problems to present. Although the period from 1689 to the 1850s is often seen as the period of emerging state bureaucracy, in which the struggle against traditional forms of patronage which masked corruption or incompetence, was only gradually and partially won, it was also a period in which administrators had to achieve increasingly good and reliable results to service a fleet that campaigned intensively across the globe. Much depended on the capability of individual administrators. Dr Roger Morriss has been one of the most prolific writers on the naval administration of the eighteenth and early nineteenth centuries. Administrators at different levels in the hierarchies and different geographical locations had their own problems. Morriss' examination of the work of the agent for transports at Portsmouth and Southampton, Captain Daniel Woodriff, is an important illustration of the richness of information and analysis about operational capabilities that can be extracted from the papers of one official.

For historians the role of individuals in organisations is an issue fraught with difficulty. The biographer inevitably puts the personality at centre stage, usually leaving the significance of the organisational context to be inferred or left as a passive factor responding to their subject's actions or thoughts. Over recent decades, historians of administration and organisation, like Roger Morriss, have done a great deal to correct this emphasis on the hero leader as the unique determinant of organisational success by placing the individual firmly into the administrative and operational context within which he operated. However, we still have many issues to examine. Organisations are made up of individuals and understanding how people behave in groups or organisations is an essential element of understanding any organisation, its leadership and performance.[22] Comparative studies of morale, training, hygiene and communication are beginning to illuminate our understanding of differentials in the performance of navies. Much of this comparative work takes its starting point from the potential clash of arms between the navies being examined. Less attention has been paid to the more prosaic influence of organisational management systems on individual performance on a day-to-day basis – a situation which has been studied extensively in business organisations. The impact of reward systems, comparative physical conditions and social status are all grist to the mill of the business organisation development specialists. Some of their work is now spilling over into naval history. These subjects are essential to the study of morale, mutiny and desertion. Sometimes seen as having origins primarily in radical ideologies opposed to the leadership elites, such assertions have to be moderated by an understanding of the social and economic expectations of leaders and followers. Groups involved in social crises are seldom homogeneous, stable and exclusive. Leaders and followers can belong to multiple groups with fluid roles and expectations which defy a neat classification into one or other side of a conflict. The Invergordon Mutiny of 1931 has attracted significant attention as representative of lower-deck feeling in relation to government policy in the face of a worsening fiscal and financial crisis. What has been less fully explored is the perceptions of the middle-ranking naval officer before Invergordon. Mike Farquharson-Roberts' examination of this group delves into the changing conditions of the service experienced by these officers between 1919 and 1931 and adds another dimension to our understanding of the tensions within the Royal Navy at this time.

As our understanding of the life and labour of seamen increases, some of the older myths are being demolished. For example, we now know that, despite the popular image of the press gang, many sailors on British warships were volunteers.[23] Nevertheless, in wartime there were never enough seamen to man the ships of the Royal Navy. Seamen were attracted to the merchant service in which wages rose in response to this additional demand. Service on merchantmen would become more dangerous in wartime, and an alternative was to serve on a privateer. Privateering, the licensing of private ships

---

[22] For an overview of this approach, see M. M. Chemers, 'Leadership Effectiveness: Functional, Constructivist and Empirical Perspectives', in D.van Knippenberg and M. A. Hogg (eds), *Leadership and Power: Identity Processes in Groups and Organizations* (London, 2003), pp. 5–17.

[23] N. Rodger, *The Wooden World: An Anatomy of the Georgian Navy* (London, 1986), pp. 153–63.

as ships of war during hostilities, was an important element in eighteenth-century seapower. Joining a privateer had its advantages and disadvantages to the seaman. Managing his expectations and leading him posed different problems for the master of a privateer compared with the commander of a royal warship or merchantman. David J. Starkey has worked for many years on privateering, its impact on the British economy and the labour market for seamen. His analysis of the management processes involved illustrates the unusual manner in which the risks and rewards were balanced in order to maintain an effective voyage. It adds another dimension to how seamen encountered and accommodated the possibilities of earning a living from the sea in times of war.

The Evolution of Management Training in the Royal Navy

During the eighteenth century training in leadership or management was very much based on an apprenticeship model. It was not a distinct form of education, but it was expected that the aspirant officer would obtain the requirements for command through a blend of learning the technical skills of seamanship and navigation, observing the demeanour of his commander or tutor, and demanding the level of social deference to which his station in life entitled him. As the nineteenth century progressed, the Royal Navy had to change. The demands of technology were obvious to anyone who could look at a ship. Ships of iron and steel, powered by steam and electricity, demanded different skills and more technical specialisms. From the seaman, traditionally employed only for the life of the commission of the ship, the navy now needed a more permanent commitment. Long service, new specialisations and changing attitudes to discipline on shore required changes to managing and leading men at sea.[24] Oliver Walton's examination of the changing code of discipline illuminates the intentions of the reforms of the 1860s and 1870s, along with its intended and unintended consequences, as officers and ratings adjusted to the new system. Change was also coming to the officer corps of the Royal Navy in these decades. Mary Jones has examined how officers adapted as the relative independence of commanders in the dispersed old sailing navy of the mid-century gave way to the more centrally controlled systems of the early years of the twentieth century. On the whole, the Royal Navy managed the

---

[24] O. Walton, '"A Great Improvement in the Sailor's Feeling towards the Naval Service": Recruiting Seamen for the Royal Navy, 1815–1853', *Journal for Maritime Research* 12:1 (2010), 27–57. See also G. A. Miller, 'From Jack Tar to Bluejacket: Impressment, Manning and the Development of Continuous Service in the Royal Navy, 1815–1853' (unpublished Ph.D. dissertation, King's College, London, 2011).

transformation of the disciplinary system and command relations effectively, and it did so without a great deal of change in the social attitudes of either the officer corps or the seamen. The increasingly specialised technical demands of the service fragmented the officer corps in some ways and, in the case of the engineer officer, introduced an element of social tension. However, the idea that the officer was primarily a leader of men, rather than a technician, endured. Yet, in this technologically advanced navy, the training for leadership was largely ignored. For the cadet and midshipman, the development of their leadership skills and experience depended very heavily on the chance example provided by the officers under whom they served and learned. Besides this, the leadership and team work experienced in boat work under sail and oar was the most important element in the curriculum for cadets between 1919 and 1939. However, as Elinor Romans explains, it was a training that was not systematically developed once the cadet took a midshipman's berth, despite the importance of small boat work in the day-to-day routine of warships. Leadership was expected of a naval officer and, on the whole, the Royal Navy got the leaders it needed. The role formal training played in this success is still something that needs further investigation.

This collection deals with a single theme – naval leadership and management. The essays have been selected for the variety of subjects, sources, questions, approaches and styles they use in order to illustrate just how rich and important field it is. They only cover a fraction of the potential field, but it is enough to suggest that the sources and questions can take us much further. Traditionally, history has been used to illustrate leadership, usually by example of heroic deeds. Biography remains the most popular means of engaging the public with history. For the public at large, the human dimension makes dry and abstract historical themes more palatable and comprehensible. For scholars of leadership, other than historians, biography most commonly serves to provide the content of case studies to support a pre-determined set of 'lessons'.[25] There is nothing wrong with this, given the vital human element in decision-making. However, history is far better used by the historian and other scholars as the focus of study in which the complex interplay of context, specific situation, personal capabilities and emotions can be laid out (in so far as the evidence allows) to inform a rich picture of leadership or management performance. Naval history and historians can contribute more to leadership studies. Just as students of leadership provide historians with theoretical

---

[25] The case method, which emerged in the United States in the early years of the twentieth century, owed a great deal to attempts to take forward the codification and rationalisation of knowledge, which had become so important in the rise of historical studies since the 1880s. See M. P. McNair and A. C. Hersum (eds), *The Case Method at the Harvard Business School* (New York, 1954), particularly pp. 15–33.

propositions to stimulate and encourage their own archival researches, so the historian provides the crucial, in-depth empirical testing of these ideas in real contexts. It is a symbiotic relationship of theory and empirical research such as this that provides each generation with its new questions and tentative answers.

Naval history will continue to develop and thrive as it evolves to pose new questions and provide answers to successive generations. Michael Duffy's encouragement of the highest standards of historical scholarship and his willingness to encourage people of all ages and levels of experience to contribute to the field of naval history has done much to enliven and expand the subject. It is hoped that these essays prove that the scholars who have worked with him, or who have been trained by him, share his commitment.

LEADERSHIP: THE PLACE OF THE HERO

1

Admiral Rainier's Management Challenges, 1794–1805

Peter Ward

At the end of the eighteenth century the East Indies Command was a junior one, warranting a commodore in peacetime and a rear admiral during times of war. Yet it had two elements which made it unique amongst all the challenges that faced Royal Naval flag officers around the globe. Firstly, there was its enormous size, over 30 million square miles with a journey of 15,000 to 16,000 miles between Britain and the farthest reaches of the station. The time taken for the various routes is explored in the section 'Communication and Intelligence' below. But the timing meant that, to all intents, its commander operated independently. The second element was the East India Company, a joint stock company that provided the government for all British possessions in the East Indies, not just India. This organisation provided the navy with all its dockyard facilities and ordnance, many of its naval supplies, and some auxiliary warships and marines.

The purpose of this chapter is to describe how Admiral Peter Rainier, through superior management skills, established an effective organisation which ensured his ships could be at sea for extended periods, and which, continued to be effective as the squadron expanded. Rainier had a reputation as a 'fighting captain', earned during the American Revolution, but for the last nine years of his command he saw no shots fired in anger. His reputation therefore rests on his success as the archetypical managerial flag officer which fits the theme of this collection. The various subordinate Admiralty Boards had little experience of providing support at such a distance from Britain and therefore Rainier had to arrange the majority of his own financial and logistics infrastructure for himself, largely in conjunction with the East India Company. Coincidentally he had to be a Commander-in-Chief of an operational, fighting naval squadron.

The East Indies Station

Commodore Peter Rainier sailed for the East Indies in 1794.[1] He had previously served there eleven years during the Seven Years War and American Revolution, but he had no experience of multi-vessel command. The East Indies Station had no Royal Naval infrastructure, indeed, there were no warships, apart from the five Rainier took with him. Rainier never had more than twenty-two vessels, including seven third rates, and 6,000 men under his command, yet, with these resources, he had to cover his vast station, it extended from the Red Sea in the north west, down the east coast of Africa, across the Indian Ocean, through the Dutch East Indies (the Indonesian Archipelago), into the Pacific to include the Philippines, and northwards through the South China Sea to Canton. Between 1796 and 1802, Britain occupied the Cape of Good Hope whose zone of influence extended into the Indian Ocean to include the French island of Mauritius, thus relieving Rainier of the need to monitor that area.

In addition to its sheer size, the wind patterns heavily influenced what Rainier could do. The major system was the monsoon, which blew from the north east over the winter six months and from the south west for the remainder of the year. Naturally the changeover did not happen on a set date, and there was a month of variability at the end of each season. Other local systems complicated matters, including the Red Sea which was impossible to enter in a sailing ship for half the year during the summer and impossible to exit during the winter. The major wind patterns meant that ships from Europe would try to enter the Indian Ocean at the beginning of the south-west trade winds and would leave to benefit from the north-east trade winds. Ships leaving Canton had to wait until at least January, when the tea harvest had been picked, before they could take advantage of a fair wind. East Indiamen, the vessels of the East India Company, heading directly from Europe to China, would head south to the 'Roaring Forties' latitudes where the winds, although often gale force, blew east to west, all the year round, before turning northwards through the Dutch East Indies. The thousands of islands which make up the Indonesian Archipelago minimised the routes available. Ships were forced to go primarily through the Straits of Malacca or Sunda when sailing between India and the East Indies, and to choose between the Straits of Bali, Lombok or Sunda when journeying between Europe and China. These pinch points made it easier for enemy commerce raiders to prey on British shipping and, conversely, for Rainier to protect it.

---

[1] Rainier was promoted rear admiral in June 1795.

Rainier and the East India Company

Recent reforms of the East India Company had formalised the pre-eminence of Calcutta over the two other presidencies of Madras and Bombay, and it was there that the governor general resided. But this did not mean that independent, and sometimes selfish, actions by the secondary presidencies no longer occurred. The governor general was a crown appointee reporting to the President of the Board of Control of the Company and the Board of Directors. As such he had command of the three armies of the presidencies, numbering 192,000 men by 1805. The Company also had its own small private navy, the Bombay Marine, which had two frigates and a number of smaller vessels, whose main duties were the suppression of piracy, convoy escort, and the carriage of official mail.

Logistically, the Company operated its own ship building and repair dry dock in Bombay, which could take three 74's simultaneously. This was the only dry dock available to the navy outside Britain. Naval supplies were therefore usually available, and there was an extensive ordnance organisation which could supply both gunpowder and naval guns. Being such a large trading venture it was also an integral part of the Indian fiscal structure which provided finance not only for Company business, but also for the regional private trade and the navy's activities.

Until 1796, Sir John Shore was the governor general and his more traditional, non-interventionist and accounting mentality was admirably suited to that of Rainier who thus experienced a constructive introduction to the complexities of Company relationships. Shore's successor, Richard Wellesley, was completely the opposite. He was an egotistical autocrat who brooked no opposition to his plans. His aim was to ensure British control of the subcontinent, and he wanted authority over the Royal Navy. These elements would all contribute to the management challenges faced by Rainier.

Britain relied heavily on the revenues generated by trade with India and China. Therefore Rainier's first responsibility was to protect the shipping both between Europe and the East Indies and also within the region itself. This latter activity was called the Country Trade and was carried out not by the Company, but by private bodies and individuals, both European and Indian. Rainier's other duty, as stated in his original orders, was to protect His Majesty's possessions in the East.[2] How he was to do this was left to his

---

[2] The National Archives (TNA), ADM 2/1347, Admiralty to Rainier, 25 February 1794.

own discretion, although he was to consult with the senior officials of the Company in assessing his priorities.

In order to achieve these objectives, Rainier needed the following ingredients; a close, positive relationship with the Company's officials, army and Marine officers, a similar relationship with the Admiralty and its subordinate Boards in London, a materials management structure that enabled the navy to be at sea for as long as possible, a financial organisation that ensured the provision of the necessary naval supplies and victuals, motivated and healthy ships' crews, and an effective communication and intelligence system enabling him to make his decisions on the best possible information obtained in the most rapid manner.

For four years Rainier had been the captain of the *Burford* (70) under Vice Admiral Hughes during the American Revolution. He had fought in each of the five fleet actions against the French Admiral Suffren off the south east coast of India. This experience had given him an understanding of the necessity for good relations with the Company, which Hughes did not have. Hughes' choices of action were often curtailed due to a lack of naval supplies and victuals. He had not been able to persuade the Company to reinforce the garrison at Trincomalee leading to its rapid capitulation to a French attack. Rainier could see that he must have good relations in order to achieve his goals. Whilst maintaining his own independence of action he went to considerable effort to communicate with the governor general, the presidents of Madras and Bombay, and senior army officers. He informed them as to how he was making dispositions of his ships and why, asking them for their opinions, sometimes telling them why he was unhappy with their actions, and asking for their help. He never went behind anyone's back, he appears to have been completely honest with them. Wellesley finally gave up his demands for control of the navy and, apart from one serious disagreement when Rainier refused to support his demands for an attack on Mauritius, their relationship was positive. Rainier was even given authority over the army by Wellesley for the planned invasion of Batavia.

Whilst Rainier might criticise others he was also keen to praise good performance and this naturally ensured a positive response when he requested the help of Bombay Marine vessels and East Indiamen which, when equipped for war, were the equivalent of a 36 gun frigate. His close relationship with Major General Stuart, the army commander, even allowed him to obtain soldiers to act as marines on naval warships.

Rainier and the Navy

Managing upwards in an organisation is just as important as managing downwards. Rainier, a self deprecating man,[3] was not one of a large band of flag officers who complained vigorously to the Admiralty if they felt they had received insufficient recognition or reward. He did not complain when his station was, for twelve months, put under the command of Sir George Elphinstone at the Cape; an exercise which added no value to Rainier's efforts but cost him £25,000 prize money which went to Elphinstone after Rainier captured the Dutch Spice Islands. He remained on good terms with successive First Lords although his primary contacts were the successive Secretaries to the Board. His main instrument was the letter. Their Lordships were regaled with every detail of the issues faced on a day-to-day basis. Nothing was omitted. But the practice seems to have been effective because Rainier always received that welcome phrase 'Their Lordships approve'. Not once in eleven years did he suffer an admonishment.

The majority of his communication was with the Navy Board which sent out naval supplies more cheaply than they could be purchased in India, such as large spars, anchors, heavy cables and copper sheathing. It was also the source of finance through the issue of navy bonds and the destination of all the invoices and receipts for purchases made on the station. By this process expenditures could be reconciled in the navy's accounts and, if necessary, reimbursed to the payee. There were many letters from Rainier complaining of the poor quality of supplies sent out from England, of the non-arrival of supplies, and of them being sent to the wrong location. The Board also felt it was receiving insufficient communication from India and therefore did not know what to send. These letters illustrate a not entirely happy relationship between the admiral and the Navy Board.

In spite of an almost religious adherence to form filling, Rainier occasionally fell foul of its strictures. Not all expenditure was covered by receipts. When the accounts could not be reconciled the Board allocated the cost of the 'missing' items to the senior officer who had authorised the purchase. Consequently, when Rainier returned home in 1805 and had to balance all his expenditures since 1794, it is not surprising that not all the books balanced. He therefore had an imprest of almost £1 million placed on his personal account. This was the Board's method of incentivising the individual

---

[3] TNA, PROB. 11/1480, Peter Rainier's will. In his will Rainier stated that the money he had acquired was more than his needs or his talents merited. He would therefore give 10 per cent of his estate to the government to help reduce the National Debt.

to rectify the situation. Negotiation over several months finally led to the imprest being lifted.

Much of the problem was caused by the fact that the officials of the Navy Board had no understanding of the conditions in the East Indies. Also with the rapid expansion of the navy, its own systems were inefficient. This caused paperwork to be lost within and between the various departments in the Admiralty.[4] It is clear that, although the Navy Board was responsible to the Admiralty for the physical maintenance and provision of warships, and the accurate accounting for naval expenditure, it had little real control over what Rainier did on his station, nor did it understand the circumstances in which he operated. But on his return to England the Board frequently asked for his advice, which helped to establish the form of a Navy Board structure in India. Thus his successors did not have to struggle with the administrative minutiae which absorbed so much of Rainier's time.

Because victualling was provided locally by a private contractor, the Honourable Basil Cochrane, Rainier directed his demands to him rather than the Victualling Board and he therefore had little to do with this organisation. Similarly, although Rainier established a hospital at Madras, medical care in other locations was provided by the Company, who supplied medicines. As already noted, ordnance was also purchased from the Company so Rainier had virtually no communication with the Ordnance Board.

Rainier's Subordinates – Command and Control

All good managers have strong values with which they motivate, teach and protect those for whom they are responsible. Fortunately Rainier's letter to his nephew has survived, which gives the newly promoted frigate captain advice on how to be a successful commander.[5] From it a clear picture of the admiral's values can be seen, relating both to the treatment of his men and to the importance of administration:

1. Muster the crew frequently to become familiar with their tempers, manners and dispositions ... from your own knowledge [not that] of your officers, many of whom are not liberal in their ideas or are too influenced by their prejudices and private animosities and resentments.
2. Consider yourself at all times their advocate when any complaint is brought against them and never proceed to punishment but on the fullest conviction of proper evidence.

---

[4] TNA, ADM 110/55, Navy Board to Marsden, 12 September 1806.
[5] National Maritime Museum (NMM): RAI/201/8, Admiral Peter Rainier to Captain Peter Rainier, 2 April 1805.

3. Be attentive to all their complaints and relieve their little wants when it is in your power.
4. Abstain from reviling them with foul or abusive language or suffer your officers to do so.
5. Few are their rights but never suffer them to be infringed by yourself or those under you.
6. Never punish with too much severity ... let them see the object is the Vice not the Man.
7. Monitor the Ship's Books, audit the Warrant Officers' Accounts to the Victualling Office. Thoroughly understand the business of the Captain's Clerk ... it requires but a very small portion of your leisure time to become perfect in it.
8. Comply with Admiralty and Naval instruction of every kind.
9. When you receive orders do not be content with a single perusal but look at them every now and then that you may not mistake their meaning.

These values, from a man born in 1741, indicate the kind of manager Rainier was. His concern for his men is demonstrated by his insistence on the best possible victuals. He even wrote that he was buying cocoa for his sick crewmen, although it was twice the cost in the West Indies.[6] He opened the first naval hospital in Madras, and his standing orders demanded that the captains and surgeons visited their sick in hospital each Monday.[7] The 1797 naval mutinies spread eastwards, being manifested by the crew of the *Trident*, but this was quelled by its captain reminding his men of all that their admiral had done for them. Several sailors were condemned to death but were pardoned by Rainier and returned to their ships on the receipt of the news of Duncan's victory at Camperdown.

The East India Company had a monopoly on all trade between Britain and the East and its sailors were legally exempted from the Press. This meant that there was an absence of available replacement skilled sailors which the navy could take from the merchant service. It could be argued that Rainier's behaviour to protect the health and wellbeing of his men was self serving, but whatever the reason, it was still the behaviour of a sensible manager to preserve the efficiency of his skilled 'human resource'. During his period in command, Rainier managed approximately forty-nine captains, commanders, and lieutenants in command. Of these five were lost at sea, two died in battle, two died of illness, one returned to Britain due to ill health and one was dismissed by court martial. Two became full admirals, two vice admirals, four rear admirals and four captains. Perhaps his largest leap of faith was to give acting Lieutenant Nesbit Willoughby command of a brig, ignoring the fact

---

[6] NMM, RAI/4, Rainier to Navy Board, 14 August 1795.
[7] National Library of Scotland, Blair Adam Papers, Rainier's General Orders, 15 February 1797.

that he had been found guilty of insubordination at a court martial consisting of Rainier's own captains and dismissed his ship. This officer went on to experience three other courts martial in a career highlighted by brilliant close combat operations on his way to becoming a rear admiral. Clearly Rainier felt he had the skill to manage a maverick because he could see Willoughby's inherent talent.

Because of the size of the station, all the captains had to be able to operate thousands of miles from support and a more senior officer. Just as the Admiralty had to trust Rainier not to take too many risks, so Rainier had to believe that his captains were 'safe pairs of hands'. This he did by issuing detailed orders which could not be misunderstood, often explaining the wider circumstances in which they were operating, in order that his officers could use their own initiative. He also showed them his trust, as when he told Captain Lucas to use his intelligence as Rainier was too far away to give any direct orders.[8] However, when his most adventurous captain, Cooke, requested permission for an operation not defined, Rainier refused, saying it was too dangerous.[9] So there were clearly limits as to how far the admiral would permit risks to be taken. And when a captain was new, he would receive detailed orders covering almost every possible eventuality to help him avoid getting into trouble.[10] The fact that his vessels could be months away from any contact with him meant that Rainier had to adapt his written orders for either a veteran experienced post captain or the most junior newly promoted commander. He had to adapt his style of management in order that it was appropriate for whatever level of experience he found in a particular commanding officer. And when he knew that a captain would be close to senior East India Company officials, such as cruising in the Sand Heads, near the governor general in Calcutta, he would avoid putting that officer in a difficult situation by telling him to take any advice offered by such an exalted person. The results of his flexible management style appear therefore to be the creation of a cadre of officers able to operate independently and who, if they were able to avoid the natural perils of the station, could expect continued employment and promotion in their later careers.

Logistics Management

Having the East India Company present at almost every location in which the navy operated was both a blessing and a curse. Warships could come

---

[8] NMM, RAI/5, Rainier to Captain Lucas, 23 October 1796.
[9] NMM, RAI/7, Rainier to Captain Cooke, 9 September 1798.
[10] NMM, RAI/7, Rainier to Lieutenant Douglas, 2 August 1799.

to depend on the Company's resources but they were not always of appropriate quality, price or specification. Occasionally promises were not kept, or supplies were not where they were expected to be. The Admiralty liked Rainier to obtain supplies from the Company, such as gunpowder and materials brought out directly from Britain as they could be paid for centrally in London, thus avoiding the use of scarce local specie in India. Rainier regularly wrote to the Admiralty about the high prices he had to pay for Company naval supplies and urged them to send out more items from Britain, or alternatively, to send out cash. He was continually looking for alternative materials, such as Indian made hemp cables, and pegu teak and fir top mast timber from Burma, both to reduce costs and for a more dependable supply. Rainier also understood that stocks of supplies should be established, ready for use as and when needed. Warehouses were established in the major ports and managed by naval administrators who were monitored closely by the admiral to ensure they maintained the most important items in stock and ensured they did not rot. The money to purchase these items was provided by the admiral through the offer for sale of navy bonds and this process allowed him to ensure that they were not paying too much.

As the recipient of what were not always the most modern ships in the navy, and having to operate in a climate which was not conducive to their longevity, Rainier was grateful for the foresight of the Company in building the dry docks at Bombay. To avoid the north-east monsoon Rainier took most of his ships around to the western coast of India which meant that, by November, he could present all the vessels requiring repair at Bombay. Of course the dockyard was not specifically available for Rainier – there were many of the Company's ships to be repaired and built. Therefore he had to ensure the support of dockyard officials in order for his ships to have priority. This meant again that he had to be on good terms with this organisation which was vital to him. The shipbuilders themselves were Parsees from northwest India. They were excellent craftsmen and Rainier praised their skills to the Admiralty, comparing them positively to the British dockyard workers. He recommended that they be given a contract to build ships for the Royal Navy, which was finally agreed. He also recommended to the Company itself that the shipbuilders be given more pay and a grant of land in Bombay. Naturally these actions ensured smooth cooperation with the navy.

The Victualling Board was the primary provider of food and drink for the navy on other stations but, apart from victuals brought out from Britain on their initial journeys, vessels on the East Indies station had to obtain their supplies locally. Rainier inherited a contract to supply victuals at the main bases on the station agreed by his predecessor, Cornwallis, and the Honourable Basil Cochrane. From an organisational point of view it was usual on all remote stations to appoint an Agent Victualler, reporting to the flag officer, who managed the suppliers of victuals. But Rainier discovered an illicit arrangement between Cochrane and the Agent Victualler which gave them pecuniary benefit from certain contracts. Rainier fired the latter but only threatened Cochrane with termination of contract. Probably realising that to replace Cochrane would involve him in a great deal of extra work which he could not afford, he thought he could ensure an honest and efficient supply of victuals by taking over the role of Agent Victualler himself and keeping a close eye on his contractor. This he did by letters of complaint about quality and non-delivery. From a modern audit point of view this was not a good idea as it laid the admiral open to questions of corruption and impropriety and the Navy Board spent much time and effort checking the accounts of both men.

Rainier's decision did, however, result in a steadily improving victualling system. The stream of complaints from the admiral became less frequent and Cochrane's organisation developed to handle the increased size of the squadron and its expansion from Canton in the east to Jeddah on the Red Sea. Some captains were even able to write to Rainier that they were supplying the Company's army with victuals which had none of its own. The success of the contract was threatened in 1803 when the Admiralty ordered Rainier to terminate Cochrane's contract and re-tender it. In the event only one other person tendered and his offer was more expensive. Therefore Cochrane was re-appointed and clearly the results were so acceptable that Rainier was able to write to Cochrane that he had not heard from the Victualling Board for fourteen months.[11] The continuity of the contract enabled Cochrane to invest in his own infrastructure and he spent much money on building warehouses, breweries, transport ships, even a canal in Madras, all of which were more factors enabling the navy to be well fed and supplied across the region.

The two men grew to be close friends although this did not stop Rainier from looking for improvements. For example, he told one captain to obtain better water casks than those he had obtained in Madagascar and recommended to Cochrane another baker he had discovered. Such was Rainier's enthusiasm that was even writing to the Victualling Board after he had retired telling them of new methods of preserving beef.

Rainier's return to England in 1805 was followed in 1806 by Cochrane. Both men had made fortunes and the Navy Board delved deeply into their accounts, asking for copies of receipts going back to 1794. As already noted, Rainier had received an imprest and now Cochrane had one for £1.4 million. Cochrane vigorously fought the charge and it took fourteen years for his accounts to be cleared. No proof was ever found that either man had been involved in corruption and the Navy Board was happy to present Rainier's

---

[11] TNA, ADM 1/175, Rainier to Cochrane, 7 March 1804.

recommendations to the Board of Enquiry concerning the future organisation of naval supplies and victualling the East Indies, and Cochrane was presented to the king in 1820 by the incorruptible Admiral Lord Keith. It is highly unlikely that either of these events would have occurred if there were the slightest hint of wrongdoing. That Rainier managed to build up a close relationship with such a complex and difficult man as Cochrane once again indicates Rainier's skill in bringing out the best in the people with whom he had to work.

The Financial Manager

Rainier's success in capturing Malacca and the Dutch Spice Islands in 1796 encouraged British merchants to expand their activities into the hitherto inaccessible islands of the Dutch East Indies. There was also a natural increase in trade between India and China in such items as cotton and opium. This activity, known as the Country Trade, had been practised for centuries by the local inhabitants, and because the Company did not participate in it, private British traders joined in enthusiastically. British and Indian merchants and bankers established a number of agency houses, such as Jardine Matheson, to finance both the cargoes and the ships necessary to carry them. Often the trade was illegal and the participants did not want to have large amounts of cash. They therefore wished to transfer their profits home in the form of bonds or bills of exchange and these bonds were provided by both the Company and the navy.

Because of the trade imbalance between Britain and China and India there was always a shortage of specie in the region and this was exacerbated by Wellesley's wars against the Indian princes. Consequently Rainier was always short of cash to buy all those items needed to keep his squadron at sea. He also needed to give cash to his captains as they sailed for remote areas of the station in order that they could purchase their own supplies. He was sent navy bonds from London at a fixed percentage interest rate to be redeemed in London at a certain date in the future. These vehicles were ideal for transmitting wealth back home without the risk of shipping actual money, but they were naturally sold at a discount. This percentage varied, dependent on the current state of war in India, the trading profits being made, and other demands for cash. Occasionally there were no takers at all and on one occasion Rainier had to ask Lord Bentinck, the President of Madras, if the Company could lend him £20,000 as no one would buy his bonds and he needed the money to keep the squadron at sea.[12]

---

[12] NMM, RAI/4, Rainier to Bentinck, 2 April 1804.

It should also be remembered that Rainier's station was not one on which Europeans could impose their own pre-eminent culture. The region consisted of several sophisticated cultures that had been in existence for centuries. This fact was nowhere better demonstrated than in the realm of finance where not only did Rainier have to acquire money in alien but highly developed markets but he had to do so in multiple currencies; the Chinese tael, the Dutch rix dollar, the Spanish dollar, the Madras star pagoda, and the rupees and sicca rupees of Bombay, Bengal and Madras, each of different value. He even engaged in currency speculation, on one occasion telling Cochrane to buy forward star pagodas as he expected their value to increase.[13]

Communications and Intelligence

Rainier's understanding of the importance of communication – with the Company's officials and officers, with the navy in London, and with his captains across the station – has already been noted. But communication was also vital in order that he could send and receive intelligence so as to allocate his resources optimally. This function can be reviewed in two parts; communication and intelligence within the station and between the East Indies and London.

Within the station virtually all communication was carried by sea. The absence of roads in India and the danger of attack meant that even between Bombay, the port of entry from Europe, and Calcutta, the governor general's residence, mail would be sent around the coast. The news of the outbreak of war in 1803 took about two months to travel between the two cities, a distance of roughly 2,600 miles. The sea journeys from Calcutta to Canton and from Madras to Manila are approximately 6,000 miles and, depending on the wind, could take three months or more. Clearly Rainier had to delegate decision making to his local senior officers whom he had trained to act with care. Neither was Rainier a commander wont to remain in one place. He understood that to be effective and to know what was happening locally, he had to see for himself. He could be in Bombay, repairing his ships and watching events in the Red Sea, he could be off Madras or Trincomalee, he could be in the Straits of Malacca or off Batavia, protecting the trade, or he could be in Canton negotiating with the Chinese authorities. An example of the difficulty of reaching the admiral can be found when Rear Admiral Edward Pellew arrived to replace him. Pellew first went to Madras to be told Rainier was at Penang. There then followed three journeys, each of 1,500

---

[13] NMM, RAI/6, Rainier to Cochrane, 28 September 1798.

miles, as they passed each other sailing between the two cities, before they finally met.[14]

Mail would normally be sent on Bombay Marine or naval vessels if it were urgent, by East Indiaman or regular merchant ship if not. Neutral vessels were sometimes entrusted with the mail if no British ones were available. Whatever method was used, Rainier was dependent on it to bring him information as to the whereabouts of enemy warships and privateers and what was in the mind of the governor general. Intelligence would also come to him from the various Company agents scattered around the region as to what was happening in their particular territory.

The Admiralty had a particular problem in communicating with Rainier. Messages were usually sent 'overland', i.e., through the Mediterranean to what is now Syria and then down the Euphrates via Baghdad and Basra and then by sea again to Bombay. Occasionally the mail would go from Alexandria to Suez and then down the Red Sea to Bombay, but politics and religion made this route less reliable than that through Basra. The average journey time between London and Bombay was three months. In case of loss, the sea route round the Cape to Bombay or Madras was used for duplicate or even triplicate mails. This journey would normally take six months, or, in a fast warship with favourable winds, four months. A warship would only be used if it were already intended to make the journey, the cost otherwise being too great. Nevertheless, the overland route was still expensive; in 1801 a letter from Bombay to London cost almost £800.[15]

As already noted, Rainier could be anywhere within his station, so once the letter reached Bombay it still had to find him, which could several more weeks. Thus the time taken for messages to meet their intended recipient was so long that the situation could have completely changed and sending specific orders was pointless. The Board had to trust that Rainier had sufficient experience, intelligence and wariness of risk that he would not endanger British interests. If a mistake caused the loss of naval capability then the time period between its occurrence, getting the news to Rainier, him writing to the Admiralty, its decision to fit out and send replacements, and their final arrival on station, would take a minimum of twelve months. This factor gave Rainier's command a unique status as being one of almost complete independence with the requirement of weighty leadership and managerial responsibility. He was on his own. In case of serious difficulty he could ask for assistance from the Company but this would not automatically be forthcoming. To a certain extent it would depend on the relationships that Rainier had built up with the

---

[14] TNA, ADM 1/174, Pellew to Admiralty, 11 December 1804.
[15] C. H. Philips (ed.), *The Correspondence of David Scott relating to Indian Affairs, 1787–1805*, Vol.1 (London, 1951), p. 126.

controllers of the powerful resources that the Company had at its disposal. The usually positive nature of these relationships demonstrates that Rainier was an effective proponent of that rare skill, the ability to manage those over whom one has no authority. The correspondence between the admiral and the governor general, the presidents of Madras and Bombay, and the senior army officers illustrates a care to maintain this vital rapport.

Conclusion

In order to achieve his goals Rainier had to manage to the optimum his two major resources of manpower and ships. With limited possibilities of replacement crews he treated his men in a manner that would be seen as perfectly reasonable in the twenty-first century and he provided them with victuals and health care as effectively as possible at that time. To use modern terminology, he also coached and trained his officers so that they could perform effectively. He cared for his vessels by obtaining the best available naval supplies from Britain and within the station and creating an infrastructure that could manage them. The obvious benefit of the Bombay dockyard was also employed to the maximum benefit by careful management of relationships with its officials.

The East Indies Station was unique, however. Its distance from London and its extent of 30 million square miles made communication and control – two vital elements of management – exceedingly difficult. Rainier and his captains had to operate independently and have the maturity and intelligence to do so. The East India Company heavily influenced what Rainier could and should do. He needed its resources and it needed the navy to protect the trade and support Wellesley's conquest of India. The assiduous care with which Rainier managed these relationships indicates a sensitive man who understood how to ensure cooperation from those whom he needed, but over whom he had no control. That trade grew in this period when French naval power was still important, that British influence in India and the region also grew, and that Rainier did not lose a single ship to enemy action during his eleven long years in command, indicates that here was a highly competent manager of both men and materials who would not be out of place as a manager in a large twenty-first-century organisation.

2

'Neglect or Treason': Leadership Failure in the Mid-Eighteenth-Century Royal Navy

Richard Harding

The traditional history of the Royal Navy is a history of heroes. Long before the emergence of professional naval history, the purpose of the past was, explicitly, to instruct the present in preferred modes on conduct. From Jesuit education to classical education, the story of great deeds provided the content, narrative structure and purpose of history. With the emergence of modern history schools in the last quarter of the nineteenth century, the central role of hero retained its hold on naval and military history. For most of the time since, the idea of leadership has been associated with the heroic central character, whose personality and capability is the determining factor in a critical situation. This is not surprising given the dominating purpose of this history in the education of the officer corps.

Even today, the heroic leader remains a powerful element within historical studies. While behaviour to be emulated is more contested today, the hero, or central character, remains a focus around which the world of the past can be understood and brought to a human scale. Whether in literature, biography or history (actual or counter-factual), personality, good or evil, engages the reader more easily than long past impersonal 'systems'. The power of Horatio Nelson, two hundred years after his death, to generate books, documentaries, dramas, societies and, ultimately, international commemoration, is testimony to the influence of heroes in the modern world.

While the cult of celebrity or personality imposes a dangerous distortion upon history, heroes play an important role in any society. Those who have achieved great things may exhibit behaviours and judgements that can inform and inspire the present day. Even heroic failures, such as Nelson's opponents at the Battle of Trafalgar, can achieve this. It properly commemorates the success of the victor and attributes such as courage, fortitude and loyalty in the vanquished. It does, however, carry with it dangers.

The accolade of heroic leadership is generally conferred on the individual after the event by the public. There are many reasons why this might happen and many modes by which it occurs. However, it is common for the precise relationship between any hero and the events in which he or she is embedded rapidly to become obscured in the fog of myth and legend. One of the important contributions of the bicentenary commemorations of the Battle of Trafalgar was to provide the forum for historians of many nations to strip away the accretion of national myth that had gathered around the event in two hundred years.

It is unusual for great leaders of the heroic mould to emerge from detailed analyses of events. In a military or naval context, the quality of leadership is usually judged in terms of operational outcomes. These outcomes are the result of a complex network of arrangements and decisions, at various stages in the conflict situation, all undertaken, inspired and overseen by leaders. Over the last half century, as analytical techniques, such as operations research and systems analysis, have progressed, so our understanding of these complex networks has produced more sophisticated explanations of success and failure, in which the heroic leader now shares acclaim with other leaders, whose leadership was important, but whose role was obscured by lack of drama or the needs of contemporary security.[1]

An interesting question emerges from this: how has this new organisational knowledge influenced our understanding of the eighteenth century? Most obviously, the emergence of 'new naval history' in the 1960s, and a little later studies of the 'fiscal-military state' which focused attention on administration, economics, and particularly taxation, have provided valuable insights into the infrastructure of naval and military organisations within which the leaders operated. There continues to be a healthy and valuable stream of research output emerging from these origins, but we still have a long way to go to understand fully the contribution of the sub-ministers, officials, financiers and merchants who led and managed these contributions.[2]

---

[1] One of the clearest examples of this is the role of Alan Turing and the other codebreakers at Bletchley Park during the Second World War, whose contribution to the Allies' success was not known to the public until 1974 and remains a contested area of historical research.

[2] The work of Daniel Baugh, David Syrett, Roger Knight and Roger Morriss is particularly noteworthy and new work covering dockyards and victualling continues to appear. The colonial history of British North America has been well served by the long-standing interest in the colonial system. More recent interest in state expenditure and military effectiveness in Europe is spreading the understanding of the structures of decision-making and influence. See, for example, C. Storr (ed.), *The Fiscal-Military State in Eighteenth Century Europe* (Farnham, 2008); H. V. Bowen and A. González Enciso (eds), *Mobilising Resources for War: Britain and Spain at Work during the Early Modern Period* (Barañáin,

Also, over the last forty years, modern studies of leadership based on social scientific methods have also provided other potential insights into leaders' behaviour, which historians are beginning to explore. However, these leadership studies sometimes pose as many problems as they answer. Their focus is usually on general aspects of the behaviour, attributes or personality of the individual leaders. The specific context provides the important stimuli that influence behaviour, but otherwise plays a generally subordinate or passive part in the explanation of events. In this respect so many of these studies serve biography better than history in that, like the traditional studies of heroic leaders, the leader is abstracted from the context.[3]

While these studies have not, generally, explicitly linked leadership performance with the capabilities existing in organisational infrastructures, they do however expand the basis for understanding the complex network within which the leader operated. This complex network can be illustrated by the great hero, Horatio Nelson. At a very personal level, Nelson's leadership depended on his own beliefs and values, influenced and moderated at any time by his state of mind and health. Nelson before Trafalgar was very different from the Nelson who commanded in the Bay of Naples in 1798 after the Battle of the Nile.[4] Beyond Nelson were the officers and crews of his squadron. Not only were their relations with Nelson important, but equally important were the physical and psychological conditions aboard each vessel which impinged on discipline, efficiency and effectiveness. Further out in this network was Nelson's relationship with the professional heads of the service. St Vincent, while not First Lord in 1805, played a particularly important role in promoting Nelson's self-confidence and continued to represent the professional ethic of the Royal Navy. The political leadership of the navy and the linkages Nelson had with the government itself were other important factors in providing Nelson with the context within which he could lead. There was also the broader naval administration, which provided the structure within which his squadron operated. Work that has been done on dockyards and

---

2006); R. T. Sánchez (ed.), *War, State and Development. Fiscal-Military States in the Eighteenth Century* (Barañáin, 2007)

[3] More recent studies of the context of leadership performance are correcting this bias. See, for example, D. van Knippenberg and M. A. Hogg (eds), *Leadership and Power: Identity Processes in Groups and Organizations* (London, 2003). For an example of how causal factors can be prioritised differently according to focus, compare K. Grint, *Leadership, Management and Command; Rethinking D-Day* (London, 2008) and R. A. Hart, 'Feeding Mars : Logistics and the German Defeat in Normandy', *War and History* 4 (1996), 418–35.

[4] Similarly, the decline of Napoleon's mental powers between Austerlitz and Waterloo have played an important role in the historiography of his career.

victualling over the last twenty years has given us a good understanding of the robustness and reach of the British naval infrastructure by 1805.

Last, but not least, there was public opinion itself, which operated on all levels of the network. At least from the early years of the eighteenth century, senior naval officers had directly appealed to public opinion by their own publications, as part of managing their relationship with the crown and society.[5] By 1805 a commander like Nelson was able to fashion his own relationship with the British public. This was not the case with most officers, whose influence on public opinion was far more limited and who felt the impact of public opinion far more often as a representative of a group, the naval officer corps. Thus, it was not just the individual or groups that formed the 'nodes' of the network that were important, but the nature of the connections between them that influenced both Nelson's leadership and the effectiveness of the network as a whole.

Furthermore, operational success depended upon far more than the direct relationship of leader and organisational context. The nature of the operational problem to be confronted was critical. The problem largely consisted of the task to be carried out and the quality of the opposition to be faced. The effectiveness of the opposition was likewise constrained or supported by the quality of its own leadership networks. To be able to understand both sides of the hill is the objective for any naval historian, albeit one that is wished more often than it is achieved. For contemporaries, their ability to appreciate the real operational problem and act upon that appreciation was essential and highlights the need to focus more attention on the command, control, communications and intelligence systems at all levels of the leadership network.

To describe the effectiveness of leadership as the result of a network is not to diminish the importance of the leader or the human contribution in the network. A dynamic network in which all variables can alter, and have an influence upon the whole makes leaders and leadership at all points central to the success of the operational task. Their task is far more complicated and the demands placed upon their capabilities more extensive than if warfare is conceived as a form of chess between opposing commanders. One only

---

[5] See, for example, Sir Hovenden Walker's *Journal or Full Account of the Late Expedition to Canada*, published in 1720. Another example is the pamphlet literature that accompanied the failure of the expeditionary force sent to the Spanish West Indies, 1741–2, and that arising from the battle off Toulon in February 1744. In 1778/9, after Admiral Augustus Keppel's failure to secure a decisive victory at the Battle of Ushant (24–27 July 1778) the dispute between him and his second in command, Vice Admiral Sir Hugh Palliser, spilled over into a full-blown political dispute in Parliament. See J. A. Davies, 'An Enquiry into Faction among British Naval Officers during the War of the American Revolution' (unpublished MA dissertation, University of Liverpool, 1964).

has to substitute Nelson for another officer, for example Sir Robert Calder, and one can see a whole range of changes in the relationships and a whole series of possibilities as to why Calder's clash with the Combined Fleet in July 1805 was both different in outcome and differently received by the public, the government and the navy itself. On the other hand, not all parts of the leadership network had to act perfectly in order to achieve dramatic operational success. As Michael Duffy has pointed out in his work on the performance of individual ships at Trafalgar, not all displayed the same Nelsonic zeal.[6] Individual leaders do make a difference, but equally important is the cumulative impact of leadership at different levels in the eventual shift in the chances of operational success.

Thinking of leadership as existing within a network also encourages the historian to look at the other side of conflict – failure as much as victory. Examining victories and the causes of victories has been the traditional role of naval history, for it was here that the useful lessons of the past may be found.[7] From the nineteenth-century penchant for the fundamental moral codes of heroes to Mahan's great exposition on the *Influence of Sea Power on History*, it was the victors whose history was told. The essential personal moral qualities or the fundamental principles of naval war were found in victory. The vanquished could usually be assumed to have lacked the moral fibre or appropriate attention to the ineluctable principles of Sea Power of their foes.

Thankfully, this is changing, but it is still very strong in contemporary naval history. It is the successful campaigns and commanders that attract the greatest attention, as if the lessons or interest of a conflict can be found only in that context. Too little attention is paid to the failures. Until the mid nineteenth century, very little contemporary attention was paid to detailed analyses of either success or failure, and even then, it was politically difficult to draw lessons from them. Consequently, for the historian, the survival of evidence regarding success and failure relies heavily on serendipity. Our analyses rely on contemporaries' personal epistolary preferences, their need to defend or make reputations, and the acclaim or condemnation from third parties.

A consequence of the tendency to focus on successful leaders and the evidence that surrounds them is to produce a direct contrast with their contemporaries. A good example of this is William Pitt the Elder. Pitt, like Nelson, was a consummate self-publicist. Pitt's political survival depended upon his ability to project himself as the voice of House of Commons. Pitt's rhetoric reflected the deeply held political and diplomatic assumptions of

---

[6] M. Duffy, "All Was Hushed Up": The Hidden Trafalgar', *Mariner's Mirror* 91 (2005), 195–215.
[7] There are exceptions to this. See, for example, E. Cohen, 'Military Misfortunes', *Military History Quarterly* (1990), 106–12.

the political nation; the efficacy of British naval power, unwavering hostility to Catholic, absolutist France and deep suspicion of Hanover. Throughout his career Pitt had to trim this rhetoric to enable him to work his way into government and maintain himself there. In government from 1757, he shared with the Duke of Newcastle and the Old Corps Whigs the conduct of a great war against France. In 1759, the Year of Victories, the war decisively moved in Britain's favour. The French navy was crushed. Quebec and Guadeloupe were taken. Over the next two years, Montreal and most of the French West Indian and East Indian Empire fell to British forces. Pitt took the lion's share of the credit for this and his colleagues, by comparison, were presented as less effectual followers of the great war leader. Pitt, whose talent supposedly brought down the empires of France and Spain, had to share some of the glory with the officers he had brought on, such as Anson, Hawke, Saunders and Wolfe. But the Pitt legend credited him with having created a new atmosphere in the navy and the army which brought these officers to a new pitch of effectiveness. By extension, those leaders who went before Pitt (and succeeded him) had allowed both services to languish.

With this interpretation of mid-eighteenth-century war policy, perhaps the nadir of British naval power was the period between 1742 and 1745. In the hands of ineffectual ministers like the Duke of Newcastle and Earl Carteret, British policy lacked the drive and focus that Pitt gave it in the 1750s. Worse still, the direction of the navy was in the hands of the Earl of Winchelsea, who presided as First Lord over 'one of the most incompetent Boards of Admiralty that have ever held office'.[8] Certainly, it is an easy conclusion to draw. The evidence of the collapse of leadership is real enough. In 1739–40 there were great hopes of quick and easy victory against Spain by decisive naval action in the West Indies, but this had come to nothing. In 1741/2, after the outbreak of the War of Austrian Succession (1740–1748), there were expectations that British naval power would hold the ring in the Mediterranean, protecting Austrian interests in Italy and encouraging Sardinian participation in a war against France and Spain. Although there were important successes, the policy foundered. Throughout there was an expectation that the Royal Navy could dominate the waters of the English Channel and the Western Approaches, but by February 1744, a French fleet had ventured into the Channel to cover an invasion of Britain from Flanders. In the same month, the Mediterranean squadron failed to inflict decisive damage upon the combined Franco-Spanish squadrons off Toulon.

That this was owing to the political leadership also has support from the archives. Winchelsea left very little correspondence, Carteret left little beyond

---

[8] H. W. Richmond, *The Navy in the War of 1739–48*, 3 vols (Cambridge, 1920), II, 145.

his official papers, Newcastle left extensive papers. All of these could be used to support the presumption of incompetent leadership. Winchelsea doubted his own abilities to act as First Lord and the Newcastle papers show that the duke faced great difficulties and anxieties in managing the war. Once in office, Carteret's papers suggest that he had little interest in, or understanding of, naval policy. The evidence of newspapers, parliamentary debates and pamphlets also support the conclusion that Britain was suffering from the collapse of naval and political leadership. However, when we look at this undoubted collapse in British naval leadership through the idea of a leadership network, the reasons for the collapse seem more nuanced than the traditional explanation based on individual incompetence suggests.

A brief outline of events gives an idea of the scale of the collapse and the causes ascribed by contemporaries. In October 1739 Britain declared war upon Spain. It was the latest twist in an Anglo-Spanish dispute over freedom of navigation in the West Indies that had rumbled on since the end of the War of Spanish Succession in 1713. Britain declared war largely because the nation and the ministry were convinced that British naval power would soon force Spain to a satisfactory peace. Part of this confidence was drawn from the example of naval leaders like Drake and Blake in previous centuries.[9] In the eyes of the British public, Spain depended upon the silver brought from Mexico and New Grenada, the Spanish navy was no match for the Royal Navy and, man for man, the Spanish seaman was no match for his British counterpart. The perceived operational problem was not great and the opposition not powerful. Thus the flow of silver could easily be cut off by naval action. This view was shared by the public, the professional leadership of the navy and the ministry.

Initially expectations were met. In March 1740, news arrived that Vice Admiral Edward Vernon had captured Porto Bello, on the isthmus of Panama, making good the claim he had made in the House of Commons over six years earlier that this port vital to the silver trade could be taken by six British ships. Very soon, however, the illusion of easy victory evaporated. Spain did not sue for peace. The stubborn action of a Spanish 70, the *Princessa*, which it took three British ships of similar size to subdue in April 1740, suggested the Spanish seaman was a far tougher opponent that popularly imagined, which raised niggling doubts about the presumed superior capability of the officers and men of the Royal Navy.

In October 1740 the great expedition to the West Indies departed and attention was focused on the expected collapse of Spanish resistance. That wait was made more anxious by the outbreak of a major war in Europe over

---

[9] *Gentleman's Magazine*, March 1738, p. 152; March 1739, p. 24; June 1740, pp. 301–7.

the Austrian Succession, but political opinion in Britain still held that victory in the West Indies, combined with support from the Royal Navy for the Austrians defending Italy against Spanish ambitions, would end the Spanish war and fulfil British obligations to Austria. Disturbingly, the navy seemed to fail to perform. British ships failed to stop a squadron from El Ferrol or the French squadron from Brest getting out into the Atlantic, bound for the West Indies. Admiral Haddock's squadron in the Mediterranean failed to prevent the Cadiz or Toulon squadrons also sailing for the Caribbean.

By mid 1741 the navy seemed stretched. Haddock had too few ships in the Mediterranean to watch Cadiz, Cartagena and Toulon. The Admiral of the Fleet, Sir John Norris, confirmed that he did not have a squadron available in home waters, should the French, whose Brest and Toulon squadrons had returned from the West Indies, declare war on Britain.[10] On 18 June 1741 news arrived in London that the expedition to the West Indies had been driven from Cartagena de las Indias. Although the reasons were unclear, Admiral Vernon's robust condemnation of his army colleagues, at least temporarily shifted blame away from the navy. In November 1741 another unexpected event occurred – 14,000 Spanish troops left Barcelona under a small Spanish escort force and arrived in Italy to attack the Austrian forces without being intercepted by Haddock.

When Parliament assembled on 1 December 1741, the naval failures provided the key to the opposition attacks on Walpole's management of the war. The initial reaction was not to blame the navy, but to seek the reason in Sir Robert Walpole's underhand policies. A long established thread of opposition rhetoric was Walpole's supposed subservience to the interests of Hanover, and even France. Their explanation of the naval failures was that they were intentional. Admiral Vernon had not been reinforced after his capture of Porto Bello. The West Indian expedition had been badly organised and led by an inexperienced general, with the intention that it should fail. British admirals had spent the year 'dancing about the sea like the master of a packet boat and another keeping his station to let loose Spain upon Hungary'. Haddock was under orders to let the Spaniards pass on their way to Italy, in exchange for French promises not to invade Hanover.[11] This was untrue, but the ministry could not explain why the navy had performed so badly. The traditional address of thanks passed the House of Lords, but in the Commons a clause thanking the King for the conduct of the war against Spain was given up without a vote.[12]

---

[10] British Library (BL), MS Add. 28133, f. 82, 27 May 1741.
[11] W. Cobbett, *Parliamentary History*, 12 (1741–1743), col. 225, 4 December 1741.
[12] *Ibid.*

In February 1742 Walpole fell from office and for a brief period confidence that the war would be vigorously prosecuted and thus successful returned. The Duke of Newcastle remained in office, but he was joined by Carteret, whose attacks on Walpole's incompetence and promises of a 'British' war encouraged confidence. Instead, it went from bad to worse. On 17 December 1741 Haddock had failed to intercept the Cadiz squadron making its way up towards Barcelona and then failed to stop that squadron, along with the Toulon squadron, escorting another Spanish army to Italy in January.[13] Reinforcements were sent out to the Mediterranean, but failed to intercept the combined Franco-Spanish squadron. Haddock was relieved of his command and replaced by Vice Admiral Thomas Mathews. Although the number of ships in the Mediterranean was rising, Mathews soon proved to be a difficult commander. He continually warned the Admiralty that he needed more ships and that a defeat would rest upon their heads.[14] He fell out with his second in command, Richard Lestock, who had preceded him to the station.

By June 1742 news arrived in London from the West Indies that Vernon's attack on Panama had failed and it was decided to recall the remnants of that force. Initially, Vernon's explanation of the failure, placing blame upon the army, had been accepted, but by now there were serious doubts about Vernon's own capability.

The following year was fairly quiet as the Royal Navy gradually adjusted its dispositions from the West Indies to the Mediterranean, but in 1744 the disappointments were staggering. In February the Admiralty was caught out by the move of the Brest squadron up the Channel towards Dunkirk to cover a French invasion of Britain. Admiral Norris failed to catch that squadron before storms drove the French out of the Channel. Faith in the Admiralty and the navy was so shaken that at the height of the crisis a motion was made in the House of Commons for 'an immediate enquiry into the Conduct of the marine and the times of fitting out and sailing of the Brest squadron' because of 'a visible neglect and slowness in our naval affairs and a want of intelligence as to the designs and motions of the enemy'. Norris' conduct was defended by Vernon and the motion failed , but the credibility of the Admiralty had been seriously compromised.[15]

The really damaging events were occurring at about the same time in the Mediterranean, news of which arrived just over a month later. A battle off Toulon (11 February. 1744) had taken place between the combined Franco-Spanish squadrons and Admiral Mathews. Despite some serious damage

---

[13] National Archive (TNA), SP42/86, f. 493, Haddock to Newcastle, 1 February 1742.
[14] TNA, SP42/93, f. 2, Mathews to Newcastle, 23 March 1742.
[15] W. Cobbett, *Parliamentary History*, 13, cols. 645–6; BL, MS Add 35337, 15 February 1744.

being inflicted on the Spanish ships, not a single enemy ship was captured or destroyed. The Combined Fleet had escaped westward and Mathews had not pursued them. Worse still, Mathews reported that during the battle, his second in command, Richard Lestock, commanding the rear division, had not come up speedily in support. Mathews suspended Lestock and sent him home.

This was the beginning of a significant decline in public confidence in the Admiralty and the navy. On 16 April the ministry was surprised by a motion for a committee of enquiry to examine the 'miscarriages' of the navy.[16] The ministry gave way in the face of furious invective delivered by Admiral Vernon against the Admiralty and the Navy Board, but was able to let the matter die at the close of the session. Mathews continued to send his demanding and threatening despatches from the Mediterranean. In September rumours that the Brest squadron was again at sea near the Channel caused a fresh flurry of alarm.[17]

Despite the fall of Carteret and the removal of Winchelsea from the Admiralty at the end of November 1744, the bad news at sea continued. In January, Captain Thomas Griffin of the *Captain* (70) led a small force of three other ships off Ushant. They fell in with two French warships and a captured British privateer. Griffin quickly recaptured the privateer. After a chase of twenty-four hours, Captain Mostyn of the *Hampton Court* (70) got up with the French warships, but failed to press home an attack. To interested observers it looked like Griffin had taken the most powerful ship in his force to retake a privateer, while Mostyn had recoiled from engaging the enemy. Mostyn was acquitted at a court martial on the grounds that his ship was smaller than the Frenchman and he would have had to engage from the windward side, potentially disabling his lower tier of guns. Vernon was infuriated and called for another enquiry to answer a simple question: If 'ships meet others of equal force, as the weather is the same for both, Did you fight or did you not?'.[18]

Vernon was reflecting a changing mood. In 1744 the Commons had been reluctant to enquire into the navy and the maritime war. The maritime war commanded great support, partly based on the deeply held conviction that the Royal Navy was unbeatable. A year later the effectiveness of the navy and its officers was much more questionable. On 26 February another motion in the Commons to enquire into the battle of Toulon was presented and this time the mood was such that the ministry could not prevent it. The enquiry lasted

---

[16] BL, MS Add 35337, f. 73, 16 April 1744.
[17] TNA, SP44/226, unfoliated, Newcastle to the Admiralty, 22 September 1744.
[18] E. Vernon, *An Enquiry into the Conduct of Captain M----n* (London, 1745), p. 23.

from 12 March to 9 April in which claim, counter-claim, charge and counter-charge were exchanged as the enquiry widened from Lestock and Mathews to implicate six captains and the lieutenants of one ship. It ended with an address to the king to court martial all of them. It did not become a party issue. The navy was too deeply established as the bulwark of the nation and the concern was widely shared that 'such discredit has been brought upon His Majesty's arms, the honour of the Nation Sacrificed and such an opportunity lost of doing the most important service to the Common Cause'.[19]

As the preparations for the courts martial progressed, Britain was rocked by other events. The defeat of the allied army at Fontenoy in early May effectively ended any hope of making gains in Flanders. The landing of the Young Pretender in Scotland in July plunged Britain into a civil war that absorbed resources and energies until April 1746.

As the rebellion progressed the navy carried out its tasks effectively, but the legacy of the leadership crisis remained. In September Captain Henry Russane of the marines was sentenced to death for cowardice in an action in July. In September the courts martial relating to Toulon opened. The lieutenants were quickly acquitted. Two captains were found guilty of failing to do their utmost and cashiered (one permanently, the other at pleasure). Another was placed on half pay and the three others were acquitted. Lestock's trial opened in March and he was acquitted in June, but in October Mathews was found guilty of being the principal cause of the failure at Toulon and dismissed. The acquittals did little to restore public confidence in the navy. During this period, a court martial was held against Captain Cosby of the sloop *Amazon* for cowardice, but the charge was dismissed on the second day. His accuser, Captain Webb of the sloop *Jamaica*, was mulcted four months pay.[20] The navy seemed divided and driven by personal ambition and animosity. In December 1745, Admiral Vernon, one of the most respected voices in the public debate on the naval war, had been dismissed from command of the squadron in the Downs, and in April 1746, after he published his correspondence with the Admiralty, he was removed from the flag list. In May 1746 the president of the court martial on Lestock, Admiral Perry Mayne, was served a writ of trespass by Lieutenant Fry of the marines. Fry had been court martialed in the West Indies, found guilty, broken and sentenced to fifteen years imprisonment. This judgment was later remitted by the king and Fry set about suing the members of the court. The Admiralty was immediately alarmed that

---

[19] BL, MS Add 29512, f. 14, Vote of the House of Commons, 11 April 1745.
[20] *Gentleman's Magazine* (1746), p. 218.

senior officers would fear that participating in courts martial could expose them to civil actions in future.[21]

By the end of 1746 events in London and at sea were beginning to revive public confidence in the navy, but it did not occur quickly nor evenly.[22] The reasons for this change of sentiment lie outside the scope of this paper. It ended a period of five years, from 1741 to 1746, in which confidence in the leadership of the Royal Navy was on a trajectory of decline. The causes ascribed to the failure were, at one level, treason or subservience to Hanover. At another level it was cowardice, personal greed, malice, neglect and incompetence. The failures took place within the wider context of God's will.[23] Human action or will was paltry against God's will or Fortune's caprice, but it was human action that incurred God's wrath or pleasure. Success or failure, therefore, lay in the personal qualities or weaknesses of the individual. These qualities were moral as well as professional. Whatever the energies applied by Lestock and Mathews to their defence or the justice of their causes, their demeanour was an important element in the outcome of their cases. Mathews lost professional and political support during the enquiry in the House of Commons. His cause was further damaged by his apparent contempt for a witness whose testimony moved others and appeared important to his own case. This contrasted with Lestock's more modest behaviour throughout the enquiry and trial.[24]

The focus on personal failure was reinforced by the process of investigation. Enquiries were not neutral examinations of events, but the result of charges of misconduct. Acts of God and Providence had their places in judgments, but it was essentially an adversarial contest in which all parties found it important to place the blame elsewhere.[25]

---

[21] TNA, SP42/30, f. 365, Corbett to Dr Paul, 16 May 1746. See also BL, MS Add 35337, f.1, Thomas Birch to Philip Yorke, 24 May 1746

[22] Both Anson and Lestock were subject to criticism for their conduct at sea. See BL, MS Add 35397, f. 41, Thomas Birch to Philip Yorke, 8 October 1746; f. 43, Thomas Birch to Philip Yorke, 16 June 1747.

[23] J. C. D. Clark, 'Providence, Predestination and Progress; or did the Enlightenment Fail?', in D. Donald and F. O'Gorman (eds), *Ordering the World in the Eighteenth Century* (Basingstoke, 2006), pp. 27–62.

[24] BL, MS Add. 35397, f. 29, Thomas Birch to Philip Yorke, 20 September 1746. The code of conduct for a naval officer was not as highly developed as it was to become by the end of the century. Adam Nicolson's *Men of Honour: Trafalgar and the Making of the English Hero* (London, 2005), is an interesting exploration of the notion of honour, but is rather general about the concept as it applied to the first half of the eighteenth century.

[25] M. Gaskill, 'The Displacement of Providence: Policing and Prosecution in the Seventeenth and Eighteenth Centuries', *Continuity and Change* 11 (1996), 341–74. This is not

Thus, for contemporaries, leadership failure was located firmly in the behaviour or qualities of individuals. However, looked at differently, it is possible to see the period 1741–1745 as one in which the leadership network failed catastrophically. At the political level, Walpole's fading grip on the ministry proved irreversible. His removal from office and replacement by Carteret in February 1742 did not solve the political problem. Carteret quickly disillusioned those who thought that the war would now be fought more vigorously against France. He never managed to work effectively with Newcastle and the Old Corps Whigs who continued to dominate the political scene. At the professional level, Wager retired with Walpole and the appointment of Winchelsea as First Lord of the Admiralty alienated the professional leadership of the navy. Norris had long thought he should be First Lord. He refused to serve on the Admiralty Board under Winchelsea and until his retirement from active service in 1744 he co-operated with the Admiralty with great reluctance. Winchelsea could never compensate for the lack of professional confidence in him or his political weakness in the face of the Old Corps.

At the operational level, Mathews took advantage of Winchelsea's weakness and made no attempt to resolve a long-standing antagonism between himself and his second in command, Lestock. Neither professional nor political pressure could be placed upon Mathews to conform to the policy identified by the Admiralty as essential.

By the end of 1745 the leadership network of the navy had broken down. The fractured network exposed weaknesses at all levels of leadership. With a solid leadership network individual weaknesses could be absorbed or compensated for with major organisational or operational consequences. Without it, the operational failures are exposed and the search for responsibility more urgent. With the focus upon the individual and palpable, causes range from neglect and incompetence through to cowardice and treason.

The recovery of the leadership network during 1746–1748 is beyond the scope of this paper. Individuals were vital to the process. Anson's role was critical – he provided a vital link between the political and professional networks – however, he could not have done it alone. Other leaders played their parts. The Duke of Bedford as First Lord of the Admiralty from December 1744 was an important part of the political settlement that resolved the crippling differences between the Pelhams and the king that had gone on since early 1742. The importance of George II himself in coming to terms with the new political leadership cannot be overestimated.

---

to suggest that analysis of operations developed much more effectively in later centuries. See J. B. A. Bailey, 'Military History and the Pathology of Lessons Learned: the Russo-Japanese War, a Case Study', W. Murray and R. H. Sinnreich, (eds), *The Past as Prologue: The Importance of History to the Military Profession* (Cambridge, 2006), pp. 170–94.

It was not just that the British leadership network recovered in this period. There was a real shift in the operational problem facing the navy. The Bourbon navies, which had stretched the Royal Navy since 1740, were becoming exhausted. The shift in French strategy during 1745 towards a policy of convoy protection relieved pressure on the Royal Navy and the 1746 campaign to recover Louisbourg effectively broke the capability of the French navy to operate extensive oceanic campaigns. Meanwhile British naval resources continued to expand and consolidate; a process which had continued even during the years of leadership failure. By 1748 the Royal Navy had a material superiority over the Bourbon fleets which had been translated into two important naval victories (the First and Second Battles of Finisterre, in May and October 1747). Coincidentally, the failure of the land campaigns in Flanders after the Battle of Fontenoy in May 1745 strengthened the naval leadership network in that political and professional support for a naval war was consolidated.

Just as the naval failures of 1739–1745 produced villains, so the recovery of the leadership network in 1746–1748 produced heroes. Anson, Hawke, Boscawen and Warren were the key personalities for the public, but the network extended far beyond them to the junior officers, politicians, administrators and contractors, who brought the political and material resources to bear on the problem. The leadership network strengthened during the 1750s and remained intact until the crisis of 1778–9 brought shades of the earlier fragmentation.[26] It recovered very quickly and had reached a high point of solidity by 1805. Nelson's death was a blow to British morale but did nothing to shake the leadership network that linked the professional and political resources that underpinned British naval dominance.

The importance of the networks that linked professional service and leadership together, and what linked them to the political leadership and the wider public has not been fully appreciated in many histories. In the eighteenth century, success or failure was as much a moral judgement on the individuals concerned as it was a reflection of the complex situations in which they found themselves. Treason, neglect or incompetence followed from moral weakness or natural ineptitude and led to disaster, just as duty, honour and innate skill accounted for victory.[27] The nineteenth- and early-twentieth-century focus on the charismatic leader derived from slightly different origins, but had the

---

[26] Davies, 'An Enquiry into Faction'.

[27] Nelson's personal life and his success in war confounded some Evangelical contemporaries and nineteenth-century historians, but the eighteenth-century concept of military success and honour was associated with innate qualities and conformity to martial codes rather than personal morality. See, for example, Maurice de Saxe, *Reveries on the Art of War* (1757), T. R. Thomas (trans. and ed.) (New York, 2007), pp. 117–20.

same effect – the leader's personal qualities dominated the situation and the outcome. Looking at conflicts from the perspective of opposing networks, the leaders remain a vital element in any analysis of naval situations. Appreciating the complexity of the context only adds to our understanding of the qualities leaders had to show, where critical leadership qualities had to be shown and how deeply those qualities had to penetrate into the navies and the societies which they served.

LEADERSHIP AND ORGANISATIONAL FRICTIONS:
CONTESTED TERRITORIES

3

Who Has Command?
The Royal Artillerymen aboard Royal Navy Warships in the French Revolutionary and Napoleonic Wars

Gareth Cole

Warfare is much more than battles, operations, admirals and generals. This was as true in the long eighteenth century as it is today. Essential to any victory, either at sea or on land, are adequate and guaranteed logistics, a firm administrative structure and clear lines of command. This chapter will examine the latter two areas during the French Revolutionary and Napoleonic Wars. It is not possible to present a full study of these in one chapter so the case study of Royal Artillerymen serving on Royal Navy warships will be used to exemplify the larger issues.

In the period under examination the military forces of Great Britain had three different, and very distinct, command structures: there was the navy run through the Admiralty; the artillery and engineers run through the Office of Ordnance; and the army run through the Commander-in-Chief and the War Office. Each of these three departments needed to communicate and co-ordinate their actions if the British war effort was to succeed. However, the true story was far more complicated than this: food and drink for the officers and men was provided by the Victualling Board,[1] transport was provided by the Transport Board[2] and weaponry was provided by the

---

[1] See R. Knight and M. Wilcox, *Sustaining the Fleet 1793–1815: War, the British Navy and the Contractor State* (Woodbridge, 2010).
[2] Established under Treasury control in 1794. Prior to this each department had requisitioned its own transports, frequently bidding against each other and consequently raising the costs. David Syrett has written numerous works and articles on this, e.g.,

Office of Ordnance.[3] In addition, the Navy Board was also involved in fitting out warships when they were commissioned.

Each of these boards was involved when artillerymen served at sea. They were fed by the Victualling Board, although as will be shown they were not part of the official crew and so were carried as supernumeraries. The tenders on which they lived were requisitioned by the Transport Board; the bomb vessels (on which this chapter will focus) were fitted out by the Navy Board; they had the master-general of the Ordnance as their colonel-in-chief; and finally, the mortars they operated were only on board the bomb vessels because of orders given by the Board of Ordnance. Thus, three government departments and numerous boards within them had to communicate successfully to get all of the necessary men and equipment on board ship.

This chapter will focus on bomb vessels in particular because these were the vessels where the two services worked most closely together at sea. This was because, until the creation of the Royal Marine Artillery (RMA) in 1804, when mortars were fitted on board the bomb vessels it was Royal Artillerymen who manned them and not seamen or marines.[4] In fact, bomb vessels were the only warships on which artillerymen were stationed.[5] It was this close working arrangement that caused many of the problems examined in this chapter, the solution to which was the Royal Marine Artillery.[6]

One of the major issues addressed is in fact the title of this chapter. Who did actually have command of the artillerymen when on board ship? For obvious reasons naval vessels had a strict hierarchy with all naval personnel on board being under the command of the commander of the vessel. Orders were expected to be obeyed without question. As shall be seen, artillerymen did not always accept the orders of the commander, nor did they see why they should, and waited for orders from their own officer, who in the case of bomb vessel detachments was usually a lieutenant in the Artillery. In addition, the Office of Ordnance did not accept that their artillerymen could be punished under

---

D. Syrett, *Shipping and Military Power in the Seven Years War: The Sails of Victory* (Exeter, 2008).

[3] See, Gareth Cole, 'The Office of Ordnance and the Arming of the Fleet in the French Revolutionary and Napoleonic Wars, 1793–1815' (unpublished Ph.D. thesis, University of Exeter, 2008).

[4] On all Royal Navy vessels the cannon and carronades were manned by the crew of the vessel, both seamen and marines.

[5] The National Archives (hereafter TNA), ADM 1/4016. Crew to Nepean, 15 September 1803.

[6] For a full history of the Royal Marine Artillery, see E. Fraser and L. G. Carr-Laughton, *The Royal Marine Artillery 1804–1923* (London, 1930). Although a very useful work on the creation and history of the RMA it has become dated and a full, modern, work on the RMA is very badly needed.

naval law and this also caused much consternation and discussion between the two departments.

Before an analysis of the cases uncovered it is necessary to describe in some detail the chains of command of the two government departments involved: the Office of Ordnance and the Admiralty.

Ordnance and Naval Chains of Command

The Office of Ordnance was headed by the master-general who at this time also sat in cabinet and was usually a senior general. If he was absent, the Ordnance could be run by the Board of Ordnance which was constituted by five principal officers: the lieutenant-general, the surveyor-general, the clerk of the Ordnance, the principal storekeeper and the clerk of Deliveries. Below this leadership level were a number of subordinate offices and departments. As far as this chapter is concerned, the important lines of communication and authority are those that originated with the master-general. As well as being head of the Ordnance, the master-general was also the colonel-in-chief of the Royal Engineers and the Royal Artillery. Thus, these two corps could trace their line of authority up to him.

As regards the line of authority of the Royal Artillery, below the master-general as colonel-in-chief was the deputy adjutant general of Artillery, an office which was established in 1795 and held throughout the period discussed in this chapter by Lieutenant General Macleod.[7] The Commissioners of Military Enquiry questioned Macleod on 27 August 1811, asking him what his duties were. As part of his answer he stated that,

> The Deputy Adjutant General is the organ through which the Master General and the Board of Ordnance issue their Orders and Regulations for the Artillery Department, and his Office is the connecting point where the various and manifold details are collected and arranged into a Military system.[8]

In addition, and of interest to this chapter, he also dealt with the correspondence 'with the Officers commanding the Artillery Detached'. As will be shown later in this chapter when discussing particular examples, Macleod was an important cog in the chain of communication.

---

[7] Lieutenant-Fireworker 1762; Second Lieutenant 1771; Captain Lieutenant and Captain 1779; Major 1795; Deputy Adjutant-General and Lieutenant Colonel in the Army 1795; Lieutenant Colonel (RA) 1797; Colonel (Army) 1797; Colonel (RA) 1804; Major-General 1809; Colonel Commandant RA and Lieutenant General 1814.

[8] British Parliamentary Papers, *Seventeenth Report of the Commissioners of Military Enquiry* (1812 Vol. IV pp. 137–246), Appendix 12. p. 231.

As Richard Harding shows in the introduction to this book, there has been a large amount written about the administration of the Royal Navy. However, much of this has ignored the Ordnance/Admiralty relationship.[9] Although the Admiralty was the main point of contact for the Ordnance, it also corresponded with the other boards, particularly the Transport Board. As this was subordinate to the Treasury and not the Admiralty, the Ordnance needed to inform the Admiralty of what had been decided.[10] However, the Ordnance was not able to write directly to the Victualling Board asking for artillerymen to receive food and drink, these orders had to come from the Admiralty. Thus, in January 1800 when artillerymen were ordered on board two tenders at Woolwich, the Admiralty was asked 'to give immediate directions to the Commissioners of the Victualling to furnish the necessary supply of Provisions for the Detachments of Artillery ordered to embark'.[11] In addition, another tender had been ordered to sail but did not have 'any Provisions on board for the Detachment of Artillery'.

Communications to naval officers were, in theory, much clearer; the Admiralty was the only part of the hierarchy that gave orders to naval officers. However, as shall be seen later, this did not stop the Admiralty issuing different orders to junior officers than those they received from their fleet commanders.

Bomb Vessels and their Tenders

Royal Navy bomb vessels were generally commanded by naval commanders and when not used in their primary role of mortar vessels they were used as convoy escort vessels even though they were not ideally suited to this role. Nelson believed that 'The Bombs are neither fit by force or sailing to convoy a Water or Wine Transport and when the Strength of the Artillery Men is taken from them I think they had better go home with the Convoys'.[12] Although bomb vessels are perhaps best known for their mortars these were by no means their sole armament. Besides the two mortars, which can be seen to be their primary weapon, these vessels carried a variety of broadside

---

[9] See, for example, D. Baugh, *British Naval Administration in the Age of Walpole* (Princeton NJ, 1965) p. 4, which states explicitly that the Ordnance will not be examined.
[10] See, for instance, TNA, ADM 1/4016. Crew to Nepean, 26 November 1803, concerning magazine keys, where the Ordnance and Transport Boards had agreed a position and the Admiralty was informed of it.
[11] TNA, ADM 1/4015, Crew to Nepean, 17 January 1800.
[12] C. White (ed.), *Nelson: The New Letters* (Woodbridge, 2005), Nelson to Melville, 2 November 1804, pp. 303–4.

armament. For example, *Thunder* was armed with eight 24pdr carronades.[13] In contrast, *Vesuvius* was armed with eight 6pdr cannon.[14] The weakness of this armament was one reason why Nelson believed them to be so poor as convoy escorts.

In addition to differing armaments the bomb vessels also varied in size and lineage. Using the numbers quoted in Rif Winfield's *British Warships in the Age of Sail* we can see that the bomb vessels ranged in size. *Vesuvius*, a purpose-built vessel first commissioned in 1778, had dimensions of 91' 6" x 27' 8" as built with a crew of sixty (later seventy) and tonnage of 302. *Thunder* was a purchased vessel, originally named *Dasher* and built in Bideford in 1800, with dimensions of 111' 3" x 27' 10" and a tonnage of 383.[15] As can be seen, these were not large vessels. As they were small vessels they also carried a small crew. According to the muster book of HM Bomb *Thunder* on 7 May 1804 she had a crew complement of sixty-seven and carried seventeen supernumeraries for victualling purposes. Of these seventeen supernumeraries, twelve were the Royal Artillery detachment which consisted of one lieutenant, one sergeant, one bombardier, eight gunners and one carpenter.[16] Thus, the artillerymen were not seen as part of the crew. Macleod certainly did not see them as such, as can be seen when he informed Lieutenant Grant that he was to take 'the charge of the Detachment and Duty as Artillery Officer *attached* [italics added] to the Terror Bomb'.[17] It was not being part of the official crew complement of the vessels that caused a number of the problems described later in this chapter.

On the occasions when the bomb vessels were fitted with their mortars they were frequently accompanied by tenders. These smaller vessels (of no more than 150 tons) carried extra shells and ordnance stores and also, and particularly of relevance to this chapter, accommodation for the artillerymen. Although they were of use some admirals did not like the tenders to sail with the fleet as they were seen as bad sailors and slowed the fleet down.[18]

Of particular interest as regards the tenders is a letter dated 27 July 1798 from Robert Crew, Secretary to the Board of Ordnance, to Evan Nepean, Secretary to the Board of Admiralty, in which he enclosed a copy of the instructions that the masters of the tenders received. The master was expected to do a number of things. Firstly, he was to proceed 'to Woolwich were [*sic*] you are to receive and accommodate on board the Commissioned, non-

---

[13] R. Winfield, *British Warships in the Age of Sail, 1793–1817* (London, 2005), p. 374.
[14] Ibid., p. 372.
[15] Ibid., pp. 372 and 374.
[16] TNA, ADM 36/15884.
[17] TNA, WO 55/1072, Macleod to Grant, 21 August 1801.
[18] See, for example, TNA, ADM 1/4016, Crew to Marsden, 23 July 1804.

commissioned Officers and Private men of the Royal Artillery'. As regards the chain of command, the Master was 'to follow and obey all orders and directions that you may from time to time receive from the Officer Commanding the detachment of Artillery on board ... also such as you may receive from the Admiral or Commander in Chief with whom you sail'.[19] Interestingly, considering the explicit nature of these instructions, the instructions do not mention the commander of the bomb vessel. Presumably the Ordnance did not consider the Master to be under his control. The Admiralty also noticed the potential problems here and on the back of the letter is a minute asking Nepean to acquaint Crew that 'their Lordships think it essential the Commanding Officer of the Tender should also be directed to obey any directions he may receive from the Commander of the bomb to which he may be attached'. Unfortunately, it has not been possible to discover whether this amendment was in fact added to the official instructions.

The tenders which were attached to the bomb vessels were procured for the Ordnance through the Transport Board. For example, on 18 February 1801, Crew wrote to Nepean stating that the Ordnance had the previous day received a letter from the Admiralty stating that the *Explosion* was without a tender. The Admiralty requested that one 'might be prepared and attached to her as speedily as possible'. Crew was under instruction to inform Nepean that 'the Board of Ordnance have engaged another tender ....which is now preparing at Woolwich'.[20] On 24 July, the tender, *Rio Nova*, was returned to Sheerness 'in a very leaky condition'.[21] Three days later Crew again wrote to Nepean stating that 'as the *Explosion*'s tender is hired by the Transport Board the payment of the expences [sic] attending her repair will be made by that Board'.[22] As all the tenders were hired through the Transport Board it is a bit strange that the Ordnance needed to inform the Admiralty of this.

That the tenders were not under Admiralty control can be seen in a letter dated 1 August 1800 from Crew to Nepean in which he stated, 'I am sorry that I am not able to give you correct information regarding the present stations of the Tenders belonging to the Bomb Ships named in your letter, as I have no regular return of those tenders before me'. He could add, however, 'I can safely assert that where the Bomb Ships are and in a State for Service the tenders are there also'.[23] By 4 August, Crew had the information to hand and could inform Nepean of the following:

---

19 TNA, ADM 1/4015, Crew to Nepean, 27 July 1798.
20 *Ibid.*, 18 February 1801.
21 *Ibid.*, 24 July 1801.
22 *Ibid.*, 27 July 1801.
23 *Ibid.*, 1 August 1800.

Table 3.1. List of bomb vessels, their tenders
and their stations, 4 August 1800

Bombs	Tenders	Stations
Sulphur	*Bilboa* [sic]	Spithead
Explosion	*Speedwell*	Sheerness
Hecla	*Judith*	Sheerness
Zebra	*Maria*	Sheerness
Volcano	*Hexham*	Plymouth

Source: TNA, ADM 1/4015. Crew to Nepean, 4 August 1800

Command, Punishment and Accommodation

This section of the chapter will discuss three main issues affecting the lives of the artillerymen aboard the bomb vessels. Firstly, and perhaps most pertinent, who actually had command of the artillerymen whilst they were on board? Secondly, if the artillerymen did misbehave could they be punished under naval law? Thirdly, there was the problem of accommodation and how the men would be quartered.

It is important to make the distinction between the theoretical as well as the actual situation on board the bomb vessels. Obviously when the vessels were on station and away from higher authorities the distinction between theory and reality could get blurred. The situation was complicated by the fact that the mortars and associated stores were signed for by the Lieutenant of Artillery and thus were in his care. On other Royal Navy ships these stores were under the care of the gunner who was under the orders of the commander of the vessel.[24]

On 19 July 1803, Crew wrote to Nepean to state that the Master General and Board of Ordnance had been shown a letter from the Admiralty where they had confirmed that

> the Lords of the Admiralty had directed Lord Keith to explain to the Commanders of the Bomb Vessels that the Detachment of the Royal Artillery embarked on board them are not to be employed on any of the Duties of the said Bomb Vessels, excepting what may have relation to the care and management of the mortars on board them.[25]

This letter had arisen out of a query from the commander of HM Bomb

---

[24] See G. Cole, 'Royal Navy Gunners in the French Revolutionary and Napoleonic Wars', *Mariner's Mirror* 95:3 (2009), 284–95.
[25] TNA, ADM 1/4016, Crew to Nepean, 19 July 1803.

Discovery to Nepean on 11 July 1803. On asking the artillery officer on board *Discovery* 'to place part of his men as centinels [*sic*], he acquainted me he had been informed by the Officers of his Corps it was not customary, that his men did not come on board to do the duty of marines, but attend to the mortars'.[26] Interestingly, Captain Joyce had previously written to his superior officer, Lord Keith, 'who referred me to their Lordship's for Instruction'. From this example, it is clear to see that the Artillery officers were very clear on their rights and those of the men under their command. They saw themselves as separate from the naval hierarchy and they were willing to disobey the instructions of a naval commander to uphold that identity. The Artillery lieutenants may have known their rights, but it is clear that neither Joyce nor even Lord Keith, the fleet commander, were as sure of theirs. Their first instinct was to go right up the chain of command to the Lords of the Admiralty.

At this juncture it must be stated that it was not only on board ship that the artillery (and engineers) saw themselves as separate and distinct. The same issue had also arisen in the Leeward Islands where a Captain Waller had been asked to do garrison duties. In this instance, Waller had done the duties as requested of him and had 'made no remonstrance with Colonel Stewart, only slightly mentioned the matter, and perform what is required of me, waiting the General's order through you'.[27] Waller believed he was within his rights not to do garrison duty from an order that had been given at Gibraltar, through the War Office, in 1766. This very clearly stated that 'the Officers of the Royal Regiment of Artillery shall not be obliged to take any other share in the Garrison Duty, than what falls within their particular branch as Artillery Officers'.[28] Once again, an artilleryman knew what he was entitled to, in this instance from an order dated thirty-seven years previously.

The Artillery lieutenant on board *Perseus*, Lieutenant Holcombe, and the commander of the Bomb, Captain Mellish, do not seem to have had a happy or constructive relationship. On 29 August, Holcombe wrote to Crew to complain that Mellish had taken it 'upon himself to give directions respecting the Mortars without consulting me'.[29] This could have untoward consequences as Holcombe went on to explain in his letter. When *Perseus* was off Boulogne and preparing to engage the French that day

> the Captain dined on board the Commodore and left orders with his Lieutenant to get every thing ready to fire and the number of shells that he thought

---

[26] TNA, WO 55/1272, Captain Joyce to Nepean, 11 July 1803.
[27] *Ibid.*, Clinton to Hadden, 23 July 1803, enclosure Captain Waller to Major Wilson, 23 April 1803.
[28] *Ibid.*, Enclosure Signed by Barrington, 15 May 15 1766.
[29] TNA, ADM 1/4016, Holcombe to Crew, 29 August 1803.

proper ... I asked for some carcasses to be got ready, but as the Captain had given no order for them they could not be hoisted up on the return of the Captain which was about 25 Minutes before we commenced firing. [30]

Holcombe also had a complaint concerning post-action events. During the action, the bed of the 10-inch mortar was damaged and he reported it to Mellish, who reported it to the Commodore. The outcome of this was a surprise to Holcombe as 'a survey was held on it by order of the Commodore, by a Lieut [sic] and his carpenter without ever asking my opinion whether it could be repaired or not'. The bed had since been transferred to a hoy and taken to a place that Holcombe assumed was Woolwich but he could not give any 'certain intelligence'. As stated earlier, Holcombe would have signed for the mortar bed and he was particularly concerned that he 'could not get any Vouchers or Receipt for it'. A day later, Crew wrote to Nepean enclosing Holcombe's letter and suggesting 'to their Lordships the necessity of giving Instructions to the Commanders of His Majesty's Bomb Vessels to observe as much Delicacy as possible in regard to interference with the management of the mortars or the stores belonging to them'.[31] This case highlights one of the problems of having two chains of command ending on board the bomb vessels. Another problem was that of punishing artillerymen.

As is well known, on board a Royal Navy vessel of this time, men were frequently punished on board ship under naval law without recourse to outside arbitration. Unfortunately for the officers and men of the bomb vessels, the Royal Artillerymen did not see themselves as being under naval law (as in fact they were not) and in fact, as shown above, they saw themselves as very distinct from the naval hierarchy. So, in theory at least, they should not have been punished by the naval officers. Such instances did, however, occur and resulted in numerous complaints to the central departments.

One such case occurred in March 1804. On 24 March the Master General, Earl Chatham, wrote to the First Lord of the Admiralty, St Vincent, stating that

> Captain Paul of His Majesty's Ship Explosion had thought fit of his own authority to punish a gunner of the Royal Artillery. I have the fullest confidence, that your Lordship will take such steps, as shall appear to you most proper to prevent the repetition of a conduct which may in its consequences prove extremely embarrassing to His Majesty's Service.

St Vincent obviously agreed with Chatham as a note on the back of the letter dated 3 April states: 'Express his Lordship's extreme concern that a

---

[30] *Ibid.*
[31] *Ibid.*, Crew to Nepean, 30 August 1803.

circumstance of so unpleasant a nature should have occurred.'[32] On 25 March, John Markham, a Lord of the Admiralty, wrote to Keith (who was Paul's commander) that, 'I am sorry to hear that Capt. Paul has flogged an Artillery man. It is very unwise and a complaint is coming to us about it, and we shall be forced to take serious notice of it.'[33] Three days after this communication to Keith an official order was sent out to all the commanders of bomb vessels stating what was to happen in future when artillerymen misbehaved. This deserves to be quoted in full.

> Whereas we think fit, in order that a regard may be paid to the discipline of the Bomb Vessel you command, by the men belonging to the Royal Artillery, who may be embarked on board her, that in the event of any such men behaving themselves improperly, they shall be confined in such manner as is usual on board HM Ships; You are in case any of the said men should so behave themselves, as to render that measure necessary, hereby required and directed to confine them accordingly; taking care if the offence should be committed during the time the said Bomb Vessel should be employed on Home Service, to transmit to our Secretary the particular circumstances of such offence in order that a proper representation thereof may be made to the Board of Ordnance; But if the Offence should be committed during the time the Bomb Vessel under your command shall be employed abroad, you are in that case to transmit an account thereof to the Commander in Chief or senior officer of HM Ships employed on the station where you may happen to be, who will communicate the same to the General Officer Commanding HM Troops there, in order that the person or persons so offending may be tried for their conduct by a Court Martial.[34]

This situation is particularly interesting as Chatham, before becoming Master-General, had been First Lord of the Admiralty. One of the captains to whom this order was sent was Captain George Cocks of HM Bomb *Thunder* who, a few months later, was serving under Nelson's command in the Mediterranean.

On 13 May, Nelson wrote to the commanders of HM Bombs *Etna*, *Thunder* and *Acheron* (the bomb vessels under his command) that, 'it is my directions that the Artillery embarked on board the Bomb-Ships do, when in port, keep watch as sentinels, and, when at sea, in the same manner as the Ship's company'.[35] This situation had arisen because Nelson had not

---

[32] *Ibid.*, Chatham to St Vincent, 24 March 1804.
[33] C. Lloyd (ed.), *The Keith Papers: Selected from the Papers of Admiral Viscount Keith. Vol. III* (Navy Records Society, 1955), Markham to Keith, 25 March 1804, pp. 149–50.
[34] TNA, ADM 2/147, Order signed by Troubridge, Markham and Neale, 28 March 1804.
[35] Sir Nicholas Harris Nicolas (ed.), *Letters and Dispatches of Vice Admiral Lord Viscount Nelson Vol. VI* (London, 1846), Nelson to the Commanding Officers of HM Bomb Ships *Etna*, *Thunder* and *Acheron*, 13 May 1804, p. 15.

wanted tenders with the bombs as they were not adequate sailors to stay with the fleet. A few days later the problems become apparent. Cocks had confined James Braid of the Royal Artillery for disobedience of orders. When ordered by Cocks, Braid had replied, 'that he was ordered neither to pull nor haul till he received that order from his own Officer'. Nelson was undoubtedly surprised by this, especially considering his letter to the captains of the bomb vessels quoted above.[36] But, as already described, he should not have been, as the artillerymen were not to be 'employed on any of the Duties of the said Bomb Vessels'. By 19 May, Nelson had discovered that the artillery officers were 'entirely ignorant of the Act of Parliament for the regulation of his Majesty's Ships, Vessels, and Forces by Sea'. He directed Cocks (and the other bomb vessel commanders) to give a copy of the Act to the respective artillery officers so that they could not plead ignorance.[37]

On 22 May Nelson wrote to William Marsden, Secretary to the Board of Admiralty, about the situation.[38] In this communication, he makes clear that he believes there should only be one commander on board Royal Navy warships, thus the artillery officers should be subordinate to the captain of the vessel. Secondly, he states that this authority will be upheld by court martial if necessary, the results of such communicated to 'the Commander-in-Chief of the Army in the Mediterranean, in order that it may be laid before the King'. Nelson's frustration at the situation was made evident on 25 May when he wrote to St Vincent that

> There is no real happiness, my dear Lord, in this world: with all content and smiles around me, up start these Artillery boys; I understand they are not beyond that age, and set us all at defiance – speaking in the most disrespectful manner of the Navy and its Commanders.[39]

The problems continued into July when Nelson replied to Lieutenant Lane RA, serving on HMS *Thunder*, who had declared that he was,

> finding it totally impossible from the difference of orders sent ... by command of the Right Honourable the Earl of Chatham, Master General, and the Honourable Board of Ordnance, with the approval of the Lords Commissioners of the Admiralty, and those given by me [Nelson] to the Commanding-Officer of the Thunder, Bomb Vessel, to agree with him on your different branches of service, and to be responsible for the mortars and stores placed in your charge, by the Board of Ordnance, and comply with their orders in every respect.

---

[36] *Ibid.*, Nelson to Captain George Cocks, 17 May 1804, p. 22.
[37] *Ibid.*, Nelson to Cocks, 19 May 1804, pp. 23–4.
[38] *Ibid.*, Nelson to William Marsden, 22 May 1804, pp. 27–8.
[39] *Ibid.*, Nelson to St Vincent, 25 May 1804, pp. 33–4.

In other words, Lane was being told one thing by the Ordnance and Admiralty and another by the local naval commander. Nelson informed Lane that his (Nelson's) orders were to 'enforce due obedience to Superior Officers'.[40] The next day, Nelson informed Marsden of his belief that 'every Land Officer (whatever his rank may be) if embarked to serve on board Ship, should most implicitly conform to, and comply with, the orders of the Captain or Commander of each Ship or Vessel'.[41]

As stated above, it was the belief of both the Ordnance and the Admiralty that artillerymen should not be punished at sea under naval law. The message had clearly not got through to the Mediterranean Station as on 8 September 1804, William Thompson, an artillery gunner on board HMS *Thunder*, was punished with '2 dozen lashes for drunkenness'.[42] Even as late as November 1804 Cocks was punishing James Braid and Thomas Patterson with two dozen lashes and William Thompson with one dozen for neglect of duty and drunkenness.[43] The crew had obviously had a good time, as two seamen were also punished on the same day. This was despite the fact that the Lords of the Admiralty were not happy that captains were punishing artillerymen, as it was seen to cause problems between the two departments and, indeed, had sent explicit orders that a different course of action was to be followed. Nelson's solution to the problem was for the navy to have its own 'Corps of Artillery'.[44]

The accommodation of the artillery officers and men also caused a number of problems. It was usual for the artillery detachment to be accommodated on board the bomb vessel's attached tender. However, in a number of cases the officer and a number of the men were required to live on board the bomb itself. Thus on 27 June 1803 Macleod received a letter from Crew informing him that the artillery detachments should embark on the tenders of the bombs that were ready to go to sea.[45] That very same day, Macleod received a further communication from Crew stating that the Lords of the Admiralty had

> signified ... that it will be of advantage to the service, that the Officers Commanding the several Detachments of Artillery allotted for the service of the Bomb Vessels, preparing for service, should, with some of their men, be embarked on board the Bombs, rather than on board the tenders.[46]

[40] *Ibid.*, Nelson to Lieutenant Lane RA, 17 July 1804, p. 113.
[41] *Ibid.*, Nelson to Marsden, 18 July 1804, p. 114.
[42] TNA, ADM 36 15884. Log of HM Bomb *Thunder*, 8 September 1804.
[43] *Ibid.*, 28 November 1804.
[44] Nicolas, *Letters and Dispatches of Nelson Vol. VI* (London, 1846), Nelson to St Vincent, 25 May 1804, pp. 33–4.
[45] TNA, WO 55/1272, Crew to Macleod, 27 June 1803.
[46] *Ibid.*, 27 June 1803.

Crew went on to ask Macleod what proportion of the detachment he thought should be on the bombs. Macleod did not answer as quickly as the Board would have liked, as on 2 July Crew was writing a reminder note to Macleod asking for an answer.[47] Later in July, Crew wrote to Nepean asking him to 'request you will move their Lordships to authorize the necessary arrangements for affording the proper accommodation for the Officer of Artillery, and the Detachment under his Command whilst they may remain onboard His Majesty's Bomb Vessel'.[48] A note on the back of the letter states that cabins would only be provided for officers, 'and that the detachment serving with him will be accommodated in the same manner as the Crews of the bombs'. It appears to have been the case that the Admiralty had asked for part of the detachment to be embarked on the bomb vessels themselves without actually thinking about the accommodation problems.

The accommodation arrangements caused problems for at least one artillery officer in 1804. In the case of the bomb vessel *Explosion* discussed earlier, the detachment commander, Captain Fraser, stated that as Gunner Brown 'got the Liquor from one of the Ship's crew … whether I may be allowed to place one sentry at each Birth [sic] of my detachments'.[49] Clearly, Fraser wanted to separate his men from the crew of the bomb as much as possible. Unfortunately, no reply to Fraser has been uncovered but he, at least, must have felt that integration was not the way forward for the two 'commands'.

Even with just the officer of the detachment needing accommodation an instance in April 1804 shows that this was not always accomplished. In that month, Crew wrote to Marsden saying that as an additional lieutenant had been appointed to the bomb *Tartarus* the artillery officer was 'very badly accommodated'. He asked that 'suitable Accommodation may be afforded Lieutenant Briscoe'.[50] The Admiralty directed Lord Keith (the admiral of the station) 'to order a proper cabin to be built for him and every accommodation to be given to him that the Ship will allow'.

Solutions

On 18 August 1804 the Royal Marine Artillery (RMA) was set up by an Order in Council. This followed an Admiralty memorial of the previous day which stated that:

---

[47] *Ibid.*, 2 July 1803.
[48] TNA, ADM 1/4016, Crew to Nepean, 19 July 1803. Macleod was informed of this representation on the same date. TNA, WO 55/1272, Crew to Macleod, 19 July 1803.
[49] TNA, ADM 1/4016, Captain Fraser to Dep. Adj. General, 17 March 1804.
[50] *Ibid.*, Crew to Marsden, 30 April 1804.

> Having taken into our consideration the inconveniences attending the embarking Detachments of Royal Artillery on board your majesty's Bomb Vessels, we are of opinion that the establishment of a Company at each of the Head Quarters of your Majesty's Royal Marine Forces under the denomination of Royal Marine Artillery, will enable us to supply your majesty's Bomb Vessels and other ships where their service may be required with proper Detachments, and to relieve those of the Royal Artillery now serving therein.

Each of the companies was to consist of 'one Captain, three First Lieutenants, five Second Lieutenants, five Serjeants [sic], five Corporals, eight Bombardiers, three Drummers and 52 Gunners'. These men were to be 'selected from the most intelligent and experienced Officers and Men of the respective Divisions'.[51]

Although the aim was to recruit the 'most intelligent and experienced', reality had to take precedence. As such, the Commanding Officer of the Chatham Division of Royal Marines was told to send to the Admiralty the names of the officers whom he thought qualified. However, he was 'to send the names of such only as are being employed at Quarters Recruiting, or in the Channel, or North Sea Fleets, are immediately forthcoming for this particular duty'.[52]

There were a number of advantages of having the RMA. Firstly, and most importantly, as members of the Royal Marines, when at sea they were under the command of the captain of the bomb vessel. This can be seen in the muster books of the bomb vessels. On the bomb vessel *Thunder*, in 1805, the number of RMA who were 'borne as part of the complement' was one lieutenant, one sergeant, one bombardier and eight gunners.[53] Not only could they be punished by the captain without another government department becoming involved but also they could help on board ship with tasks that the Royal Artillerymen had refused to do.

A rather sad example of this can be seen on board HM Bomb *Aetna* serving in the Baltic in 1807. The surgeon's log for 12 September notes that Thomas Davies, a private in the RMA, 'When assisting to weigh the anchor in a heavy gale of wind, received a blow (from one of the bars) on the face by the Capstan recoiling which fractured it in a dreadful manner'. Davies 'expired shortly after'.[54] If Davies had been a Royal Artilleryman then he would not have been on the capstan in the first place and this case shows the integration

---

[51] TNA, PC 2/165, 18 August 1804, pp. 600–1.
[52] TNA, ADM 201/31, 24 August 1804, Marsden to Lt-General Barclay.
[53] TNA, ADM 36/15884.
[54] TNA, ADM 101/81/1, Surgeon's log of HM Bomb *Aetna*.

of the RMA into the crew of the bomb vessels in a similar way to the regular marines on board any other naval vessel.

Although the creation of the RMA solved many problems for the navy and Ordnance, it also created a new one for the navy. As the Ordnance had previously supplied the artillerymen to the bombs, the navy did not seem to know how many artillerymen would be needed for each vessel. In 1806, two years after the creation of the RMA, Crew was informing Marsden that a vessel the size of HM Bomb *Lucifer* would have had two NCOs and eight gunners.[55] Similarly, on 16 March 1805, *Explosion* and *Hecla* each embarked eight gunners, one Corporal and one Serjeant.[56]

Another problem, at least as far as the Ordnance was concerned, was who was 'considered responsible for the Ordnance Stores put on Board Bomb Tenders since the Royal Artillery have been withdrawn from that Service'.[57] The memo on the back of the letter shows one of the difficulties of the Ordnance's two-headed structure and communications with the Admiralty. In January 1805 'Lord Chatham was acquainted the Gunners of the Bombs were to have charge of the stores in question'. As stated previously, the artillery lieutenant had had charge of the mortars and stores when the Royal Artillery manned the mortars. Thus, in 1805, the Admiralty had decided to bring the bomb vessels onto a similar footing as the rest of the fleet. That the Ordnance was not aware of this fact in 1810 seems rather far fetched as all gunners' accounts needed to be cleared by the Office of the Clerk of the Ordnance before either the gunner or the ship's captain was paid. It is probable that the officials in the office were aware of this but the Board may not have been. In addition, Chatham, in this instance, had clearly lived up to his reputation of either not passing information on to his subordinates or not doing his paperwork.

One problem did remain, at least until 1807. When the Admiralty wanted tenders to send out with the bomb vessels to Copenhagen they still asked the Ordnance to provide them. The Ordnance believed that as the RMA were under the Admiralty's superintendence the tenders should be acquired by the Admiralty. However, they added that on this occasion they would procure them on the Admiralty's behalf in order to save time.[58]

---

[55] TNA, ADM 1/4017, Crew to Marsden, 19 December 1806.
[56] TNA, ADM 185/62, p. 272.
[57] TNA, ADM 1/4019, Crew to John Croker, 23 November 1810.
[58] TNA, ADM 1/4018, Crew to Pole, 18 July 1807. No evidence has been uncovered in the Transport, Ordnance or Admiralty records that this issue re-appeared after 1807.

Conclusion

This chapter has shown the difficulties that arose when artillerymen and sailors operated together on board the bomb vessels in the Royal Navy. The example of the bomb vessels has been used because these were the ships where the two military commands operated most closely together. The chapter has demonstrated where the areas of friction were and also that these areas were not only on board ship but also at departmental level.

The problems which the two branches faced on this issue can be used to exemplify the problems of separated command during the period under question. Indeed, the solution that was eventually, and logically, found was to remove one of the commands from the ship with the creation of the Royal Marine Artillery in August 1804. As such, it can be seen as part of the rationalisation of the British military and government at the end of the eighteenth century. By removing one branch of the military from the equation the whole procedure for fitting and equipping bomb vessels for sea was simplified. Although not entirely successful and suffering a number of early teething problems, the advantages far outweighed these negatives. This rationalisation was also seen in the transport services being brought under one roof in 1794 with the formation of the Transport Board. Charles Middleton, whilst Comptroller of the Navy, had actually wanted to go further and bring the whole supply of ordnance under Admiralty control; thus removing the Ordnance from this service.

By creating the Royal Marine Artillery and making its servicemen part of the naval chain of command the problems of divided loyalty and separated chains of command were solved. Using existing Marine officers and men helped this integration process in that the newly created Royal Marine Artillerymen were used to working on board ship and, more importantly, were used to operating under naval command and naval law.

4

'The Marine Officer is a Raw Lad, and therefore Troublesome': Royal Naval Officers and the Officers of the Marines, 1755–1797

Britt Zerbe

The command hierarchy of a ship-of-the-line in the eighteenth century has been widely written about within recent naval historiography. However, one area that has been largely overlooked is the conflict, in relation to their place in the ship's hierarchy, between the British Marine Corps officers and their Royal Navy counterparts and their eventual acceptance. The conflict reinforces the perception of the growing authority and centralization of command by the Admiralty. From the very start of the new marine divisions in 1755, the Admiralty constructed the new command structure in such a way as to integrate the marines, yet divide them from the navy. This new command structure would create friction between the marines and navy, especially among the officer ranks. One area of contention that existed between marine and naval officers was with regard to the marine officers' social backgrounds. These social conflicts existed as a result of the majority of marine officers coming from a substantially lower class than their naval counterparts. This created hostility within the ship's wardroom, even though the marine officers had the right to sit in the wardroom because of their commissions. To cure this problem, the marine officers developed three methods by which to integrate themselves into the command hierarchy via their amphibious operational roles. The first stage of this development was to use external influences, such as army commanders, to exert influence on their naval commanders to help marines in amphibious and command matters. The second stage was to use a more cooperative approach in order to have their proper place and professionalism recognized. The final stage was the growing acceptance of the marines for their professional competence in amphibious battle. It would take nearly the entirety of the forty-seven year period from 1755 to 1802, when they were given the 'Royal' prefix, for the marines and their officers to be seen as a professionalised element and accepted by the navy.

Social and Professional Background of the Marine Officer

The birth of the new British Marine Corps establishment on 3 April 1755 was a dramatic departure from the previous marine regiments deployed in wars from 1664 to 1748. This new structure radically transformed not only the administration of the marines but also their basic command structure. The old regimental system was abolished for the more malleable grand-division structure in which there were three divisions, each in the corresponding royal dockyards of Chatham, Portsmouth and Plymouth. Each of these divisions had previously been commanded by a lieutenant colonel, one major and one adjutant. However after the reforms instituted following the Falkland Islands Crisis in 1771, this was changed to one colonel-commandant, two lieutenant colonels, two majors and two adjutants. In addition, there was one naval flag officer called Lieutenant-General in Town (i.e., London) who was to act as an adjutant-general for the entire corps. The colonel-commandants were made 'General Officers', but were also required to 'continue to do the duty of Colonels at the Head Quarters [each division]'.[1] One of the primary reasons for establishing this new command by the Admiralty was to help shed light on the ambiguity which had existed surrounding who had direct command of the divisions following the establishment of the 'Blue Colonel' system in 1760. This system was designed to be a sinecure post for naval captains who were awaiting promotion to flag rank.[2] Unfortunately the Admiralty never made this objective clear to the naval officers awarded this post under the 'Blue Colonel' system, for these naval officers felt it was their place as senior marine officers to instruct the marine divisions in their day-to-day operations. It was not until the Falkland Island Crisis that the Admiralty recognised this problem: 'under an establishment made by His late Majesty's order in Council on the 1st of February 1760, it unavoidably happens that the Care, Inspection and Command of the said Head Quarters [three divisions] is often left to officers of no higher Rank than a Lieutenant Colonel'.[3] Therefore part of the new reforms was to create Colonel-Commandants who were given full explicit command over their units, finally pushing the naval commanders with marine titles to an official sinecure post. The Admiralty eliminated the problem of

---

[1] The National Archives (TNA), ADM 2/1165, 4 April 1771, p. 485.
[2] TNA, ADM 2/1156, 1 February 1760, pp. 274–6.
[3] TNA, ADM 2/1165, 4 April 1771, p. 484.

cooperative commands with their army counterparts in operations when they requested the king to make marine officers' ranks equivalent to officers of the regiments of foot, giving the marines the same official respect for their rank.[4]

Other than these field and flag ranks, the lower level marine command structure was similar to army grenadier detachments with a captain, captain-lieutenant (usually a junior first lieutenant in command of the field officers companies), first lieutenant and second lieutenant, already placing the marines in a special class of their own.[5] When the first 210 marine officers were commissioned in April 1755, they were mostly army officers from the half-pay list. These were officers like James Patterson, who was eventually to become the first Lieutenant-General of Marines, John Mackenzie, of Belle Isle fame and one of the first Colonel-Commandants of Marines, among others.[6] Almost all of these officers had served in one of the ten marine regiments raised during the War of Austrian Succession. Following the reconstitution and placement under Admiralty control in 1755, the major difference between the officers in the new marine corps and those in the marine regiments was that their commissions were not purchased. One reason for this was the Admiralty's fear that external influence through patronage on the navy's new branch of service would mean that only men of inexperience who were politically and financially connected would be able to advance in such a system. This was a fear that both George I and George II frequently held with regard to the army, and as a result both monarchs continually put restrictions on the army's purchase system throughout the first half of the eighteenth-century.[7] This fear of undue external influence on the marine officers' hierarchy was demonstrated in 1755 when the new establishment was created. Jack Fletcher wrote to the Duke of Newcastle in 1755, asking for a major's commission in the new marine corps and explaining that he had clear experience as he had 'served in the last war',[8] but the request was rejected by the Admiralty and First Lord, Admiral Anson. Instead, all of the officers were drafted from men on the half-pay list who had held the same rank in the old marine regiments during the previous war. This list was created and their names presented to the king the

---

[4] Ibid., p. 485.
[5] G. H. Hennessy and A. J. Donald (eds), *General H. E. Blumberg, Royal Marine Records from 1755 to 1914*, Royal Marines Historical Society Publication No. 2 (Eastney, 1979), p. 2.
[6] TNA, ADM 1/5116/1, 2 April 1755, pp. 30–6.
[7] A. Bruce, *The Purchase System in the British Army, 1660–1871*, Royal Historical Society Studies in History, No. 20 (London, 1980), pp. 13, 26–7; S. Conway, 'The Mobilization of Manpower for Britain's Mid-Eighteenth-Century Wars', *Historical Research* 77 (2004), p. 396.
[8] British Library (BL), MS Add. 32861, fol. 518, Jack Fletcher to Newcastle.

day before he officially re-established the marines on 3 April 1755.[9] However, soon these 210 officers began to die, or to be promoted, returned to half-pay or discharged from the service for other reasons. A new method of finding potential marine officers needed to be established.

The new officer recruits were therefore drawn from a different social background than their predecessors; for the marines was considered by many a second rate place in the military pantheon for aristocratic or upper-gentry sons. Those upper-gentry boys who were interested in military service were more likely to join the navy or army as these services held superior social and political status. The other two services also had the further incentive of quicker and more readily available chances for advancement, especially to flag or general officer rank. One historian has found that 'of the 523 marine officers recorded as serving in 1759, a mere seven bore titles'.[10] This ratio did not change throughout the forty-seven years from its establishment until the creation of the Royal Marines in 1802.

Like the other services, the marines still needed a relatively educated pool from which to draw upon for potential officers. The only other area from which they could draw their recruits was the sons of the lower-gentry and merchant classes. For example, Henry Norton Gamble, the son of a Leicester alderman and grocer, received his commission in the marines during the War of American Independence.[11] Another officer of a similar background who received his commission was Andrew Burn (eventually made Major-General of Marines), this time in the Seven Years War. Burn's grandfather was a 'pious clergyman of the church of Scotland' and his father, who drew 'his fortune at sea', was a merchant with various shipping concerns. Burn had a different background from other officers, for he started his career at sea as a purser on a 'Man of War'; the clerk on a ship along with a variety of other jobs related to the sea.[12] Finally in May 1761 he received his commission in the marines. The perception of marine officers coming from non-nobility backgrounds was recognized by various civilian contemporaries alike. George Farquhar, in his play *The Recruiting Officer*, wrote a dialogue in which two recruiting officers are boasting of their successes in finding men:

---

[9] TNA, ADM 1/5116/1, 2 April 1755, pp. 29, 34.

[10] S. Conway, *War, State, and Society in Mid-Eighteenth-Century Britain and Ireland* (Oxford, 2006), p. 76.

[11] S. Conway, *The British Isles and the War of American Independence* (Oxford, 2000), p. 36; M. Balderston and D. Syrett (eds), *The Lost War: Letters from British Officers during the American Revolution* (New York, 1975), pp. 112–18.

[12] O. Gregory (ed.), *Memoirs of the Life of the Late Major-General Andrew Burn, of the Royal Marines*, Vol. I (London, 1815), pp. XIV, 15.

Plume: Well, what Success?

Kite: I sent away a *Shoemaker* and a *Taylor* already; one to be a Captain of Marines and the other a Major of Dragoons[13]

While this play is a satire directed at the entire military recruiting system, it reveals the contemporary impression that marine officers were commonly recruited from the middling classes.

Another potential way for marine officers to be brought into the service was through the practice of marine and army officers being able to trade their commission for one in the army. Marine officer Lieutenant Charles Shearer was just one example of such a trade. Shearer gave up his commission in the marines so that he could join one of the army units, then forming under Lord Loudoun's command, which was ordered to Portugal during 1762–1763. Lieutenant Shearer's military career is fascinating, for he served all over the world within various units; initially with General Whitmore's Regiment, then transferring his commission to the marines, where he served in the Senegal and Guadeloupe operations.[14] Unfortunately since there was no purchase system in the marines, army officers had to take their new commission at the bottom rank of second lieutenant.

None of the above should minimize the importance of the most valuable element of officer recruitment in all eighteenth century military and civil promotions – that of patronage. While the Admiralty actively tried to minimize most forms of external influence, this did not mean that they did not exert their own internal influence on who was commissioned. The members of the Admiralty Board were one potential source of patronage for young men awaiting a marine commission. Thomas Marmaduke Wybourn, an orphan, was nineteen in 1795 when he received his commission in the Plymouth Division. Wybourn was able to secure his commission with the help of his powerful patron, the Earl Spencer, who was first Lord of the Admiralty at the time.[15] Naval officers were another group with a certain level of patronage over marine commissions, and men like Nelson and Collingwood (both held sinecure posts as marine officers), among others, used the system to put their people into open placements.[16] In addition to the Admiralty Board and naval officers, marine officers were another group with considerable power of patronage for new commissions. Division commanders and those senior

---

[13] G. Farquhar, *The Recruiting Officer: A Comedy* (London, 1755), p. 63.
[14] BL, MS Add. 44068, fols. 153, 155, 161, Lt. Charles Shearer to Lord Loudoun.
[15] A. Petrides and J. Downs (eds), *Sea Soldier: An Officer of Marines with Duncan, Nelson, Collingwood and Cockburn* (Tunbridge Wells, 2000), p. xi.
[16] E. Hughes (ed.), *The Private Correspondence of Admiral Lord Collingwood*, Navy Records Society 98 (London, 1957), p. 34, Collingwood to his sister, 17 February 1793,

Marine officers in operations overseas regularly had their appointments of new officers confirmed by the Admiralty. Officer confirmation in overseas operations had always been a privilege of naval commanders-in-chief within their stations, so the practice was not unique to the marines. Marine Major Mason in Senegal was promised a commission for his choice, in his case Mr Eagle,. Unfortunately Eagle was too late to be on the list for that year but was promised to be the first name on the list for the following year.[17]

This is not to say that others did not have any recourse to get their people commissions in the marines. Andrew Burn, for example, was given his commission due to the influence of Sir Henry Erskine, the army commander and MP for Ayr.[18] Some nobles possessed significant influence within the Admiralty, which they were able to utilize to get their favourites a commission in the marines. Basil Feilding, 6th Earl of Denbigh, had great influence with the Admiralty of 1774–1784, largely due to his close friendship with the then First Lord, the Earl of Sandwich.[19] The Earl of Denbigh was able to get commissions for an array of family members and friends such as John (marines) and Edward (navy) Bowater and William Fielding (marines), among many others. The process through which the Earl of Denbigh received these commissions only reaffirmed the solidity of the Admiralty's control. Each request was directly sent to the First Lord or the Secretary of the Admiralty, and was then reviewed before being accepted. Denbigh's family was seen at the time to possess a suitable military heritage, and their local political power was also of great help.[20]

As the service matured, a large number of marine officers increasingly began to come from family backgrounds steeped in naval or marine service. William Patterson served as a Volunteer during the operations against Belle Isle and received his commission for his action. Patterson was also the son of the first adjutant of the corps, General James Patterson. William Pitcairn was the son of marine Major John Pitcairn, who gained fame during the War of American Independence. Another example is Lieutenant Richard Caunter, who, when he died in 1795 from 'complications of disorders', had one of his sons serving as a lieutenant of the marines in the East Indies.[21] There were also men whose fathers were naval officers, such as William Feilding, who was the son of Admiral Feilding. Others like Cuthbert Collingwood were

---

[17] TNA, ADM 2/1155, 27 October 1758, p. 126; TNA, ADM 2/1156, 15 January 1760, p. 233,

[18] Gregory, *Memoirs of the life of the late Major-General Andrew Burns*, p. 71,

[19] N. Rodger, *The Insatiable Earl: A Life of John Montagu, 4th Earl of Sandwich* (London, 1994).

[20] Warwick Record Office, CR2017/C244, Letter book of the 6th Earl of Denbigh.

[21] TNA, ADM 1/3337, 12 February 1804, p. 324.

able to get relatives, such as his cousin, a commission.[22] As the marines aged, the families of the existing officer corps unofficially became the main pool of potential officers. The First Lord of the Admiralty, Admiral St Vincent, re-emphasized the point of using sons of former officers and enlisted marines in a letter to Sir William Heathcote in 1803:

> I fear your application in favour of Mr. Steele for a Commission in the Royal Marines is too late, the list having been made out some time and chiefly composed of the Sons and near Relations of Officers, who, I am persuaded you will agree with me should be preferred to all others.[23]

This practice, as an unofficial policy, is further confirmed in the same year by a marine officer writing to the *Naval Chronicle*. In his letter he discusses that upon recently looking at a new list of marine officers, he saw many 'gentlemen so appointed were relatives of some of the brave men of that corps who fell gloriously during the late war'. He continued to confirm this in the same manner as St Vincent: 'and where could we expect to find better Officers than the sons of those heroes who has so nobly shed their blood for their country's cause'.[24] This should not be seen as an alien practice, for the king[s] many times tried to follow the same policy by recruiting many non-purchase army commissions from martial families, but the scale was never to be as significant as that in the marines.[25]

Another area that was a pool for marine officers was the enlisted ranks. These men had progressed through the NCO ranks and were usually given the commission in recognition of heroic action in battle or in security to the state. John Hardy was promoted to second lieutenant in the Second Marine battalion in North America after the Battle of Bunker Hill, but he had nearly twenty years of experience before the battle.[26] Battle was not the only way to promotion, however. Preventing mutiny was another area in which promotion to officer could be gained. Two sergeants from the Plymouth Division were promoted to second lieutenant for their loyalty in helping to prevent the Plymouth Marine Barracks mutiny on 28 May 1797.[27]

---

[22] Hughes, *Private Correspondence of Admiral Lord Collingwood*, p. 34, Collingwood to his sister, 17 February 1793.
[23] David Bonner Smith (ed.), *The Letters of Lord St. Vincent*, Vol. II, Navy Records Society 61 (London, 1926), p. 155, St Vincent to Sir William Heathcote, 4 July 1803.
[24] *The Naval Chronicle*, Vol. 10 (July to December 1803), pp. 67–8. 'To the Editor of the Naval Chronicle', 22 July 1803.
[25] J. A. Houlding, *Fit for Service: The Training of the British Army, 1715–1795* (Oxford, 1981), p. 103.
[26] TNA, ADM 158/3, Chatham Description Books, 4th Company.
[27] TNA, ADM 1/1186 18 July 1797, 517, Letter from ADM to Gen. Bowater; A. J.

One last area for finding potential marine officers was doomed to failure from the start because it was exerted by outside influences. This attempt demonstrated the strict control by the Admiralty over the marine corps and its full departure from the old army model of the marine regiments. Major-General Simon Fraser, of 71st Highland Regiment fame, offered to raise a battalion of marines for the king if his men were given the choice of the officers of this battalion. These men were to be given four months' leave from their army units, in which time they were to recruit a set number of men. This was a practice in the British Army of the eighteenth century whereby entire companies, battalions and even regiments were raised with the understanding that the men raising them would be made lieutenant, captain, major or colonel of their respectively sized units. This was commonly practised in times of emergency or at the beginning of war when the need for troops was great, and many of the Highland regiments were raised via this method. While the king granted the request, the Admiralty created obstacles to prevent this loss of patronage power over its marines. First, the Admiralty denied leave to Lieutenant Duncanson of the marines, who was due to receive a lieutenancy in Fraser's new battalion. Then, when after the allotted time the officers were unsuccessful in raising their agreed quotas numbers, the Admiralty had a second excuse to refuse General Fraser's battalion. Finally, to allay any complaints from the king, the Admiralty mentioned 'that since the late augmentation of the Marines to Eighty Men a Company the number of Officers allowed to each have not been sufficient to carry on the service in the manner they are desirous of'.[28] Therefore, instead of forming new marine units the Admiralty made the argument that it would be better to increase the officer establishment of each company.

Relations between Marine and Royal Navy Officers

From the beginning marine officers were explicitly ordered to 'obey the orders of the Captain or Commanding Officer of the Ship, and also the Commanding Officer of the Watch for His Majesty's Service'.[29] This strict command was given in direct response to a recurrent problem that arose when the combined forces of the army and navy were placed within the small confines of the wooden world. Army officers felt that it was their right to give orders and punishments to their personnel when on board ship. Conversely, the ship's

Donald and J. D. Ladd (eds), *G. H. Blumberg, Royal Marine Records: Part II, 1793–1836*, Royal Marines Historical Society Publication No. 4 (Eastney, 1982) p. 10.
[28] TNA, ADM 2/1169, 6 January 1776, pp. 152–3, Admiralty to Lord Barrington.
[29] TNA, ADM 2/1152, 24 July 1755, p. 147, Article 3, 'Rules and Instructions relating to Marines serving on board His Majesty's Ships'.

captain felt that it was his right to command and punish all on his ship.[30] In the Rules and Regulations governing marine and naval officers, there was a clause clearly stating: 'Marine Officers are, upon all Occasions, to be treated, as well by the Captain of the Ship, as by all other Officers and People belonging to her, with the Decency and Regard due to the Commissions they bear'.[31] This made clear to the captain and other naval officers that, regardless of the marine officers' backgrounds or professional knowledge, they were to be treated as equals.

This was easier said than done. Some naval officers felt marines and their officers were at least an annoyance and at worst a subversive element to the harmony of a ship. This also bred feelings by some that marines were little more than unskilled landsmen and could not be trusted. In 1797, after the naval mutinies at Spithead and the Nore, Admiral Patton wrote in a letter to a friend:

Let us now suppose the ship to have such a degree of motion as discomposes landmen and let us suppose the officers of this ship depending on the marines for protection from the irritated seamen; where is the security? In such a case it is well known that three seamen are absolutely superior in force to ten landmen, whatever the colour of their coats or their state of discipline on shore.[32]

Others further derided the marine officers. One published pamphlet giving advice to naval officers stated that 'if the marine officer is a raw lad, and therefore troublesome, as no one can dictate to you what steps you ought to take in carrying on service'. This was a reaction to the fact that many newly commissioned marine officers were quite young, between 16 and 19 years old. Unlike their naval colleagues they did not have years of learning at sea prior to being commissioned, nor did they have to take the test obligatory for naval lieutenants. The author goes on to exclaim against the marine officers who resented naval officers who 'impose duties on his people which may appear to him to be forbid by his instructions from head quarters [marine divisions]'.[33] In the view of this author, a naval officer would know how to instruct marines better than their own officers.

This author also goes on to talk about subversive elements inherent in the marines: 'there is a little jealousy existing between the sailors and marines, it

---

[30] M. Duffy, *Soldiers, Sugar, and Seapower: The British Expeditions to the West Indies and the War Against Revolutionary France* (Oxford, 1987), pp. 186–7.
[31] TNA, ADM 2/1152, 24 July 1755, p. 147. Article 4, 'Rules and Instructions relating to Marines serving on board His Majesty's Ships'.
[32] B. Lavery (ed.), *Shipboard Life and Organisation, 1731–1815* (Aldershot, 1998), pp. 633–4, Observations on the State of Discipline in the Navy.
[33] Anonymous, *Advice to the Officers of the British Navy* (London, 1785), p. 45.

will be to your interest, by humbling the later, to flatter the stronger number of seamen'.[34] He goes on to deride the marines for their sense of discipline, and even encourages naval officers to belittle them by reminding them they are neither soldiers nor sailors. The incompetence of young marine officers is not entirely off the mark; for the commanding marine officer in Portsmouth in 1775 asked for Admiral Sir James Douglas to inform ships' captains to be diligent in making sure they prevented marine officers from being negligent in their duties.[35] This statement, while confirming the above critique in some areas, demonstrates the ever greater encroachment on the ship captains' authority because they had to be told by the commanding marine officer through the local commanding naval officer. While it was the marine commanding officers who were asking for this to be carried out, the senior marine officers on ships were not inexperienced men, as all marine detachments from first to sixth rate were to have as their senior officer either a captain or a first lieutenant. Second lieutenants should not be seen in the context of naval lieutenants, but instead as similar in rank to midshipmen, who were given limited responsibilities while on ship.

Marine officers also publicly expressed their concerns about their poor treatment by certain naval officers. In 1757 an anonymous marine officer wrote a twenty-page published letter to the Admiralty. In it he said his reasons for writing:

> I take the liberty to express my good wishes, for the benefit of my kindred corps ... that gentlemen engaged on the same duty, for the same good King ... may have, according to their rank, an equal right with the sea officers to the conveniencies [sic] the ship affords, and that they may all be considered as part owners of the vessels they serve in ...[36]

While this officer conceded Admiral Patton's point 'that those who are not bred to the sea, cannot carry *their sea legs and stomachs on board with them like sailors* [sic]', he goes on to comment about the poor treatment of marine lieutenants, being relegated to 'speak to the Boatswain and Carpenter to take them into their mess'. This practice was explicitly prohibited in the regulations issued to all ships' captains. However, this policy clashed with the common principle of 'my ship, my cabin, my boat, my marine officer', the impact of

---

[34] Ibid., p. 22.
[35] W. G. Perrin (ed.), *The Keith Papers, Vol. I*, Navy Record Society Vol. 62, (London, 1927), p. 25, Sir James Douglas to Elphinstone, 28 November 1775.
[36] Officer, *A Letter, to the Right Honourable the Lords of the Admiralty; Setting forth the Inconveniences and Hardships, the Marine Officers are Subject to, who Serve on Board the Fleet* (London, 1757), p. 2.

which was twofold. First, the marine officer was of a lower class than naval officers, and secondly it was to put the marine officer in his place on ship.[37]

The majority of the letter is concerned with the issue of proper accommodation onboard ship. Marine officers' accommodation, according to the author, was usually 'between two guns, about seven foot long and four foot wide'.[38] This problem was recognized by the Admiralty, as they had given the Navy Board commands to either prepare canvas berths or cabins in which the marine officers were to sleep. They even prevented ships from sailing until they had made proper accommodation, even for lower level marine lieutenants. In 1759 on HMS *Fortune*, Lieutenant Huckle wrote to the Admiralty stating that no accommodation existed for him. The Admiralty ordered Vice Admiral Holburne at Portsmouth to 'enquire into what he sets forth, and report to the Lords' before the ship could leave.[39] This was not uncommon, for HMS *Neptune*, *Essex* and *Royal* were prevented from sailing by Commissioner Hughes in Portsmouth until the proper accommodation was provided for their marines.[40] All of these ships, including HMS *Fortune* above, were sloops, and were therefore limited in space. Many of the navy's ships-of-the-line had the space for cabins and many were already constructed. This is why there were few complaints from marines on ships-of-the-line in the fleet.

An additional area of friction that existed between marine and naval officers was the ability to request individual marine officers for service on a particular ship. One privilege held by all naval captains was the ability to appoint a number of their own ship's officers and crew. The Admiralty prevented captains from carrying over this privilege to marines – a clear infringement upon a ship captain's authority and patronage. The Admiralty reinforced their position to Captain Taylor of HMS *Seahorse*, in that the 'Lords never interfere in the Appointment of Marine Officers to Ships'.[41] Instead, the Admiralty allowed each division commander to decide which officers and men would embark on which ships. The amount of men that could be embarked remained the prerogative of the navy.

The Maturing of the Marine-Navy Relationship

How then did the marine officers overcome some of the command issues and become more accepted by the naval officers? One prominent catalyst for the

[37] Officer, *A Letter to the Right Honourable the Lords of the Admiralty*, pp. 2, 6, 7.
[38] *Ibid.*, p. 4.
[39] TNA, ADM 96/3, 1759, p. 5; Article 7, 'Rules and Instructions relating to Marines serving on board His Majesty's Ships'; TNA, ADM 2/1156, 23 August 1759, p. 61.
[40] TNA, ADM 106/1123, 26 January 1763, p. 38, Hughes to Navy Board,
[41] TNA, ADM 2/1154, 9 May 1757, p. 048.

transformation of ideas and feelings about the marines was their increased competence and fighting effectiveness. This section will look at three separate operations, all ashore, to illustrate how naval officers' perceptions changed over time. The first action is the 1761 operation against Belle Isle. The land forces component of this expedition was commanded by Major-General Studholme Hodgson of the army, with 8,339 soldiers under his command. The naval forces were commanded by Commodore Augustus Keppel, who had fifteen ships-of-the-line along with nearly a hundred other ships ranging from transports to bomb vessels. This force also provided large detachments of seamen to be used ashore, and over 1,000 marines (under the command of Lieutenant Colonel John Mackenzie) from the various ships.[42] If amphibious operations were to be very successful in the eighteenth century, like the Martinique (1761) and Havana (1762) operations, they needed to have a high level of inter-service cooperation between the naval and army commanders. The day before the operation against Belle Isle began, General Hodgson and Commodore Keppel travelled 'to the Northern Part of the Island, to be as well informed of the strength of the Enemies (sic) works'.[43] The operations would last nearly two months, and the marines were to play a pivotal role throughout. On the initial day, Captain Stanhope led battalions from Grey's and Stuart's regiments along with 500 marines, with the objective being to 'divert the Enemy from the principal object'.[44] On 13 May they led the assault against the redoubt on the outskirts of the town of Le Palais. Then on 7 June they were given the honour of leading the successful assault against the key redoubt for the citadel of Le Palais. This operation cost the marines dearly. They made up 10 per cent of the total of 303 men killed, and 13 per cent of the 523 wounded. These statistics are more striking considering that only a tenth of the total forces were composed of marines, indicating they were in the thick of the action throughout the campaign.[45]

The importance of this battle is not in the action itself, but in the operational perception of the marines by the army and the navy, and their subsequent reporting of the action back home. From 13 April until 9 May, Commodore Keppel, when writing to the Admiralty, only spoke of the actions, the issues and losses of the navy personnel. But throughout this campaign General Hodgson consistently wrote to Commodore Keppel informing him of the best practices to take with his marines. For example, on 9 May, 'Major General Hodgson having represented to me the necessity of a proper person to act as

---

[42] F. J. Hebbert, 'The Belle-Ile Expedition of 1761', *Journal of the Society of Army Historical Research* 64 (1986), 81–93, pp. 82, 84.
[43] TNA, ADM 1/91, 13 April 1761, pp. 1–2.
[44] *Ibid.*, p. 5.
[45] TNA, ADM 1/91, 8 June 1761, p. 1.

Brigade Major to the Corps of Marines', Keppel then requested the appointment of Captain Chalmers to fill the post and agreed to have the army supply the marines with surplus camp equipage.[46] This recommendation shows the lack of understanding, not only among local navy commanders, but more importantly the Admiralty, about the needs of an amphibious force to be effective in fighting on land. Another area about which Hodgson wrote to Keppel was with regard to the bravery and heroism of the marines under the command of Lieutenant Colonel Mackenzie. There are some vague hints that the marines were asking Hodgson to compel Keppel to advocate on their behalf to the Admiralty and government. A demonstration of this is to compare Keppel's first commentary about the marines' attack on the city's redoubts on 13 May with his later more glowing report of 7 June. Keppel made the first notice very matter of fact and brief, only a few short lines of a six page report. However, concerning the marines leading the assault on the main redoubt around the citadel of Le Palais, his tenor changed. In the after-action dispatch, which was quickly made public, Keppel devoted his account entirely to the marines' actions. He even reveals where the pressure was coming from; 'Major General Hodgson, by his constant approbation of the behaviour of the battalion of marines ... gives me the pleasing satisfaction of acquainting you of ... the goodness and spirited behaviour of that corps'.[47] This suggests that the marines, while still a relatively new element, had to receive their advocacy and linkage to the public, government and naval officer corps from external sources. Keppel only belatedly recognized his duty to congratulate and extol the marines for their heroism.

The second example demonstrates the cooperative nature of the marine officer. Following the 1773 tea party which began the embargo of Boston Harbour, the city was a hotbed of the rebellious activity in the colonies. On Monday 3 October 1774, the Admiralty was consulted on 'whether two or three ships of war, with as large a detachment from the Marines as can be conveniently accommodated' should be sent immediately to Boston.[48] The battalion of marines that was formed for this expedition to America would be under the command of Major John Pitcairn. The battalion arrived six weeks after leaving Portsmouth, in late October 1774. At first Admiral Graves did not want to land the marines, but after Major Pitcairn's constant requests to

---

[46] *Ibid.*, 9 May 1761, pp. 1–2.

[47] *Ibid.*, 17 May 1761, p. 1; *General Evening Post* (London), Saturday, 13 June 1761; Officer, *An Impartial Narrative of the Reduction of Belle Isle* (London, 1761), pp. 41–2.

[48] G. R. Barnes and J. H. Owen (eds), *The Sandwich Papers, Vol. I*, Navy Record Society 69 (London, 1932), p. 55, Minute of Cabinet,

both the Admiralty and his division commander, Graves relented and allowed the marines to land.[49]

Pitcairn was so concerned about the ambiguities of his command authority that he personally requested Colonel-Commandant Mackenzie, Chatham Division, to petition Sandwich in the hope of promoting him lieutenant colonel. Writing to Colonel-Commandant Mackenzie, Pitcairn stated that this promotion 'would have saved me the mortification of being commanded by several majors that are much younger officers than I'.[50] He never received this promotion, a demonstration of the lack of promotion for Marines in general. However his demeanour and skilful politicking convinced the commander in Boston, General Gage, never to place Pitcairn under the command of anyone below the rank of lieutenant colonel; a clear testament to Gage's trust in Pitcairn. Major Pitcairn felt Admiral Graves, whom he described as 'but a weak man with infinite pride', was frequently trying to undermine his command authority. Graves had kept a large body of marines on his ships so that he could use them in his enlarged ship-searching operations in Boston harbour. Pitcairn tried repeatedly to extract his men from the ships in order to fill his battalion, but 'you may easily immagine [sic] his [Graves'] behaviour on this occasion was not the most polite'.[51] One issue used by the Admiral to keep the marines under his direct command was his concern regarding who should victual the battalion while ashore. As time wore on, even General Gage was getting tired of requesting that the supernumerary marines on board the squadron be landed at Boston. He, like Pitcairn, felt they would be useless unless they were disciplined 'this winter in a manner to enable them to act on shore with the rest of the King's troops'.[52] Graves only relented after Pitcairn, 'saying everything I could to the Admiral', refuted the Admiral's objections by showing that his men would welcome being equal with the army. Graves eventually released 390 of the marines.[53]

Pitcairn's orders throughout were very clear; he was to have sole command of the battalion and was to land them as soon as possible. This was reinforced in his instructions regarding the purchase of winter wear, 'the Marines under *your command* [my emphasis] should be landing in the *Winter*'.[54] Pitcairn also understood the political and command minefield he was navigating, and persistently tried to stay in Admiral Graves' good graces, no matter how

---

[49] BL, MS Add. 39190, f. 204–6, Pitcairn to Mackenzie, 5–10 December 1774.
[50] *Ibid.*
[51] BL, MS Add. 39190, f. 207, Pitcairn to Mackenzie, 20 December 1774,
[52] TNA, ADM 1/485, p. 3, Graves to ADM, 8 January 1775.
[53] BL, MS Add. 39190, f. 208, Pitcairn to Mackenzie, 20 December 1774.
[54] TNA, ADM 2/1168, p. 278, ADM to Pitcairn, 28 November 1774.

'absurdly he behaves'. This problem was still not fully resolved by February, when writing to Sandwich he states:

> I have but a small battalion on shore: there are still fifty of the supernumeraries that were ordered out on board ship, this hurts the appearance of the battalion greatly, as they are the best of our men and ten of them belong to our light infantry company. I have spoken often to the Admiral about this, but to no effect; it was much against his inclinations that he landed any of us.[55]

Some of Pitcairn's correspondence eventually paid off, for on the 20 January the Admiralty ordered Admiral Graves to 'cause not only all supernumerary Marines but as many of those which are born[e] as part of the ships complements and can be spared from the duty of the ships to be landed'.[56]

On 18 April 1775, General Thomas Gage ordered 700 men under Lieutenant Colonel Francis Smith and Major Pitcairn, made up mostly of regimental and marine grenadier and light infantry companies, to seize arms and ammunition stores in Concord. These men were split into two different units, one under Pitcairn was to go to Lexington, and then later to meet up with the larger column on the march to Concord.[57] Pitcairn repeatedly worked amongst the forces of government, army and navy, but at all times he kept his marines together and under his personal command. Pitcairn's diligence and experience was rewarded by being appointed the second-in-command in the operations against Lexington and Concord, in which he perished, while winning the marines a position in the battle line at Bunker Hill, next to the light and grenadier companies.

The last stage for the marine officers was their full acceptance into the naval fold as professionals in their field. This example originates from the night before the landings at Tenerife on 21 July 1797. Of the 1,000 men assembled by Rear-Admiral Horatio Nelson for the next day's operations, 250 were marines under the command of Captain Thomas Oldfield.[58] Oldfield had been an officer in the marines since the War of American Independence, and by the time of Tenerife had nearly twenty years experience in amphibious operations throughout the world.[59] Nelson declared Captain Oldfield 'is a

---

[55] Barnes and Owen, *The Sandwich Papers*, pp. 57–8, Pitcairn to Sandwich, 14 February 1775.
[56] TNA, ADM 2/1168, ADM to Graves, 20 January 1775, p. 326.
[57] A. French, 'The British Expedition to Concord, Massachusetts, in 1775', *Journal of the American Military History Foundation* 1:1 (1937), p. 5.
[58] N. H. Nicolas, *The Dispatches and Letters of Vice Admiral Lord Viscount Nelson*, Vol. 2, 1795–1797 (London, 1845), p. 416. The Following Regulations are Recommended by Rear-Admiral Nelson, 17 July 1797,
[59] War Office, *A List of the Officers of the Army, and Marines; with an Index …* (London, 1785), p. 163.

very worthy man' and Oldfield's marines 'a most excellent body of men'.[60] The illuminating part of this operation was Nelson's council of war and who was invited to plan the upcoming strategy. In Nelson's 'Detail of the Proceedings of the Expedition', he stated that before the landing he called together 'Captains Troubridge and Bowen with Captain Oldfield of the Marines ... to consult with me what was best to be done and were of opinion they could possess themselves of the heights'.[61] This is a fundamental shift in perception from Keppel, for it was a clear sign of the growing interdependence of the two services in carrying out quick amphibious operations. Calling a marine officer into the council of war along with two other ship's captains demonstrated Nelson's level of confidence in the marines as a professional body.

While the marine officers were socially inferior to most of the men in the naval officer corps, they were able to integrate with the naval officers through time and operational experience. Marine officers, who in some cases were being barred, though unofficially, from the wardrooms of ships, and who had continual problems with accommodation, were faced with two problems. The first problem was the feeling that marine officers were professionally incompetent and the second related to the perception that they were too young. These problems, and that of social inferiority, were gradually overcome by the growing operational competence of the marines. At first they used the influence of external forces, then, with time, they were able to use cooperative political powers to exert influence on operations and senior officers. Finally their position was confirmed with the acceptance of marine officers' opinions in the councils of war. As time went on, marine officers were not only accepted by their naval counterparts, but they also began to be considered equals by their professional brothers in the other two services of the time.

---

[60] Nicolas, *The Dispatches and Letters of Vice Admiral Lord Viscount Nelson*, p. 393, To Admiral Sir John Jervis, 7 June 1797; J. Sugden, *Nelson: A Dream of Glory* (London, 2005), p. 733.
[61] G. P. B. Naish (ed.), *Nelson's Letters to His Wife and Other Documents, 1785–1831*. Navy Record Society 100 (London, 1958), pp. 371–2, 'A Detail of the Proceedings of the Expedition against the Town of Santa Cruz in the Island of Teneriffe'.

MANAGEMENT CAPABILITY AND
THE EXERCISE OF NAVAL POWER

5

High Exertions and Difficult Cases: The Work of the Transport Agent at Portsmouth and Southampton, 1795–1797

Roger Morriss

In 1987 the Clarendon Press published Michael Duffy's book, *Soldiers, Sugar and Sea Power. The British Expeditions to the West Indies and the War Against Revolutionary France*.[1] The book revealed the achievements and the tragedy of Britain's 'blue water' policy in the French Revolutionary War. This paper aims to complement his book by revealing some of the administrative efforts that facilitated the expeditions. Its principal source is a copybook of letters received by Captain Daniel Woodriff, agent for transports at Portsmouth and Southampton from 1795 to 1797.[2] His work is here placed in its broader context, which indicates how the British state developed to project its power by sea, and how that capability stemmed from the heart of the state's central bureaucracy.

Historiographically, with regard to the transport service of Great Britain, we live in the wake of David Syrett's work on the American War of Independence, the Seven Years War and War of Austrian Succession.[3] David emphasised the problems of competition between the naval boards, the Treasury and Ordnance departments for the hire of ships, their different procedures

---

[1] M. Duffy, *Soldiers, Sugar and Seapower. The British Expeditions to the West Indies and the War Against Revolutionary France* (Oxford, 1987).
[2] The National Archives (TNA): ADM.108/28; a collection of Woodriff's other personal papers survive in the National Maritime Museum.
[3] D. Syrett, *Shipping and the American War 1775–83. A Study of British Transport Organization* (London, 1970); D. Syrett, *Shipping and Military Power in the Seven Years War. The Sails of Victory* (Exeter, 2008); D. Syrett, 'Towards Dettingen: The Conveyancing of the British Army to Flanders in 1742', *Journal of the Society for Army Historical Research* 84 (2006), 316–26.

which meant owners could pick and choose the terms that most suited them, and the shortages of transports that developed. He especially accentuated the views of Sir Charles Middleton who, as Comptroller of the Navy Board, was responsible for the hire and equipment of troop transports for the Treasury and took over the supply and despatch of army victuallers. It was Middleton's view that there should be just one board hiring and supplying transports to all the boards that needed them. His desire, heavily represented to the Commissioners on Fees during the 1780s, was implemented in July 1794.[4]

The new Transport Board commenced effective management of the transport service from 1 September 1794. It completely relieved the Treasury, Navy, Victualling and Ordnance Boards of their main individual needs to hire shipping. This eradicated competition, standardising terms and conditions of hire.[5] It removed the burden of inspecting ships tendered for transports from the Navy Board's dockyard officers, for the Transport Board appointed its own professional staff to survey, measure, value and report on ships offered for hire. The Victualling Board's Hoytaker was also relieved of his duty of inspecting and hiring ships to act as victuallers. The only duties remaining to him were the occasional hire of small craft for shipments of provisions to the outports, attendance upon the issue and return of food into store, and account-keeping of provisions on board ships in the Thames.[6]

The re-organisation of 1794 was thus a significant one. It began a new era in transport provision. David Syrett's work suggested that reform would bring about advances in efficiency. As this paper will show, however, central reorganisation did not remove the necessity for unremitting work on the part of the Transport Board's agents in making ready ships for service and lading them with troops and horses – in effect bringing order out of chaos. This feature of the transport service remained as demanding and arduous as it had been earlier in the eighteenth century.[7] Neither did rationalisation of central management remove the environmental and human challenges of managing ships. As this paper will show, naval and army personnel remained as demanding to deal with while storms and winter weather exacerbated the work of despatching ships.

---

[4] M. E. Condon, 'The Administration of the Transport Service during the War against Revolutionary France, 1793–1802' (unpublished Ph.D. thesis, University of London, 1968), p. 35.
[5] For records of ships hired, 1806–11, see TNA: ADM. 108/150.
[6] 'Eleventh Report of the Commissioners for Revising and Digesting the Civil Affairs of the Navy', 18, cited in Condon, 'The Administration of the Transport Service', p. 62.
[7] P. K. Watson, 'The Commission for Victualling the Navy, the Commission for Sick and Wounded Seamen and Prisoners of War, the Commission for Transports, 1702–14' (unpublished Ph.D. thesis, University of London, 1965), pp. 263–70.

THE WORK OF THE TRANSPORT AGENT

Nevertheless the reorganisation of 1794 made a significant impact. Rationalisation enhanced the speed with which large numbers of transports could be assembled and despatched. As this paper will show, this effect derived as much from the political status of the new Board as from its successful engagement with the economics of ship management. In 1794 the Transport Board claimed an independence, indeed an authority, in shipping matters from other boards which permitted it to streamline procedures and create for the British armed forces a bureaucratic machine for the supply of shipping. Underpinned by the experience and teamwork of officials, both central commissioners and local agents, the resulting service formed the foundation of Britain's military expansion overseas during the French Revolutionary and Napoleonic Wars.

These central bureaucratic developments will be examined later. First, this paper considers the business of managing transports at the level of the transport agent in 1795–7. Work in the main embarkation ports was arduous, challenging and at times chaotic, and probably never more so than during the mid 1790s. The Transport Board took up its responsibilities at the back end of the expedition of Lieutenant-General Sir Charles Grey and Vice-Admiral Sir John Jervis in 1793–4 which succeeded in taking Martinique and St Lucia, but failed to take Guadeloupe as sickness and death eroded the army's manpower. The despatch of reinforcements in 1794/5 took transports which, with the necessity to retrieve men from the continent, left the Transport Board looking for more ships. The determination to despatch a second, even larger, expedition in 1795 under Major-General Sir Ralph Abercromby and Rear Admiral Hugh Cloberry Christian really taxed the resources and organisation of the new board.

The Abercromby-Christian expedition demanded the transportation between November 1795 and March 1796 of over 30,800 men which, when scraped together, eventually included a large number of foreign troops and about 6,000 cavalry. At the rate of two tons to a man, the Transport Board had to produce 60–70,000 tons of shipping, which was over 250 transports, by the end of 1795. With horses, artillery, ammunition, engineers and medical stores, baggage and provisions, the expedition eventually required about 100,000 tons of shipping, about 370 ships.[8]

In 1795 the main expeditionary force had to embark from Southampton, with supplementary contingents and ordnance joining it from Cork and the River Thames. One of the officers brought in to sort and prepare the necessary tonnage was Captain Daniel Woodriff. He qualified as a naval lieutenant at the end of the American War of Independence and was promoted Commander in September 1795. By then, on account of 'long services in the

---

[8] Duffy, *Soldiers, Sugar and Seapower*, pp. 184–96.

transport line of duty', he had acquired a reputation for 'high exertions in difficult cases'. It was for this reason the commissioner for transports working at Portsmouth, Captain John Schank,[9] said in October 1795 that Woodriff was appointed agent at Portsmouth and Southampton.[10] Woodriff's appointment was one of a number, all of which permitted the management of the range of tasks involved in despatching transports.

The initial problem facing the Portsmouth office was that the troop transports employed by the Transport Board had become scattered everywhere between the Isle of Wight and Southampton. Many had 'secreted themselves in different places and not made reports, either where they were, or the state of the ships'. Moreover those arriving continued to disperse, beyond the capacity of the single commissioner of transports at Portsmouth to control. Woodriff was thus appointed to deliver the orders of the Transport Board to the ship masters, who were to obey Woodriff as the representative of the Board, while he collected returns of the state and condition of the ships. For this purpose, Woodriff was equipped with a small sailing vessel and toured the outer reaches of Southampton Water.

While he was so engaged, in October 1795 came an influx of transports from the River Elbe with the Hanoverian regiments. Many carried horses, which had in some cases to be transferred to other ships for shipment to the West Indies. Horses did not travel well and had to be disembarked, while Woodriff had to decide which other vessels should be prepared for them. In view of the sickness sustained on the earlier Grey-Jervis expedition, he was also required to assist – and ensure all masters and other agents assisted – Sir Jerome Fitzpatrick who had been appointed by the Secretary of State to inspect the cleanliness and ventilation of transports in the interests of the health of the soldiers and animals who were to occupy them.[11]

Early November 1795 was spent supervising embarkations. On 16 November 18,742 officers and men sailed with Abercromby and Christian from Spithead. However, gales on the 17–18 November scattered the convoy and much of the expedition put back to Spithead. In a second departure, 12,000 troops sailed again with Christian on 9 December but they were struck by another violent storm and confronted by adverse westerly gales. After three weeks at sea, Christian remained no more than three days sail from Spithead and returned on 29 January 1796. Eventually, Abercromby

---

[9] Succeeded by Captain Charles Patton early in 1797.
[10] D. Syrett and R. L. DiNado (eds), *The Commissioned Sea Officers of the Royal Navy 1660–1815*, Navy Records Society (Scolar Press, Aldershot, 1994), p. 479.
[11] TNA, ADM.108/28, 11 October 1795.

sailed successfully on 14 February, while Christian remained until 20 March to take out the reserve. He eventually reached Barbados on 21 April 1796.[12]

After the first abortive departure, Woodriff was ordered up to Southampton early in December 1795 to take charge of all the remaining vessels there. Some were regular long-term transports; others were under short-term contracts of various expiry dates. Woodriff had to examine their charter parties to see which could be sent abroad and which retained for use between England and the continent. There was a local transport agent, Mr Young, who assisted him. While there, he was able to live on shore or afloat, hoisting a pendant, as the nature of his work demanded.[13] Sorting long-term from short-term, Woodriff embarked troops and sent transports to Spithead as they became ready. At Spithead two other captains, Lane and Poulden, mustered and liaised with Admiral Christian to ensure the transports received their sailing directions. In some vessels, Woodriff was able to load 'foreign victuals' that came with the soldiers from the Elbe – though Patton at Portsmouth had 'doubts as to the propriety of the measure'. Otherwise the provisions from Germany were sold,[14] lodged at Northam, or sent to Deptford in ships proceeding to the Thames, while empty water casks were collected by Dutch hoys probably for storage at Portsmouth.[15]

Following the return of the second sailing, the transports regrouped and some replenished. By mid March 1796 the vessels were virtually complete and ready for their third departure. Some foreign troops, notably the greater part of Choiseul's hussars, declined to serve in the West Indies and had to be embarked from the Isle of Wight for Hamburg. Woodriff was instructed to use the ships under short-term 'four month' hire for this purpose. They would bring back to England some foreign recruits for the British army and stores from Hamburg that belonged to the British government. The four ships allotted to this purpose were prepared under the supervision of a Lieutenant Kent and hurried to Spithead where the embarkation was managed by another transport agent, Lieutenant Baker. Otherwise 'all foreign ships and transports engaged for three or four months' were discharged, a task with which a Lieutenant Wheatley was appointed to assist Woodriff.[16]

---

[12] Duffy, *Soldiers, Sugar and Seapower*, pp. 203–16.
[13] TNA, ADM.108/28, 4 December 1795.
[14] The Board's letter to Woodriff of 1 April 1796 instructed him 'to prepare the Hay for sale by auction, in lots as small as may be most convenient, and to put it on shore for that purpose as soon as possible'.
[15] TNA, ADM. 108/28, 18, 21 March 1796.
[16] Duffy, *Soldiers, Sugar and Seapower*, p. 196; TNA: ADM. 108/28, 18, 21, 22 March 1796.

By the end of March 1796 the main expedition had finally been dispatched to the West Indies, but there was to be no peace for Woodriff. 'We are going to be very busy again', he was advised from Portsmouth, 'having no less than 4,000 British troops to embark for different places, and shipping to provide for 1,200 men which are to embark at Cork. The Secretary of State is determined the transports shall not long remain idle nor any of the officers under the Board.'

Immediately, Lieutenants Wheatley and Flinn were ordered to Lymington to embark 1,000 men of the 33rd Regiment on East India ships if they arrived in time from the Thames; if not, the troops were to be landed on the Isle of Wight.[17] From Southampton, the 90th Regiment was to embark 'at one ton and half per man' for Gibraltar, for which no porter or potatoes was allowed; the transports were to await convoy in Stoke's Bay. A stock-check of 'spare beds, and other stores such as windsails, hoses etc' ready for the supply of transports was needed. Finally, in order to bring them into useful service, the 'Dutch Hoys' were to be examined and a report made to the Board on their condition, manning, rig, equipment and efficiency of operation.[18]

Despite this pressure of business, Woodriff was deprived of assistance. The two subordinate lieutenants were ordered to accompany the transports, Wheatley to Gibraltar, and Flinn to the West Indies. Meanwhile two ships sent to receive troops at Southampton each required refitting and cleaning. Captain Joshua Mulock wrote from Cowes warning Woodriff with regard to the *Jane*: 'The joiners have been very negligent, the cabins being scarcely all fitted. So much for Easter Holidays.'[19] Simultaneously, Captain Charles Lane wrote from Portsmouth that he understood the *St Mary's Planter* 'must be whitewashed and fumigated, after the nasty fellows that have been on board of her'.[20]

At the end of 1796 another expedition, this time to occupy Trinidad and Puerto Rico, demanded Woodriff's exertions. With the foothold on French St Domingue, this expedition was intended to give Britain control of the largest islands in the West Indies. Having returned to England, Abercromby departed again on 15 November 1796, and the rest of the expedition a month later. However, yet again, finding enough ships for the troops proved a problem, especially as the 'Inspector of Foreign Troops' [Transports]' (probably Sir Jerome Fitzpatrick, mentioned earlier) objected to crowding on

---

[17] For the embarkation of troops in East India ships, see J. H. Thomas, *The East India Company and the Provinces in the Eighteenth Century*. Vol. I *Portsmouth and the East India Company 1700–1815* (Lampeter, 1999), pp. 223–49.
[18] TNA, ADM.108/28, 24,26,27,28,29 March 1796.
[19] TNA, ADM.108/28, 30, 31 March 1796.
[20] TNA, ADM. 108/28, 30,31 March, 1 April 1796.

THE WORK OF THE TRANSPORT AGENT

the ships destined for St Domingue. There was a scramble to find another ship and many complaints of officers and stores left behind. On Christmas Eve 1796 Woodriff was required to report 'by return of post' the stores and names, ranks and number of officers 'actually embarked' or remaining to be embarked. For each, he had to detail the government office, with date, from which an application for passage came – in order that the Transport Board could 'report to Mr Secretary Dundas whether any delays or negligence may have occurred in completing the late expedition so far as may implicate the agents of the Board'.[21]

Otherwise, the business of equipping and despatching transports was settling into a routine. 'Horse ships' were largely completed with stalls, horse gear and most of their water, provisions, and forage before they left the River Thames. The supervising agent at Blackwall, Captain Rains, had at least five lieutenants under him, each employed afloat completing ships. The final boatload or so of ballast was often left wanting, because its provision 'would be an excuse for the master to detain the ships for many days at Blackwall'. Anyway better ballast could be had near Southampton where 'in the creek on the upper side of Calshot castle any number of ships can be ballasted with great ease'. Oats and forage were also sometimes deficient. But Rains had to use every fair wind to get the vessels down and out of the Thames. Easterly winds, thick fogs and 'frost in the Thames' detained them, as did the occasional accident: the stern of the *Betsy* was 'entirely stove in by a ship falling on board of her' and required the carpenters to effect repairs.[22]

The ships on their way from the Thames to Portsmouth were listed periodically to Woodriff by the secretary to the Transport Board. One list of eighteen horse ships 'for Portugal' indicates an average individual tonnage of 324 tons, the largest 429 tons, the smallest 255 tons. Each took between thirty and forty-four horses, and the same number of riders.[23] The horse transports were more than usually incomplete: only nine had all their fittings, provisions and forage. They had been hurried out of the Thames from 'apprehension of the ice blocking them up'. Captain Schank thought that fumigation was 'not absolutely necessary' in such cold weather and left it to Woodriff 'to burn a few devils and white wash them' if he thought it necessary.

For these horse transports, Woodriff had to buy pressed hay and oats, and employ a specialist to inspect the fodder before concluding his purchases.

---

[21] Duffy, *Soldiers, Sugar and Seapower*, pp. 270–4; TNA, ADM. 108/28, 24 December 1796.
[22] Lieutenants Parke, Pemberton, Lamb and Hay were mentioned on the 28 December, Parke and Boyce on 4 January 1796. TNA, ADM. 108/28, 23 December 1795, 4 January 1796.
[23] TNA, ADM. 108/28, 28 December 1796.

Because he had to deal with the cavalry when they embarked at Southampton, the Board left 'entirely' to his judgement the final fitting of the ships. The Board simply recommended he adopt 'any mode proposed by the cavalry officers for the safety of the horses – if you see no material objection thereto'. He was allowed funds to purchase the articles 'usual on former occasions to provide them with'. In addition, large quantities of horse shoes in sets, with proportions of nails, were sent overland from London to Southampton by 'Russel and Kent's Waggon': there were twenty-three casks containing 800 sets of horse shoes and 76,800 nails in one load.[24]

The failure to complete the transports in the Thames increased the pressure of work upon Woodriff. He was prompted to submit regulations 'for facilitating embarkation of the cavalry' which were approved by the Transport Board. Yet the Board, anxious about the progress of transports preparing for Portugal, required him to submit a daily progress report 'till the whole embarkation is completed and the ships ready for sea'. The Board itself was under pressure to economise, and this pressure was transferred to their agent at Southampton. Woodriff was required to make a 'general return' of all the persons, vessels and storehouses employed by him, their costs, and his opinion where reductions might be made.[25]

Economies in 1797 meant that fewer vessels were available. One small one had to be found solely for a voyage to Holland under a flag of truce with thirty-six prisoners of war. Troops destined for Martinique that could not be squeezed into tonnage under hire had to be found passages on merchant ships congregating at Spithead for convoy to the West Indies. One consignment of 156 recruits to reinforce the garrison in the Channel Islands went by transport under standard long-term charter. For such short voyages, however, it was more economical to use ships one way on short-term charter. To achieve an even greater saving, for the next voyage to the Channel Islands the Board instructed Woodriff to negotiate 'freight' with the masters of 'passage boats' to take 150 invalids from Hilsea barracks to Guernsey and Jersey.

For these invalids, the Board did not want to crowd more than one man to one ton burthen, and anticipated the cost at ten or twelve shillings per man or woman, half the price for children, and 'officers in proportion'. The navy had to supply the 'blankets, or some kind of bedding', for which the masters had to be accountable. But to keep the arrangement simple and avoid the Victualling Board having to provide provisions in bulk, the masters were expected to supply victuals at an extra 1s 3d per man. The Board gave Woodriff authority

---

[24] TNA, ADM.108/28, 22 December 1796, 4, 11, 14, 15, 21 January 1797.
[25] TNA, ADM. 108/28, 4, 10, 13 January 1797.

to fix an agreement on the best terms possible, but stipulated it would have nothing to do with convoy or insurance.[26]

While receiving such directions direct from London, Woodriff's workload was increased by demands at short notice from Portsmouth. When, on account of strong winds, the Portsmouth transport commissioner was unable to inspect ships at the request of the Board, he asked Woodriff to do it. Demands for the 'loan' of vessels came from Portsmouth too. Regiments had to be shipped from Portsmouth to the Isle of Wight. That was no great distance, but army officers expected shipping to be ready for a particular day and time; and, although accommodation for 400 to 500 men could be estimated, the amount of regimental baggage could not. While the Portsmouth port admiral might spare one or two cutters, Woodriff was expected to supply one or two gunboats or some other craft.[27]

In all these tasks, Woodriff appears to have been capable of executing his duties with promptitude and good sense. He also appears to have been capable of exercising authority with discretion. For example, the master of the *Adventure* transport complained of Captain Barton (probably the naval Barton of that rank[28]) taking his jolly boat for half an hour and keeping it for the whole day; then taking it the following day to go to the Isle of Wight. Captain Barton insisted 'he would have a boat when he wanted it', but the ship master was also without his launch and yawl which were employed getting water and forage. As the ship master pointed out, had a man fallen overboard or a signal been made, he could not have answered it. Indignantly he claimed, 'it is more than my charter specifies, that boats are for pleasure when actual service is required'. Unwilling to confront Barton itself, the Transport Board asked Woodriff to take steps 'to prevent the delay' which might result to His Majesty's service from Barton's conduct in the future.[29]

As the local manager, representative and eyes of the Transport Board at Southampton, Woodriff managed ships with efficiency and men with discretion, and was clearly perfectly acquainted with the clauses of charter parties and the regulation of transports. Paradoxically, in view of his experience and ability, Woodriff was moved from Southampton to Norfolk in March 1797, to become responsible for the movements of prisoners of war between Lynn Regis and the prison camp at Norman Cross. He was to remain there until February 1800. Promoted from commander to captain in 1802, he was made a CB in 1832.[30]

---

[26] TNA, ADM. 108/28, 24 December 1796, 25, 26, 27 January, 18 February 1797.
[27] TNA, ADM. 108/28, 27 January, 18 February 1797.
[28] Robert Barton, RN: captain 1794, rear-admiral in 1812.
[29] TNA, ADM. 108/28, 26 January 1797.
[30] TNA, ADM. 108/28; *Commissioned Sea Officers of the Royal Navy*, p. 479.

Woodriff's forte was the ability to impose order on the shipping in Southampton Water. What contribution did this ability make to the capacity of the Transport Board to assemble, prepare and despatch ships on overseas expeditions? We should remember Woodriff was just one of a corps of agents employed by the Transport Board: at Deptford, Woolwich, Gravesend, Dover, Deal, Portsmouth, Cowes, Southampton, Plymouth, Bristol, Guernsey, Waterford, Cork, Liverpool and Leith. In addition there were agents working afloat, at Spithead and with large contingents of transports on expeditions.

The great value of these local agents was their ability to turn ships from one use to another, to turn them around with the minimum delay, to manage cleaning, fitting, equipment and embarkations efficiently, so that ships under hire were used with economy and for the purposes demanded by government. As Woodriff's work showed, moreover, the transport agent was expected to handle all the problems of a miscellaneous nature that occurred at the main rendezvous. Experience and teamwork facilitated this task, and not only at the ports. There is no question that the Transport service as formed in 1794 benefitted from experience accrued by its commissioners during the American War of Independence, experience indeed which continued to develop through the wars from 1793.

How did this team of experienced commissioners and agents make for efficiency in the provision of transportation? The first expedient was to hire on a broad front. Such was the pace of preparations for the expeditions of the French Revolutionary War that ships were hired on a large scale even before their specific use was decided – to carry troops, victuals or stores as the board's surveyors recommended. The Transport Board hired ships from far more owners than the other boards before 1794 had been able to do. In the American War, the Navy Board (the board hiring the greatest number of ships) had taken up transports from as many as seventy-two contractors, with one-third of its vessels from a single owner or broker.[31] Yet by 1801 the Transport Board had contracts with over 300 owners. It was helped by the start of ship registration in 1788, which identified vessels suitable for hire, and simplified the process by a decision to take their registered tonnage as their size instead of measuring them. In consequence, the work and cost of surveying vessels before hire was reduced.[32]

Economies of scale, speed of hire, and the flexible conversion of ships from one use to another gave the Transport Board a higher rate of output than its predecessors. In 1776 ships to convey 27,000 troops, their provisions and

---

[31] William L. Clements Library, University of Michigan, Shelburne Papers, vol. 151, 24 October 1782. D. Syrett, 'The Victualling Board Charters Shipping', *Historical Research* 68 (1995), 212–24.

[32] Condon, 'The Administration of the Transport Service', pp. 312–14.

ordnance to America had taken nine months to hire and despatch. In 1795 the ships needed to convey a greater number, 30,800, on the first Christian-Abercromby expedition to the West Indies took only three months.[33]

Many of the ships in 1795 were already under hire. But four years later, the Transport Board achieved a greater, and more measurable, pace. The Helder expedition in 1799 demanded the conveyance of 46,000 men from England and the Baltic to north Holland. Preparations were begun at the end of June 1799. Within a month the Transport Board had allotted 44,000 tons of transport to the task, three-quarters of which had been newly hired into government service. After three months the Board had collected, fitted and despatched 90,000 tons of shipping; that was nearly six per cent of all the tonnage available in the United Kingdom, taken up at a rate of 30,000 tons (or more than 100 ships) a month.[34] At the rate of two tons of shipping per soldier, the Transport board had the ability to convey to the continent at least 15,000 men on average every month. Of course the Helder was closer to England than the West Indies and in 1799 the shorter distance permitted some transports to make three successive trips carrying troops. The rate of conveyance nevertheless indicates an impressive facility for amphibious operations.[35]

Of these operations, the work of the transport agent, like Captain Daniel Woodriff, was an integral and essential part. Yet, as Woodriff's work in Southampton Water suggested, the business of despatching transports, the pressures for efficiency and economy, and the tensions that existed with navy and army personnel were not new. What, then, did the new board possess that permitted it to manage war pressures and achieve logistical feats that lay at the foundation of Britain's amphibious capability after 1794? It possessed three qualities which it fiercely maintained: its reputation, independence and authority.

From the beginning the Transport Board established a reputation for scrupulous administrative integrity. Within a month of its establishment, the Transport Board ruled in August 1794 that any employee having any interest, direct or indirect, in any ship hired as a transport would be dismissed forthwith.[36] The ruling came five days after the master of a naval victualler, owned by the Victualling Board's former Hoytaker, claimed freight for £1,409 which

---

[33] Ibid., pp. 315–16, 319. See also Duffy, *Soldiers, Sugar and Seapower*, pp. 184–96
[34] Calculated at 270 tons per ship.
[35] Condon, 'The Administration of the Transport Service', p. 317.
[36] TNA, ADM. 108/31, 26 August 1794, cited in Condon, 'The Administration of the Transport Service', p. 62.

that Board could not sanction, having no knowledge of the terms upon which part of the sum was earned.[37]

With this new beginning, the Transport Board assumed an independence from the earlier proceedings of the other existing naval boards. Established by the Treasury, the Transport Board received the king's commands directly from the Secretary for War and Colonies rather than from the Admiralty. Indeed, though a formality, it was the Transport Board that reminded the Admiralty of cabinet decisions at the same time as it requested convoy for the vessels – the Transport Board having already by then directed the masters of transports where to embark troops, ordered its own local agents to manage these embarkations, and instructed those agents to await orders from the Admiralty regarding convoy.[38]

This independence imparted some authority, but for the rest the Transport Board had to fight. Within two weeks of its first official meeting an important demarcation dispute arose with the Victualling Board over which of them should direct and control the transports once they were laden with provisions. The Victualling Board based its claim on previous directions from the Admiralty: the situation before July 1794. But the Admiralty decided the Transport Board should henceforward direct transports when and where to proceed at the same time as it requested convoy. The task of the Victualling Board was accordingly reduced to just that of supplying the appropriate provisions to troop transports and victuallers.[39] The same reasoning was applied to the Navy and Ordnance Boards. The Transport Board provided tonnage according to the stores the other boards had to convey and the Transport Board informed the Admiralty when the ships were ready to sail.[40]

The authority of the new commissioners permitted it to transact business with the other boards on equal, if not superior, terms. This was vital to the efficiency of its administrative role. For, although it served the other boards, it also required their assistance and cooperation. For example, initially the

---

[37] NMM, ADM.DP/14, 21 August 1794; the ship was the *Crescent*, James Loring master, owned by Messrs St Barbe, Green and Bignall.

[38] TNA, ADM. 1/3730, 6 September 1794, cited in Condon, 'The Administration of the Transport Service', pp. 60–1.

[39] Having laden the transport *Active* and given her master directions to proceed to Spithead, the Victualling Board claimed 'a right to send out provisions, and by that right to give their directions for the movements of the transports, not admitting that the Transport Board had any power to do more than to hire in the first instance'. Meanwhile the Transport Board claimed 'the victualling service should extend no further than ... receiving ... the species of provisions they had occasion to embark'. TNA, ADM.1/3730, 17, 20 September 1794; ADM.108/31, 17 September 1794.

[40] TNA, ADM. 1/3730, 20 October 1794; in Condon, 'The Administration of the Transport Service', pp. 66–7.

Treasury or the Secretary for War corresponded with both the Transport and Victualling Boards to secure provisions for troop transports and the army victuallers.[41] But in September 1794, to save repeated directions to the Victualling Board, the Secretary for War requested the Admiralty order the Victualling Board to comply automatically with demands for the supply of provisions from the Transport Board. This the Admiralty did and the Victualling Board needed no prompting from a senior board thereafter.[42]

This cooperation at board level, the reputation, independence and authority of the Transport Board, combined with the high exertions of its agents in the ports where transports were assembled and despatched, gave the British state a bureaucratic organisation that directly addressed the need for a large-scale, efficient transport service. There can be no doubt that the effectiveness of this service underpinned the amphibious military operations mounted by the British state during the French Revolutionary and Napoleonic Wars. The work of Captain Daniel Woodriff possessed neither the drama nor the excitement of military combat, but it was representative of the efforts made by individuals within the state's bureaucracy that ensured Britain's military operations overseas during the French wars were successful. Woodriff's work was not much different to the efforts that had been made in the ports during the American War of Independence and previous hostilities, but after 1794 they were part of a new and developing structure that ensured shipping and all other resources were made available to the British armed forces on a large scale. These efforts, and their new structural context, deserve and need to be recognised as a vital part of British military and imperial history.

---

[41] For an example of this coordination, see TNA, ADM.109/102, 19 September 1794, cited in Condon, 'The Administration of the Transport Service', p. 63.
[42] TNA, ADM.1/4162, 3 September 1794, cited in Condon, 'The Administration of the Transport Service', p. 64.

6

Forgotten or Ignored, the Officers at Invergordon: 'We are doing this for you as well you know'

Mike Farquharson-Roberts

This chapter looks at a forgotten part of the Royal Navy of the 1920s and 1930s – its junior executive officers. Most junior regular naval officers are always in the background; only when they become commanders, captains and flag officers do they move forward on the stage. Otherwise they are almost a 'dull, slight, cloudy naught'.[1] What of these officers; how were they trained and how were their careers managed? In particular, what of their morale and personal concerns?

First, a note on sources and in particular Admiralty Fleet Orders (AFOs) as they were known after 1923.[2] These were the Admiralty's way of communicating with the navy, and up to four thousand a year were issued. They came out weekly in six sections, the second covering personnel issues. Being promulgated policy, they can be regarded, in modern terms, as a management bulletin board.

This study concentrates on lieutenants and lieutenant-commanders. Properly speaking the latter was a senior officer. However, until very recently a lieutenant-commander was no more than a senior lieutenant; promotion from lieutenant to lieutenant-commander was automatic at eight years seniority. Scrutiny of the personnel records of 20 per cent of officers commissioned between the two world wars, 494 records,[3] shows that only two of those still serving were not promoted eight years after becoming lieutenant; one because

---

[1] G. Keynes (ed.), *The Poetical Works of Rupert Brooke* (London, 1946) p. 44.
[2] Prior to that they were issued as either Admiralty Weekly Orders (AWOs) or Monthly Orders (MOs).
[3] The author has been allowed access to officers' personal records by the Second Sea Lord, subject to the constraints of the University of Exeter ethical approval and individual

he had lost two years seniority at court martial and the other because he submitted his resignation just before the eight-year point and he left the navy three months later. The remainder were promoted automatically. Lieutenants were a 'lump of labour', as Lambert has pointed out:

> The navy need a large supply of capable officers for junior command, watch-keeping, managing the men and imposing order. It required relatively few captains to exercise the independent command of ships. Rather than overeducate those who would not rise beyond lieutenant, the navy took in boys, and trained them for this specific rank, relying on chance and opportunity to select those who would become the next generation of leaders.[4]

Lieutenants and lieutenant-commanders were and are the middle management 'worker bees' and leaders of the navy. What tends to be forgotten is that leaders need to be led; it is a very rare person who does not need inspiration and leadership, and this paper will show that is precisely what the navy got wrong through the 1920s. This is done by looking at the morale and motivation of naval officers in the years after the First World War leading up to the Invergordon mutiny in September 1931 and then briefly looking at some episodes in the mutiny itself, which can fairly claim to be the oddest mutiny in the history of the Royal Navy. However, this chapter is not about Invergordon; it is about the officers, and will draw on some post-Invergordon sources to make some points.

The Royal Navy between the Two World Wars

Between the wars the Admiralty was headed by the First Lord of the Admiralty, a civilian political appointee. The professional head of the Royal Navy was the First Sea Lord[5]; from the First World War up to the Invergordon mutiny the office was held successively by Admirals Sir Rosslyn Wemyss (1917–1919), the Earl Beatty (1919–1927), Sir Charles Madden (1927–1930) and Sir Frederick Field (1930–1933).

When they were members of the Admiralty Board, officers did not wear uniform. They even visited ships and naval shore establishments in plain clothes (that is, civilian clothes). Service Board members on appointment went onto half pay, as if they were un-employed by the navy, and were given

---

confidentiality. These records are available on request. Subsequent references to these records are 'Second Sea Lord, Officers' personal records'.
[4] A. Lambert, *Admirals: The Naval Commanders Who Made Britain Great* (London, 2008), pp. 160–1.
[5] Also holding the post of 'Chief of the Naval Staff'.

a civil service salary. It would have been difficult for them to see themselves as other than civil servants, and certainly Admiral Lord Chatfield, Field's successor and previously a Board member, put it they were 'a body who had left their naval sympathies as well as their uniforms behind them and who, with their civil clothes, had put on also a civil mind'.[6]

In the years after the First World War, what did the Board do to motivate its officers? It is difficult to prove a negative, but apart from the introduction of the pay scale in 1919 up until 1930, the Admiralty Board did nothing significant to improve the lot of the generality of the officer corps, admittedly during a period of severe retrenchment.[7] Beatty was First Sea Lord for most of the 1920s and was mainly concerned with materiel matters.[8] Madden crippled his standing from the start with a childish row over seniority which he insisted on taking to the Prime Minister. On losing the argument he lost, at the same time, his authority in Whitehall.[9] Only when Field became First Sea Lord and started a whole series of reforms did things start to improve, but these had not had time to have any effect on officer morale or mood by the time of Invergordon.

Pay and Allowances

The 1919 pay scale was originally announced as a First World War 'bonus', recognizing that sailors had been underpaid in comparison with industrial workers even before the First World War, let alone the pay increases and inflation during the war.[10] For ratings and, to a lesser extent, officers, the basic pay was only a significant part, not the totality, of their pay. There were many additional allowances.[11] Some were patently a cause of bad feeling, but to only to small segments of the officer community, for example, submariners stopped getting submarine pay while ashore on staff course; a significant cut in their income.[12]

There was one allowance, or rather its absence, that caused a lot of bad feeling across the officer corps. All eligible members of the Armed Forces

---

6   Admiral of the Fleet Lord Chatfield, *The Navy and Defence. Volume 2, It Might Happen Again* (London, 1947) p. 58.
7   There were minor changes and improvements, and some tinkering with allowances.
8   And justifying his performance at the Battle of Jutland.
9   S. Roskill, *Hankey: Man of Secrets. Volume ii, 1919–1931* (London, 1972), pp. 445–6.
10 AWO 407a/19 *Bonus to Naval Officers and Men*.
11 For example, two shillings (10 pence) per week for playing the harmonium or a penny a day if in charge of the library.
12 AFO 1381/25 *Submarine Officers and Naval Observers – Allowance while undergoing staff courses*.

were entitled to a marriage allowance, except Royal Naval officers.[13] This was given to naval ratings and even dominion naval officers. AFOs updating the allowance for Canadian officers usefully included the rate in sterling to aid in paying officers serving attached to the Royal Navy, which given the public nature of AFOs can only have rubbed salt into the wound.[14]

Beatty himself initially did not support the recommendation of his own Grand Fleet committee that there should be a marriage allowance, but later, in 1924, he tried to get one for naval officers.[15] How hard he tried it is difficult to determine from the extant papers, certainly Roskill was not impressed with his efforts:

> When the struggle over the marriage allowance was in progress, sea going officers commonly expressed the view that Admiral Beatty, having married an extremely wealthy wife, did not view the problems of less favoured individuals sympathetically.[16]

Officers had been told that 20 per cent of their pay was variable, i.e., subject to cuts. Officers, and officers alone, underwent a pay cut in 1924 of 5½ per cent attributable to the fall in the cost of living.[17] How the cost of living was estimated has been the subject of much debate, suffice it to say that most authors seem to think the basket was weighted against the middle class, such as the officers. Curiously, at exactly the same time, civil service pay was increased, because of an increase in the cost of living, but judged over a slightly different time period.[18] This would have meant of course that Board members had a pay rise while all their officers had a pay cut. For ratings the only significant change in their pay came in 1925. At that point all new entrants to the Royal Navy, officers and ratings, were put on the lower pay scale, but those on the 1919 scale were unaffected until Invergordon.[19] It did mean however that there was a two-tier pay structure.

In 1927 officers had a further pay cut. The reasoning of the AFO and the mechanism was, at best, arcane (and with a fine disregard for rules regarding mixing percentages and fractions):

---

[13] There was an age qualification.
[14] AWO 2718/19 *RCN and RCNVR Marriage Allowance*.
[15] While CinC Grand Fleet he had established a series of committees, effectively a shadow naval staff.
[16] S. Roskill, *Naval Policy Between the Wars: The Period of Anglo-American Antagonism* (New York, 1968), p. 449.
[17] AFO 1701/24 *Officers' Pay in 1924 – Revision of Rates*.
[18] A. Richardson and A. Hurd (eds), *Brassey's Naval and Shipping Annual 1925* (London, 1925), p. 157.
[19] AFO 2858/25 *Officers' Pay – Revised Rates for New Entrants*.

THE OFFICERS AT INVERGORDON

The rates of pay, retired pay etc., ruling from 1ˢᵗ July, 1927, until 30ᵗʰ June 1930, will accordingly be, approximately, 80 per cent. plus 74/107 ½ of 20 per cent. of the standard rates *i.e.* 93.77 per cent. of the standard rates.[20]

This pay scale was to be in force until 30 June 1930, meaning that officers' pay would be reviewed triennially. Despite this in 1929 a further pay cut was announced and at the same time it was announced that officers' pay would now be reviewed annually. There was another pay cut in July 1930, and officers were told that 20 per cent of their pay was to be regarded as variable, that is, subject to cuts. This meant 20 per cent of each year's pay rate, not 20 per cent of the starting pay in 1919, which is what had been said in 1924. In February 1931 a further 8 per cent pay cut was announced with the actual pay rates promulgated in May 1931. Then in September 1931 came the pay cut that precipitated the Invergordon mutiny. The pay cut for ratings was to be a one off cut,[21] but for officers, what was eventually announced, after the mutiny was over, was a further 3 per cent on top of the 8 per cent, already promulgated, backdated to the end of September, with the added sting in the tail that they were to have their pay rate reviewed six monthly thereafter.[22]

Redundancies

It is popularly believed that there was only one major redundancy round for officers after the First World War, the so called 'Geddes axe'.[23] In fact there was a continuous series of badly handled redundancy programmes throughout the 1920s and into the 1930s. Immediately after the war the 'Reconstruction Committee', charged with reducing manpower numbers, did not know how large the post-war fleet would be but nonetheless decided with amazing precision as to the numbers of officers to be made redundant.

It is very interesting to look at the management weight put on various ranks. The Admiralty Board minute discussing and agreeing the compulsory redundancy round for the more junior officers, that is lieutenant-commanders and below, runs to four lines. Having made this decision the Board then

---

[20] AFO 26/27 *Officers' Emoluments – Revision on account of Variation in the Cost of Living.*
[21] AFO 2239/31 *Pay of Naval Ratings and Royal Marines – Revised Rates for Men at present in Receipt of pre-Octobers 1925, Rates – Allotments and Pensions.*
[22] AFO 2238 /31 *Officers' Emoluments – Revision of, on account of Need for Economy in National Expenditure;* AFO 2409/31 *Officers' Emoluments – Revision on account of Need for Economy in National Expenditure.*
[23] Cmd 1581 *First Interim Report of Committee on National Expenditure.*

Table 6.1. Ranks and numbers of officers to be made redundant

Commanders	189
Lieutenant-Commanders/Lieutenants	283
Sub-Lieutenants/Mates/Midshipmen	398
Cadets	347
Captains	95
Warrant Officers	800

Source: TNA, ADM 116/1888.

turned to discussing the surplus of captains – the minute is an entire foolscap page long and does not reach a decision.[24]

The redundancy programme itself was not well managed. Cadets and midshipmen, or rather their parents,[25] were sent a letter by the Board saying in essence go now and take £400 to start a new career or, if you choose not to go and we then choose to make you redundant, you will get nothing.[26] This was hardly a scheme designed to retain the best, nor did it. One cadet was made redundant at the very end of his time. His sister (*in loco parentis*) wrote to the Admiralty asking for confirmation that the Dartmouth education was equivalent to that of a public school. Armed with the confirmatory letter, he then applied for Public School Special Entry and, because of the differing regulations for the two officer entry streams, he ended up senior to his Dartmouth term mates, retiring in 1954 a highly decorated and successful officer.[27]

Chatfield as Assistant Chief of the Naval Staff (ACNS) was in charge of the redundancy scheme, and was obviously very touchy about the criticisms of it. Even years later he insisted: 'There was not a single case of any officer being axed in preference to any other except from the standpoint of Service ability'.[28]

How were the officers chosen to be made redundant? Special confidential reports known as 'Form S206' were called for. However, these reports only allowed officers to be graded as 'outstanding', 'above average', 'average' or 'below average'. Of the 494 officers whose reports were examined, only three were graded outstanding and that on one occasion each,[29] so in reality the Board had very little to go on when choosing between officers to make redundant.

[24] TNA, ADM 116/1888.
[25] Being under twenty-one they were minors.
[26] AWO 906/20 *Midshipmen RN – Grant for Voluntary Withdrawals – Report 19.9.*
[27] Second Sea Lord, Officers' personal records.
[28] Admiral of the Fleet Lord Chatfield, *The Navy and Defence* (London, 1942), p. 199.
[29] Reports were made annually or on change of appointment or of Commanding Officer

It only serves to illustrate that then and well into the latter half of the twentieth century the personnel management systems for officers were, at best, old fashioned. Each officer was managed from a ledger partially abstracted onto a foolscap card in a landscape or horizontal format with their name somewhere near the top. The ledger pages were approximately in order of seniority as a cadet, but there appear to have been no indexing systems so that appointing officers would have to work from notes, personal knowledge and the 'I've got just the job for you' style of appointing well known to generations of naval officers. Without going into details, such as the absence of service numbers[30] which would allow tabulation and mechanical data management systems such as the Hollerith punch card system widely used elsewhere by the end of the 1920s,[31] personnel management was very hit and miss, and could only be done by fairly extreme rigidity. For example, officers were not allowed to ask for a given appointment or change one once received.[32] This was not, as stated, for disciplinary reasons, but because the system could not cope with such changes.

Thus, even by contemporary standards, the Admiralty Board, did not have the proper personnel management tools to carry out a measured redundancy programme in slow time, let alone the rushed process that actually happened. This cannot have improved its standing in the eyes of the officer corps.

Unfortunately the officers being made redundant were given little support. The king sent them a message in 1922:

> I have learned with great regret that the necessary reduction of the Royal Navy entails the retirement this year of a large number of Officers and Men who took part in the labours and perils of the War and contributed so largely to its victorious issue. As their King I desire to express to them my high appreciation of their devoted service, and deep sympathy with them in the enforced termination of their careers in the Navy; that life so dear to them, as it was to me and in which many of them have gained distinction both in Peace and War.[33]

There were no further words of support from management, there was no statement made by politicians or Service members of the Board of Admiralty. The Admiralty promulgated some efforts to find jobs for the surplus officers. Some junior officers were offered transfer to the Royal Air Force, or into the engineering branch which was in shortage.[34] For officers who had been

---

[30] Officers in the Royal Navy did not have service numbers until the 1960s.
[31] N. Rankin, *Churchill's Wizards: The British Genius for Deception 1914–1945* (London, 2008), p. 274.
[32] AWO 264/20 *Appointments – Officers.*
[33] AFO 1970/22 *Capital Reduction of personnel – Message from H.M. The King.*
[34] AFO 173/23 *Royal Air Force Offer of Short Service Commissions to Surplus Officers.*

through the 'Cambridge course', Cambridge University was prepared to allow this as being equivalent to two terms of residential training.[35] The University of London offered eased terms of entry, as did the University of Bristol which waived its requirement that first-year undergraduates must reside in a hall of residence.[36]

Otherwise, apart from three places in the Chinese Maritime Customs service, the only support offered was agricultural training, help with emigration or agriculture overseas.[37] At the end of 1922 the Admiralty Board sought further sources of employment:

> Their Lordships would be glad if Officers, who hear of any appointments or opportunities of employment outside the Service, suitable for retired Officers, would communicate details of the same *direct* [italicised in the original] to the Secretary of the Admiralty'[38]

The Geddes axe was not the end of it. Obviously, the officer corps was nervous because when in 1926 a committee was convened to consider 'the policy to be pursued in future with regard to the executive' the Admiralty Board went so far as to specifically deny that further redundancies were in the offing.[39] However, later the same year it announced a further redundancy round, stating that unless the surpluses were removed long periods of unemployment would be necessary, which would of course be time spent on half pay.[40] At the very least, this cannot have enhanced the credibility of the Board in the eyes of the officer corps.

There was another redundancy round in 1929, followed by a further one in February 1931, seven months before Invergordon, which would have made one in six lieutenant-commanders of seniority of 1923 to 1931 redundant.[41] Overall, as one commentator summed matters up: 'the Government of Great Britain ... "axed" many naval officers who became garage-owners, poultry-keepers or farmers until they went bankrupt, as they mostly did'.[42] This not

---

[35] Comprising two terms at Cambridge, this had been introduced after the First World War to broaden the education of officers who had been sent prematurely to war; AWO 1809/22 *Retired Officers who have been through the Cambridge Course, Further Study.*
[36] AWO 2114/22 *Officers Retiring under Special Scheme – Facilities for Study at London University.*
[37] AWO 2894/22 *Surplus Junior Executive Officers – Vacancies in the Chinese Maritime Customs Service*; AWO 2336/22 *Surplus Officers – Courses in Agriculture.*
[38] AWO 3335/22 *Retired Officers – Reports as to Opportunities of Employment.*
[39] AFO 5/26 *Committee on the List of Executive Officers of the Royal Navy.*
[40] After two years on half pay, there was a mechanism for compulsory redundancy.
[41] AFO 1036/29 *Lieutenant-Commanders RN – Special Terms of Retirement*; AFO 289/31 *Lieutenants and Lieutenant-Commanders RN – Special Terms of Retirement.*
[42] P. Gibbs, *Across the Frontiers* (London, 1938), p. 19.

only affected the officers made redundant; they left friends behind in the service who must have been all too well aware of what was happening to their ex-colleagues.

Morale

What else happened to affect morale before the Invergordon mutiny? The navy had probably got used to the fact by 1931 that the service was not the centre of attention it had been before the First World War, that the eight battleships ordered in 1909 as part of the 'We want eight and we won't wait' public furore had gone for scrapping with barely any attention paid by the media. It was not so much that the navy had a low public standing, it just didn't have one at all; social histories of the period barely mention the Royal Navy. However there were a couple of significant incidents that did bring the navy unwelcome public attention. The first, the *Royal Oak* affair, was 'a farce that was to bring a deep blush to the navy's face',[43] started with an episode at a ball on board HMS *Royal Oak* in front of civilian guests. A difference between three officers which should have been resolved within the chain of command led to a very public court martial, and the press had a field day. Then there was a mutiny in HMS *Lucia* in January 1931. She was a German prize converted in 1915 to be a submarine depot ship. The Admiralty Board acted entirely properly, but unfortunately political intervention made it look as though they had been driven by political considerations, by the requirements of a Labour First Lord to look good to the trades unions.[44]

HMS *Lucia* itself was illustrative of another factor that impinged on officer morale. The vessel was old in 1923 when the Admiralty Board had considered replacing it; by 1931 it was described by the Court of Enquiry into the mutiny as having very poor facilities for the crew. *Lucia* continued to serve until 1946. This was an extreme case, but a lot of ships in the fleet were very old, very tired and very out of date, which made for a poor working environment.

Promotion

Throughout the 1920s officers' promotion chances progressively worsened. An officer was expected by the navy to join at the age of 13½ with the intention of making it his life's career, but if he was not promoted commander

---

[43] R. Glenton, *The Royal Oak Affair: The Saga of Admiral Collard and Bandmaster Barnacle* (London, 1991), p. 17.
[44] M. A. Farquharson-Roberts, 'The *Lucia* Mutiny: A Failure of the Royal Navy's Internal Communications', *RUSI Journal* 154:2 (2009), 104–7.

by the age of forty-five the navy ended that career. As has been shown, the navy considered the list of lieutenant-commanders overborne, and thus their percentage chance of being promoted steadily reduced during the 1920s. This had an unfortunate effect; officers were scared stiff of doing something wrong and so tended not to show initiative. An extract from an officer's confidential report in 1932 serves to illustrate this point.

> [He] has erred tactlessly in this ship with my predecessor & was given a well-deserved black mark, but the whole episode occurred due to his sense of zeal & duty – a lazy or cowardly Offr. Would have done nothing & thus received no black mark; it is unfortunately true already that [lieutenant-commanders] think it necessary, due to the limited chances of promotion, to avoid any semblance of a black mark, & this is re-acting disastrously on initiative ...[45]

This may be taken with the opinion of Admiral Kelly in his report after the Invergordon mutiny:

> It is abundantly clear also that the present system of training and appointment of Officers is in many ways unsatisfactory ... To give all these Officers employment of a character suitable to their age and seniority is not possible ... and the efficiency of Officers of all ranks therefore suffers.[46]

The Invergordon Mutiny

This study does not seek to re-examine the whole mutiny, but rather to look at one or two occurrences and features. Lieutenant Elkins had commanded the patrol[47] ashore and, coming off shore the night before the mutiny, he was bumped into by a slightly drunk three-badge man[48] off HMS *Rodney* who, according to Lieutenant Elkins, said 'We are doing this for you as well as ourselves.'[49] The following morning Lieutenant Elkins was woken by his servant and told 'The hands refused to fall in this morning Sir'. Lieutenant Elkins's reaction to being told the ratings had mutinied was to have a bath and go down to the wardroom for breakfast where he was told by the steward 'as far as he knew everything would be as usual'. In fact in HMS *Norfolk* one steward on his own initiative decided to join the mutiny. His messmates dissuaded him and he turned to with two black eyes. The whole mutiny was characterised by the sailors showing exaggerated marks of respect to their

---

[45] Second Sea Lord, Officers' personal records.
[46] TNA, ADM 178/129.
[47] The navy not having a police force apart from a small 'regulating branch', the 'patrol' made up of duty personnel carries out this function.
[48] The 'badges' indicate that he had at least twelve years' service.
[49] D. Divine, *Mutiny at Invergordon* (London, 1970), p. 142.

officers and apparently the officers going out of their way to avoid giving orders to individual ratings; what would normally be an order was phrased as a request. Thus individuals could not be charged with mutiny.[50] Apart from the steward in *Norfolk*, the only firm imposition of discipline that I can find occurred among the Royal Marines. In HMS *Rodney* the marines refused to turn to and the subaltern, Lieutenant Campbell-Hardy, an officer who later became known, even outside the corps, for his rather direct approach to life, went to their mess deck (known as the Marine barracks), and told the marines, 'I would like to remind you that you are all sworn men and if you are not present at the next muster of hands I will see that you are shot.'[51]

In the aftermath of the mutiny confidential reports were requested from commanding officers on their heads of department and from admirals on their captains. Rear Admiral Wilfred Tomkinson, acting Commander in Chief Atlantic Fleet, commenting on the captain of HMS *Nelson* wrote that he had 'made the astonishing suggestion that the [second in command of the ship] should proceed to the Admiralty owing to his knowledge of the feelings of the men'.[52] While it certainly was an astonishing suggestion, the implication must be that the captain, a decorated officer, commanding one of the Royal Navy's two newest battleships, felt that the Admiralty needed to be told how the men felt.

When the mutiny was over the Board of Admiralty wrote to all commanders in chief setting out the events of the mutiny and asking for their comments. Admiral Sir Reginald Tyrwhitt was commander-in-chief of the Nore command. He was a distinguished, brave and extremely capable officer who had been knighted while serving as a Commodore, i.e., a substantive captain afloat, during the First World War, an accolade unique in the twentieth century. His letter to the Board concluded

> 9. In conclusion I cannot emphasise too strongly how deeply I feel that the most urgent need of the Navy today, compared to which all suggested changes are trivial, is that the absolute confidence of Officers and Men in the Admiralty be restored.
>
> I have the honour to be,
Sir,
Your obedient Servant,
[Reginald Tyrwhitt][53]

For an Admiral to write in that tone to the Board of Admiralty was bad

---

[50] B. Whinney, *The U-Boat Peril: A Fight for Survival* (London, 1986), p. 30.
[51] *Ibid.*, p. 29. Sailors do not take an oath of loyalty, marines do.
[52] TNA, ADM 156/71.
[53] TNA, ADM 1/27410.

enough, but the reaction of the Board was worse. The Secretary to the Admiralty Board wrote (and other members of the Board agreed)

> It seems to me quite wrong that an officer in the position of the Commander-in-Chief should quote such views as he ascribes to officers and men in this letter, and should say that rightly or wrongly these views are to his knowledge being expressed. I suggest that it should be made clear to him not only that his views on what is involved in Service discipline do not meet with the approval of the Board, but that They look to an officer in his position severely to discourage officers and men, and particularly officers, from allowing such views to permeate the Service. [initialled by Secretary to the Board, Oswyn Murray][54]

A midshipman who was at Invergordon stated that at the time of the mutiny, officer morale was 'appalling'.[55] All the indications are that at Invergordon the officers were at the least sympathetic with the mutineers; indeed that they probably felt that they had had a worse deal than the lower deck.

Invergordon, Officer Morale and a Herzberg Analysis

Frederick Herzberg was an extremely highly regarded occupational psychologist particularly interested in the mechanisms employers use to motivate employees.[56] Naval officers were and are employees; while they wear uniforms to work, they are employees nonetheless. Herzberg put forward a 'two factor' theory of employee motivation; the first factor was what he termed hygiene, the second was motivation. This theory continues to be very highly regarded by occupational psychologists today and his book is the most requested reprint in the 'Harvard Business Review Classics' series. Herzberg claimed that although it was essential to get the 'hygiene' aspects of employment right, employers could not expect credit from their employees for doing so. To get them wrong undermines morale and productivity, but getting them right only provides the basic platform upon which employers can build future morale/productivity. These hygiene aspects are usually listed as 'Pay and Benefits', 'Company Policy/Administration', 'Physical environment' and 'Relationships with co-workers'. For naval officers, the Admiralty signally failed to achieve these; their pay and benefits were poor, the Admiralty Board was seen as distant and out of touch, they were mostly serving in outdated, even decrepit, ships. Only the relationships between members of the Service can be seen as being satisfactory.

---

[54] TNA, ADM 1/27410.
[55] Vice Admiral Sir Louis Le Bailly, letter to the author dated 3 August 2009.
[56] F. Herzberg, *One More Time, How Do You Motivate Employees?* (Boston MA, 2003).

Herzberg's 'motivational' factors are those for which an employer can claim credit, and which make an employee feel good as well. They are 'Achievement', 'Recognition', 'Work itself', 'Responsibility', 'Promotion' and 'Growth'. The vast majority of naval officers in the period up to the Invergordon mutiny possibly felt that none of the foregoing applied to them. Regrettably, the navy, or rather the Board of Admiralty, had forgotten that even in peace time its leaders needed to be motivated and led rather than managed.

7

'To Excite the Whole Company to Courage and Bravery': The Incentivisation of British Privateering Crews, 1702–1815

David J. Starkey

Privateering has been viewed from various perspectives by academic researchers. Historians have tended to focus on the economic and military significance of privateering in particular nations or ports during particular wars or epochs. This not only reflects the character of a business that was generally authorised by, and in theory benefited, nation states during time of war, but also the fact that the documentary evidence underpinning most historical studies was generated by national institutions, chiefly prize courts and admiralties. Within these confines, much of the research effort has been expended on establishing the scale of privateering, generally in terms of the number of vessels commissioned and prizes taken. This has revealed a good deal about the level and impact – in quantitative terms – of private commerce-raiding undertaken in a range of contexts. Much is known, for example, about the private forces set forth by the English during the 1585–1603 and 1625–30 conflicts,[1] the Spaniards operating out of Netherlandish ports from 1621 to 1648,[2] the Scots during the 1513–1713 period,[3] the French during the wars of Louis XIV,[4] the British in the five wars in which they engaged as belligerents

---

[1] K. R. Andrews, *Elizabethan Privateering: English Privateering during the Spanish War, 1585–1603* (Cambridge, 1964); J. C. Appleby, 'English Privateering during the Spanish and French Wars, 1625–1630' (unpublished Ph.D. thesis, University of Hull, 1983).
[2] R. A. Stradling, *The Armada of Flanders: Spanish Maritime Policy and European War, 1568–1668* (Cambridge, 1992).
[3] S. Murdoch, *The Terror of the Seas: Scottish Maritime Warfare, 1513–1713* (Leiden, 2010).
[4] J. S. Bromley, 'The French Privateering War, 1702–13', in J. S. Bromley, *Corsairs and Navies* (London, 1987), pp. 213–42.

between 1702 and 1783,[5] the British American colonists in the 1740s[6] and the Americans during the 1812–14 war.[7]

Scholars from other disciplines have adopted more theoretical approaches. Thomson, for instance, has examined privateering in the context of the monopolisation of violence at sea by nation states, a long-term gradual process that was largely accomplished by the nineteenth century. She contends that private forces were only effective if they were poorly regulated, which led to piracy and other 'unintended consequences'.[8] Economists have viewed privateering as a form of private enterprise that might function more efficiently as a means of waging war than public sector providers in the contemporary world.[9] Micro-economic studies into the organisation and management of privateering 'firms' have also been undertaken, with Benjamin and Thornberg assessing the extent to which tournament theory explained the success of the Royal Navy and privateers in the eighteenth century,[10] and Gifford analysing the relative cost structures of shipping, whaling and – by proxy – privateering companies.[11]

The aim of this chapter is to meld some of these theoretical perspectives with empirical evidence to explain the organisational structure deployed by those who promoted privateering ventures in the British Isles during the 1689–1815 period. The chapter is divided into three main parts. After surveying the scale, purpose and management of privateering ventures in the long eighteenth century, attention is afforded to the incentives that were deployed to motivate and control crews, and the tensions that marked relations between the parties engaged in privateering firms. It is argued that an unorthodox business form emerged to mitigate the managerial problems that were inherent in private commerce-raiding enterprise. This structure, in line

---

[5] D. J. Starkey, *British Privateering Enterprise in the Eighteenth Century* (Exeter, 1990).

[6] C. E. Swanson, *Predators and Prizes: American Privateering and Imperial Warfare, 1739–1748* (Columbia SC, 1991); C. E. Swanson, 'American Privateering and Imperial Warfare, 1739–1748', *William and Mary Quarterly* 42 (1985), 357–82.

[7] J. R. Garitee, *The Republic's Private Navy: The American Privateering Business as Practiced by Baltimore during the War of 1812* (Middletown CT, 1977); F. M. Kert, *Prize and Prejudice: Privateering and Naval Prize in Atlantic Canada in the War of 1812* (St John's NL, 1997).

[8] J. E. Thomson, *Mercenaries, Pirates and Sovereigns: State-Building and Extraterritorial Violence in Early Modern Europe* (Princeton, 1994).

[9] L. J. Sechrest, 'Public Goods and Private Solutions in Maritime History', *Quarterly Journal of Austrian Economics* 7 (2004), 3–27.

[10] D. K. Benjamin and C. Thornberg, 'Organization and Incentives in the Age of Sail', *Explorations in Economic History* 44 (2007), 317–41.

[11] A. Gifford jr., 'The Economic Organization of 17th- through mid 19th-Century Whaling and Shipping', *Journal of Economic Behavior and Organization* 20 (1993), 137–50.

with management theory, was based on incentivisation through profit sharing. But it was neither a structure that promoters devised through an objective planning process, nor a constant feature of privateering throughout the era, as is implied in the 'steady-state' analyses of economists. Rather, it was an organisational mode that evolved out of earlier customary practices and was shaped by the statutory devices that increasingly regulated the British shipping industry. It changed, moreover, according to the fluctuating prospects that motivated privateer owners and privateersmen during the course of the eighteenth century.

The Privateering Business: Extent, Objectives and Managerial Challenges

Complemented and corroborated by contemporary newspapers, Admiralty archives, business accounts, voyage narratives and other primary sources, the records of the High Court of Admiralty reveal much about the extent and objectives of British privateering enterprise during the long eighteenth century.[12] This court issued licences empowering private individuals to deploy their vessels to 'take, sink, burn or otherwise annoy' seaborne properties belonging to citizens of designated sovereign states at war with Britain, and also, in 1777–83, the American colonists 'now in rebellion' and operating in contravention of the 1775 Prohibition of Trade Act.[13] It was in this court, moreover, that the majority of the captures effected by these licensed vessels were adjudicated, with the ownership of those lawfully confiscated being formally transferred to the captor. Estimates gleaned from the archive generated by these legal proceedings indicate that approximately 10,500 privately-owned vessels were licensed during seven wars in which Britain engaged as a belligerent between 1702 and 1815. As Table 7.1 indicates, the number of vessels licensed in each conflict ranged from 98 in the comparatively brief anti-Spanish conflict of 1718–1720 to 2,676 in the American Revolutionary War, when Britain fought against the American rebels, France, Spain and the United Provinces. In terms of their operational bases, these vessels belonged to over 100 ports and havens around the coasts of the British Isles and in the colonies, with London, Bristol, Liverpool and the Channel Islands the most prominent. They also varied greatly in respect of size, with some of the largest privately-owned vessels afloat – notably East Indiamen, a number of which were declared to be over 1500 tons burthen when commissioned in the 1793–

---

[12] The National Archives, Kew, London (TNA), High Court of Admiralty (HCA) Archive.
[13] TNA, HCA 26/60.

Table 7.1: Licensed vessels by war and region, 1702–1815

	1702–12	1718–20	1739–48	1756–62	1777–83	1793–1801	1803–15
London	671	61	614	648	719	580	599
Bristol	157	17	132	253	203	61	33
Liverpool	31	0	79	246	390	630	401
Channel Islands	207	1	85	128	223	172	229
East England	11	0	44	73	135	33	40
SE England	36	1	61	116	243	58	95
SW England	59	3	74	62	283	69	151
Wales & NW England	9	0	8	28	80	65	46
West Scotland	6	0	8	22	216	34	113
East Scotland	11	1	0	9	32	18	31
Ireland	28	0	15	40	81	14	6
Overseas bases	34	6	27	30	35	30	22
Port unknown	83	8	44	24	36	31	44
Total	1343	98	1191	1679	2676	1795	1810

Source: The National Archives, HCA 25/14–209; HCA 26/4–104. See D. J. Starkey, *British Privateering Enterprise in the Eighteenth Century* (Exeter, 1990), pp. 89, 113, 121, 165, 200–1, 322–3.

1815 conflicts – furnished with the same warlike and prize-taking powers as the sloops of less than 10 tons burthen fitted out in Jersey and Guernsey.[14]

Although the precise objectives of licensed vessels are rarely specified in the court's documents, evidence derived from these and other records indicates that the privateering business comprised two principal modes of operation. First, there was the private ship-of-war.[15] Such a vessel was invariably manned by a crew that was large in relation to its tonnage and prepared to seize enemy vessels by force and navigate prizes taken by dint of such actions to a home or neutral port. It carried no cargo and was set forth to cruise the shipping lanes with the sole objective of locating and seizing ships and cargoes that would in due course, and according to due process of law, become the property of the captors. In eighteenth-century Britain, this profitable opportunity was embraced by the owners and crews of various types of private ship-of-war. At one end of a broad spectrum of scale and ambition there were the comparatively diminutive craft that set out from the Channel Islands and the ports of south-east and south-west England to cruise in the Chops of the Channel and the coastal waters of Brittany and Normandy with the aim of capturing French merchantmen and fishing craft, as well as neutral traders suspected of carrying cargoes belonging to citizens of an enemy state. Such vessels were generally from 20 to 80 tons burden, armed with four or six low-calibre carriage guns and an array of anti-personnel weapons, and manned by at least twenty-five men. Larger, more powerful 'deep-water' vessels fitted out chiefly in London and Bristol, but also in a range of smaller ports, were despatched to cruise in the Western Approaches, the Bay of Biscay and off the Iberian Peninsula, where they endeavoured to intercept homeward-bound French West Indiamen or Spanish register ships. Dubbed 'stout ships' and 'privateers of force' by newspaper correspondents and advertisers, these vessels measured between 250 and 600 tons burthen and were generally equipped with twenty or more carriage guns and manned by complements of at least 100 men, with some exceeding 250. Similar in scale, but distinguished by their operational scope, were a handful of vessels that embarked for the Pacific, intent on attacking Spanish settlements in South America and capturing the Manila Galleon in its annual passage from the Philippines to Acapulco.[16] Such 'expeditions' comprised consortships of at least two ships commanded by privateering luminaries such as William Dampier, Woodes

---

[14] Starkey, *British Privateering*, 39–40, 53–5.
[15] Ibid., 35–48.
[16] See B. M. H. Rogers, 'Dampier's Voyage of 1703', *Mariner's Mirror* 10 (1924), 367–81; C. D. Lee, 'Alexander Selkirk and the Last Voyage of the *Cinque Ports Gally*', *Mariner's Mirror* 73 (1987), 385–99; B. M. H. Rogers, 'Woodes Rogers's Privateering Voyage', *Mariner's Mirror* 19 (1933), 196–211.

Rogers and George Shelvocke, and were marked by acts of heroism, cowardice and opportunism – together with singular occurrences like the marooning and rescue of Alexander Selkirk, and the shooting of what was to become the 'Ancient Mariner's' albatross – that filled the pages of the immensely popular narratives published by some of those who survived to tell their highly subjective and somewhat apologetic tales.[17]

The second type of licensed vessel was the commissioned merchantman, sometimes known as a 'letter of marque'.[18] This was a dual-purpose vessel, in that it was set forth both to convey a cargo and to prey upon the enemy's seaborne property. The balance between these two objectives varied considerably. Many of these vessels were primarily intent on delivering goods to a set destination, but were furnished with a privateering licence so that their owners and crews might profit from the capture of enemy-owned property encountered en route, either by chance or as a consequence of a successful defensive action against an assailant. In essence, the *modus operandi* and capability of such vessels differed little from the trading activity in which they generally engaged in peacetime. As few coastal and short-sea traders sailed with licences, this strand of the privateering business largely comprised vessels bound for the Mediterranean, the Caribbean, North America, Africa, India and China. It therefore included slavers, West Indiamen, colonial traders, whalers and the vessels of the Hudson's Bay and East India companies, nearly all of which were granted licences for their long distance voyages in wartime.[19] Also engaged in cargo conveyance, but in a particular wartime capacity, were the privately-owned vessels hired by state departments such as the Navy Board, the Victualling Office and His Majesty's Transport Service, which equipped them with privateering licences for their passages to overseas theatres of conflict with the tools of war in their holds.[20] Prize-taking was more central to the objectives of another breed of commissioned merchantman, which was described in newspaper reports and advertisements as engaging in a 'cruising voyage' or departing 'on a cruise and a voyage'.[21] This was a clear signal to readers and potential recruits that the vessel was sailing with a rela-

---

[17] P. Edwards, *The Story of the Voyage: Sea-Narratives in Eighteenth Century England* (Cambridge, 1994).

[18] See Starkey, *British Privateering*, 48–55.

[19] With regard to East Indiamen, this assertion is based on a comparison of the letter of marque declarations (TNA, HCA 26) with C. Hardy, *Register of Ships Employed in the Service of the Honourable United East India Company (1799)*, 2 volumes.

[20] See D. Syrett, *Shipping and the American War, 1775–1783: A Study of British Transport Organisation* (London, 1970); D. Syrett, *Shipping and Military Power in the Seven Years War: The Sails of Victory* (Exeter, 2008).

[21] For example, see advertisements in *Felix Farley's Bristol Journal*, August–October 1778.

tively large crew – generally to the Caribbean – in search of prizes, but would take a cargo aboard if her primary quest proved fruitless.[22]

Although Britain's licensed vessels were diverse in purpose and practice, they were all imbued with a predatory capability by virtue of the letter of marque or privateer commission they carried. To those who promoted, managed and worked these vessels, nearly all of whom were primarily engaged in shipping and sea-related occupations, this prize-taking dimension presented particular difficulties. An obvious challenge lay in the legal basis of privateering, for this branch of the shipping industry was governed by a distinctive set of laws, rules and regulations. Shipowners and seafarers therefore became privateer owners and privateersmen in respect of the predatory element of their business, a change in identity that reflected the fact that shipping cargoes and taking prizes were located in different legal frameworks and conducted according to different codes of practice. Unfamiliarity with, or ignorance of, the rules of the prize game could lead to costly delays, court hearings and criminal penalties. In December 1780, for instance, the sudden onset of the Fourth Anglo-Dutch war encouraged a number of vessels to take Dutch merchantmen before licences had formally been issued, these seizures being condemned as droits and perquisites of the Admiralty rather than good and lawful prize to the captors.[23] Likewise, those who sailed with privateering licences were obliged to observe instructions issued by the Admiralty regarding their behaviour at sea and the proper means by which properties should be taken and returned to land, where evidence concerning their ownership, voyage, cargo and nationality was to be gathered from the interrogation of witnesses according to a set of prescribed questions.[24] The papers of the Prize and Prize Appeals courts – divisions of the High Court of Admiralty that specialised in such matters – indicate that some privateer owners and privateersmen suffered financial and other losses due to their proven failure to abide by these legal and behavioural guidelines.[25]

Mounting a privateering venture entailed the assembly of resources that were extraordinary in the context of the eighteenth-century shipping industry. Intrinsic to all licensed ventures was a fighting capability. Whereas such a

---

[22] Such newspaper accounts are corroborated by the muster rolls submitted by commanders of such vessels on returning to their home port. For Liverpool from 1778 to 1780, see TNA, BT98/38–43; for Bristol, 1777–1783, see the Hospital Bill Muster Rolls held by the Society of Merchant Venturers, Clifton, Bristol.
[23] Huntington Library, San Marino, California, HM 55650, Correspondence between George Gosling, an Admiralty Court Proctor, and various merchants, 1778–87.
[24] A copy of the 'Instruction to Commanders of Private Ships-of-War' pertaining in the American Revolutionary War is included in the opening pages of TNA, HCA 26/60.
[25] TNA, HCA 32, 42, 45.

capacity was vital if the offensive objective of the private ship-of-war was to be realised, it was also necessary if the 'letter of marque' was effectively to defend its cargo or make prize of properties it might encounter, whether by design or chance. Acquiring a vessel to undertake such activities rarely posed problems for privateering promoters. 'Letters of marque' were generally merchantmen engaged in commercial work that was similar in many respects to their peacetime occupations. The majority of private ships-of-war, moreover, were merchant vessels converted into fighting vessels by virtue of the installation of additional carriage and swivel guns, and the strengthening of the hulls with extra planking and the 'sides being filled ... in such a manner as to be shot-proof'.[26] On occasion, naval vessels were purchased and despatched on cruises by private owners, while a few new-built vessels, most notably the Bristol circumnavigators, *Duke* and *Dutchess*, were designed for predatory purposes. Preparing a vessel to fight also obliged promoters to purchase armaments and ammunition – carriage guns, swivels, carronades, cutlasses, muskets and stinkpots – as well as the food, provisions and stores that were essential to the functioning of any sea-going vessel.

Such essential supplies might be unusually costly, for the main weapon of private ships-of-war and 'letters of marque' was the manpower required to fire the guns, board the enemy or repel his boarders, and steer prizes and prisoners to a friendly port. Relatively large crews were therefore shipped aboard licensed vessels. While substantial complements might have been key to the execution of the venture, they also posed a range of problems to the managers of ventures in which they enlisted. Recruiting complements that might comprise well over 100 men was inevitably difficult in wartime when the demands of the navy led to shortages of seafaring labour, while remuneration might prove expensive at times when wages in the shipping industry were two or three times higher than their peacetime rate. Large crews, moreover, exerted pressure on the space aboard ship, and overcrowding could ensue, especially when prisoners from captured vessels came aboard. Such conditions – large numbers of men, not all of whom were 'used to the sea', in confined conditions intent on committing acts of violence for their own gain – raised the spectre of ill-discipline. While this was a major threat to the mission of every licensed vessel, whether its purpose was prize-taking or cargo conveyance, it was especially acute in 'deep-water' private ships-of-war and the vessels engaged in 'expeditions' to the South Seas. These predators not only carried extraordinarily large complements, but also promised to generate exceptional returns through the capture of prizes while cruising in the shipping lanes rather than sailing for a set destination. Inherent in this

---

26 *Exeter Flying Post*, 5 March 1779, Recruiting notice for the *Dragon Privateer*.

modus operandi were logistical and communication difficulties, particularly in the more distant cruising grounds, as the problems encountered in the refit of the *Royal Family* private ships-of-war in Lisbon amply demonstrated.[27] At the same time, the landing of a valuable prize tended to attract criminal elements on land while the captors remained at sea.[28] In such circumstances, the scope for opportunism amongst those engaged in these ventures was much greater than in peacetime trading ventures. Well publicised instances of opportunistic behaviour, like that of the managers of the *Royal Family* squadron,[29] led to a further managerial problem – the mutual mistrust of privateer owners and privateersmen.

In seeking solutions to the extraordinary managerial difficulties with which they were confronted, those who invested capital – both financial and human – in the privateering business adopted particular incentive schemes that lay at the core of the organisational structure of their ventures.

Incentives and Organisational Structures

Privateering represented a business opportunity for those willing to invest their productive resources in the quest for prize. The incentive to make such an investment lay in the prospect of a substantial return, for windfall profits might be earned if a valuable enemy vessel was seized and condemned as lawful prize in the Admiralty Court. But such returns were by no means guaranteed. While the enemy might prove elusive, he might protect his trade adequately, forcibly resist attempts to take his property, or fit out his own vessels-of-war to make prize of would-be assailants. Moreover, the natural hazards of the sea and the weather inevitably threatened the success of the commerce-raiding enterprise. The leadership and management of the venture constituted further risks, for an inept commander, conflict among the crew at sea, or disharmony between shipowners and seafarers, threatened to jeopardise the efficiency and profitability of the venture. By the same token, effective organisation and co-ordination of effort ashore and afloat enhanced the chance of generating significant gains.

To realise the profitable potential of prize-taking, those who initiated privateering ventures required an organisational structure that was appropriate to

---

[27] H. S. Vaughan (ed.), *The Voyages and Cruises of Commodore Walker* (1760, repr. 1928), 137–50.

[28] See the 'Petition of Several Persons who lately served on board the *Prince Frederick* and *Duke* private ships of war', *Journal of the House of Commons* (1749), 941.

[29] See James Goddard's open letter to the Houses of Parliament, printed in the *Gazatteer and London Daily Advertiser*, 29 June 1756.

the market in which their vessel was designed to operate. In Britain, articles of agreement – which were a statutory requirement from 1729 – defined this organisational structure, just as they did in the commercial ventures undertaken in the shipping industry as a whole. These were contracts prepared by the promoters of the venture, and signed by members of the ship's company as they enlisted, their purpose being to establish the object of the business, the obligations of the various parties to the agreement and the distribution of rewards between these parties. Reflecting the particular risks that were intrinsic to prize-taking activity, however, the contracts drawn up by initiators of privateering ventures differed from the norm in various respects, while there were variations within the commerce-raiding business in line with the objective, scale and character of the venture.

With regard to licensed merchantmen, the main obstacle to the success of the venture – aside from natural hazards – was enemy action, for these cargo-carrying vessels were more prey than predator in the context of eighteenth-century conflicts. Accordingly, in seeking to defend their properties, owners of vessels and cargoes adjusted the conventional organisational structure of shipping ventures by acquiring privateering licences and appending a prize-taking dimension to the voyage. In so doing, they sought to encourage the seafarers in their employ to resist the efforts of enemy naval and privateering vessels to seize assets that belonged to the shipowner and merchant rather than the crew. The incentive offered to 'excite the whole company to courage and bravery' in defending other people's property was the prospect of a share in the proceeds of any assailant that might not only be rebuffed but also captured. This essentially defensive device – which enabled shipowners to insure their vessels and despatch them to 'run' ahead of a convoy – insinuated further risks and opportunities into the venture. On the one hand, it might encourage the crew to deviate from its primary duty of conveying a cargo to a specific destination by sailing in search of prizes, a risk that could only be countered by strong leadership at sea. This was evident in 1744, when the crew of the *Hudson's Bay Frigat*, a commissioned Hudson's Bay vessel, had their hopes of taking a significant prize dashed by the stoicism of a captain who refused to alter the transoceanic course prescribed by his employers.[30] On the other hand, the provision of a licence might enhance the flexibility of operations, which was notably evident by the most aggressive of 'letters of marque' – ships such as the *Lyon*, *Hercules*, *Ann Gally* and *Chambers*, which were all bound from Bristol on a 'cruise and a voyage' to Jamaica,[31] their mission being to load cargoes if prize-taking prospects were poor.

---

[30] B. Wilson, *The Great Company, 1667–1871* (London, 1900), pp. 326–7.
[31] *Felix Farley's Bristol Journal*, 26 September 1778.

Although the commercial dimension of the 'letter of marque' venture was administered in the manner of an orthodox trading voyage – with wages paid to the crew as recompense for their cargo-handling and shiphandling work – the prize-taking element of the venture was managed according to the same organisational form that was deployed in the overtly predatory private ship-of-war. This business structure was marked by three distinctive features.[32] First, seamen were generally recruited on a 'no purchase, no pay' basis; that is, they agreed to serve for a share in the proceeds of any prizes their labour returned rather than a fixed monthly or lump-sum wage, which was the standard system of remuneration in the shipping industry. The provision of comparatively generous welfare payments and productivity bonuses was the second unusual aspect of privateering agreements. Generally, a pre-determined sliding scale of welfare payments was agreed. Accordingly, a privateersmen who lost an eye or a limb in carrying out his duty would receive a set amount of compensation, while rewards were to be paid to the privateersman who first sighted a vessel that was ultimately condemned as good prize, or to the man who was first to board a prize. Third, decisions as to who should be awarded welfare and bonus payments were generally made by councils comprising the commander and representatives of the officers and men aboard the private ship-of-war at the time of the action. In vessels such as the *Boscawen* of Dartmouth, the whole crew was to be consulted about such matters. While such collective decision-making mechanisms did not extend to the objectives, execution and strategy of the cruise, they were extraordinary in relation to the management systems that prevailed aboard contemporary merchant and naval ships, where the captain and senior officers made the key decisions.

One explanation as to why privateering articles contained these unusual provisions lay in the market for seafarers. Privateers, especially private ships-of-war, were labour-intensive vessels, and as the demand for seafaring labour was invariably high in wartime, promoters of 'letters of marque' and private ships-of-war were obliged to seek comparatively large crews in a highly competitive market.[33] The laws of supply and demand therefore dictated that inducements to enlist had to be offered, and these took the form of cash sums, or bounties, paid on enlistment, the provision of good accommodation aboard ship, and assurances from the managers of the venture that 'they will take care that each brave Tar shall have his exact share of all Prizes as a just

---

[32] The following section is based on the Articles of Agreement of over forty licensed vessels held in TNA, ADM 43.

[33] D. J. Starkey, 'War and the Market for Seafarers, 1736–1792', in L. R. Fischer and H. Nordvik (eds), *Shipping and Trade: Essays in International Maritime Economic History* (Pontefract, 1990), pp. 25–42.

reward for their Bravery'[34] – an indication of the distrust that sometimes marked relations between owners and crews. Nevertheless, profit sharing was the most important incentive, for it afforded many seafarers a once-in-a-lifetime opportunity to share in the gains of a commercial venture. Although this opportunity involved the very real risk that nothing would be gained if the cruise proved barren, many eighteenth-century British seafarers were willing to take such a gamble because privateering offered them a rare chance to raise the ceiling imposed on their earnings by the payment of wages. By enlisting in a privateer, the seafarer automatically incurred a minimum opportunity cost of 22s 6d per month, which was the net rate of pay in the navy and notionally represented the extent of the privateersman's financial investment in the enterprise. Against this, he might hope to bring home prize money worth many times the value of his forsaken wages. For example, for a minimum investment of £6 15s in the six-month cruise of the *Duke* and the *Prince Frederick* in 1745 able seamen returned with over £400 each – the equivalent of over ten years' work in a merchantman paying the exceptionally high rates of £3 per month.[35] For a similar investment in the *Mentor* of Liverpool in 1778, each able seafarer earned £109 – at least three years' worth of wages.[36] In another example, the fifteen men who shipped aboard the *Snap Dragon* of Dartmouth in 1781 were rewarded with a share in at least £7,000 in return for three months' work.[37]

The profit sharing incentive was also geared to the cost structure and operational efficiency of the prize-taking venture. In conceding a share in profits to the workforce, privateer promoters were relieved of the burden of wage payments, which might have been prohibitively high in ventures that required relatively large crews – many of which exceeded 100 men – at high wartime rates of pay. Shipowners also needed to recruit labour on a shareholding basis to mitigate the high costs of monitoring the efforts of the workforce. Supervision of labour costs money, but in projects where all have a common interest in maximising returns these costs, in theory, are much reduced. Any privateersman neglecting his duties would be damaging his own interests. In this respect, private ships-of-war resembled whalers and fishing vessels, which were likewise organised on profit sharing basis for very similar reasons, as Gifford points out:

> whereas monitoring ... played a large part in seeing that the day-to-day aspects of sailing the ship went smoothly, monitoring alone was insufficient to induce efficient effort on a whaling ship. The crew of a whaling ship was involved in

---

[34] *Exeter Flying Post*, 28 August 1778, recruiting notice for the *Favourite*.
[35] *Journal of the House of Commons*, 26 (1750), pp. 104–5.
[36] TNA, C114/36.
[37] TNA, C124/bundle, LH8.

all aspects of whaling. They played a major role in finding, chasing, killing, and processing the economic sustenance of a whaling voyage: whales and whale oil. They performed many tasks that were difficult to monitor effectively, such as standing lookout for whales in the crow's nest, rowing strenuously as part of a team for up to ten miles in the chase, facing danger by coming in close contact with the whale for the harpooning and the kill and staying up all night to render the whale blubber into oil only to resume the hunt the next day. The share system was a substitute for monitoring of these activities which would have been prohibitively costly.[38]

Although prize-sharing might have mitigated the costs of monitoring, it did not mean that individual privateersmen were left to regulate their own performance. Indeed, premia were paid by promoters of privateering ventures for the services of leaders, whose roles aboard ship included the maintenance of good order and the effective deployment of labour. Such inducements often assumed the form of shares in the ownership of the vessel, as well as a relatively large part of the crew's portion of the prize fund. For instance, George Walker, commodore of the *Royal Family* squadron of private ships-of-war, was allocated fourteen shares in the crew's moiety of prize proceeds, whereas able seamen owned a single share and ordinary sailors three-quarters or half a share. Walker also stood to gain 5 per cent of the profits due to his appointment as quartermaster of the fleet. Mates, or lieutenants as they were generally called in the muster rolls of private ships-of-war, and specialist crew members such as boatswains, carpenters, gunners and surgeons, normally owned a relatively high shareholding, ranging from four to seven shares in the case of the *Royal Family*.[39] Incentives on this scale were offered to attract experienced and well respected seafarers to command predatory ventures, which was especially important in a tight labour market, for the good reputation of a captain represented a form of 'brand name capital' that would encourage seafarers to enlist aboard his ship.[40] This is evident from recruitment notices posted in newspapers; for instance, in seeking to attract seafarers to serve aboard the *Mars Privateer*, the owners informed readers that the commander, William Scott, 'has already been remarkably successful in the last privateer he commanded'.[41] Once at sea, the ability of a commander to ready his crew for action by regular drill practice,[42] to deal

---

[38] Gifford, 'Economic Organization', p. 146.
[39] TNA, ADM 43/13.
[40] Gifford, 'Economic Organization', pp. 140–1.
[41] *Exeter Flying Post*, 18 February 1780.
[42] John Engledue, commander of the *Southwell* of Bristol, was instructed to train his men regularly in the use of small arms and great guns. Avon County Library, papers of the *Southwell* Privateer, 24651.

effectively and swiftly with ill discipline,[43] and to motivate his men to perform at optimal levels were significant operational assets.[44]

In seeking solutions to the managerial difficulties arising from the belligerent purpose of private ships-of-war and 'letters of marque', privateering entrepreneurs endeavoured to recruit an experienced, astute and inspirational commander. This strategy accorded with Gifford's contention that the acquisition of 'brand name capital' was a significant means of attracting labour and managing the crew at sea. The deployment of financial incentives to enlist labour and, more importantly, to stimulate the prize-taking efforts of the ship's people supports Benjamin and Thornberg's assertion that 'incentives matter'.[45] Although it is frequently stated or implied in the articles of agreement of privateering ventures that 'harmony', 'goodwill' and 'co-operation' were central to the organisational structures of such enterprises, in practice the relationship of the parties engaged in these business forms was beset by tensions.

Structural Tensions

Venturers attempted to manage the high risks intrinsic in privateering enterprise through articles of agreement.[46] In essence, these management devices derived from two interacting sources. First, there were customary rights and practices. These had their origins in the Middle Ages and included the right to inflict reprisals on transgressors, the right to pillage prizes and the principle that underpinned the ancient adage that 'freight is the mother of wages'. Another customary stream emanated from the Caribbean, which was the cradle of a loose set of customs and practices that evolved in the middle decades of the seventeenth century. This 'custom of the coast' evolved from the fusion of the 'rugged individualism' and rough frontier democracy of the *boucaniers* of St Dominigue, with the radical beliefs of political and religious refugees from England, France and the Netherlands.[47] Second,

---

[43] Woodes Rogers's swiftness in punishing malcontents in the early stages of the *Duke's* South Sea voyage was part of his managerial strategy. See J. W. D. Powell, *Bristol Privateers and Ships of War* (Bristol, 1930), p. 106.

[44] George Walker emphasised the importance of motivating his crew and keeping their spirits high. See Vaughan, *Voyages and Cruises*.

[45] D. K. Benjamin and C. F. Thornberg, 'Comment: Rules, Monitoring, and Incentives in the Age of Sail', *Explorations in Economic History* 40 (2003), 195.

[46] This section is based on the articles of agreement held in TNA, ADM 43.

[47] See C. Hill, 'Radical Pirates?', in C. Hill, *The Collected Essays of Christopher Hill, III, People and Ideas in Seventeenth Century England* (Brighton, 1986), pp. 161–87; J. S. Bromley, 'Outlaws at Sea, 1660–1720: Liberty, Equality and Fraternity among the Caribbean Freebooters', in J. S. Bromley, *Corsairs and Navies* (London, 1987), pp. 1–20.

contracts, which increasingly governed transactions in the shipping industry as the eighteenth century progressed, were also germane to the formulation of privateering articles of agreement. Accordingly, as in conventional commercial voyages, the articles were agreed between vessel owners and seafarers, and invariably included clauses relating to discipline, punishment and desertion, while the workforce was organised along hierarchical lines.

Customary rights and contractual obligations co-existed uneasily in the eighteenth-century shipping industry, with seafarers generally in favour of custom and shipowners increasingly seeking to enhance the extent and legal hold of contracts. Tension between the two relational forms was clearly apparent in the privateering business, chiefly in respect of property ownership and earnings. Private ships-of-war and letters of marque were owned by merchants, shipowners and other investors who engaged the services of seafarers to work their vessels. Nevertheless, in some privateering agreements, provision was made for the generation of a return even if the cruise yielded no prize. In such cases, it was agreed that the vessel should be sold, the proceeds of the sale comprising a common stock to be distributed between the owners and seafarers engaged in the venture. Such an arrangement prevailed in the *Winchelsea* of London, a large private ship-of-war of 550 tons and 300 men set forth to cruise in the East Indies in 1744. When they returned empty handed a year later, however, the managers reverted to type and refused to share the proceeds of the disposal of their property with the crew, precipitating a riot in the London inn where the decision was announced.[48]

While the returns of privateering ventures were divided between privateer owners and the ship's company, the proportion received by the respective parties varied according to a number of factors, the most important of which was the wage that was paid to the workforce. This issue was invariably dealt with in the articles of agreement that governed the conduct of the venture. Accordingly, in many of these documents, it was explicitly stated that seafarers had no right to wages; instead, a share in any prizes taken remunerated these men. In other agreements – for instance, those relating to long, dangerous cruises in the Pacific, those pertaining to cargo-carrying 'letter of marque' voyages, and those made in particular ports, notably the Channel Islands – the wage to be paid was precisely stipulated. Generally, full wages – that is, remuneration at the market price – were paid to seafarers working in 'letters of marque', while those shipping aboard private ships-of-war might serve for part-wages and a share in the portion of prizes owned by the crew, which was usually 25 per cent of the total, to take account of the payment of a wage.

[48] TNA, C103/130.

Tension was sometimes evident if a cruise proved successful. Once a vessel had been taken, condemned in the prize court, and the prize goods duly sold, the distribution of the rewards permitted the shipowner to claw back some of the fixed and variable costs incurred in the promotion of the venture. The division of the booty was detailed in the articles of agreement. Normally a prize fund, or general account, consisting of the gross proceeds of prizes taken, was established. But it was the net proceeds of the venture that were divided between the various parties to the contract, with the difference between gross and net returns often being contested by the captors. In numerous agreements, the seafarer was obliged to contribute to the costs of mounting the successful venture – costs which were normally borne by shipowners in other maritime trades. It was clearly in the owner's interest to pay as many items of cost as possible out of the joint account – and in the framing of the various articles of agreement, the desire to spread the financial burden towards the seafarer is widely apparent. The charges shared in this way varied. In all cases, the costs of handling and condemning prizes were paid out of the joint account. In many contracts, it was further stipulated that any costs or damages awarded against the venturers by the prize court should come out of the prize fund. It was usual that the encouragements and benefits paid to stimulate the crew's diligence should be borne by all – thus the brave or vigilant seafarer was given a bonus which derived, in part, from his own earnings. This was fairly marginal to the individual's rewards – a guinea was normally paid to the seamen who first sighted a prize vessel, while a benefit of £10 to £15 was generally paid for each limb or eye lost in combat. But in some cases a similar principle extended to the fitting out costs of the entrepreneur. The owners of the *Swift*, for instance, were to be re-imbursed the charge of victualling the ship out of the first prize taken. The *Lowestoff*'s promoters could draw out of the first prize taken the whole charge of the warlike stores and victuals shipped aboard, while in the case of the *Surprize* of London the bulk of the outfitting costs were to be repaid to the owners, as the articles indicated:

> Out of the neat produce of prizes there shall in the first place be deducted and re-imbursed all every and whatsoever sums as shall have been laid out and expended in victualling the said Privateer and in furnishing her with powder, shott and medicines.

In other ventures, the promoters were granted rights to part of the crew's share in the prize fund. In Bristol, for instance, a share in the men's half of the proceeds was generally allocated to the owners for each of the carriage guns fitted, a device that effectively shifted some of the seafarer's earnings to the pockets of the ship's owners. A more substantial transfer came from the agency fee charged, for in most articles the owners stipulated that they themselves should act as agents for the venture, thereby placing a levy of 2½ to 5 per cent on the seafarer's portion of the prize fund.

In general, an inverse relationship between the wage level and the proportion of the profits owned by the workforce prevailed in British private ships-of-war. Accordingly, if no wages were to be paid, the crew normally agreed to accept one half of the proceeds of any prizes taken, while complements engaged on a 'part wage, part share' basis owned a quarter, a sixth or an eighth of the prize proceeds. Common to all privateering agreements, however, was the principle that the men's share in prizes should be divided in line with the rank of the individual crew member. Commanders of private ships-of-war might own twelve, sixteen or more shares, while mates, boatswains, gunners, carpenters and other specialists might be allocated half of that number, and able seamen received just a single share. Such a division reflected the hierarchical structure of the private ship-of-war's crew, and was also evident in the disciplinary provisions that applied to the prosecution of predatory enterprises. According to the 'custom of the coast', such measures extended only as far as punishing those crew members who embezzled or stole prize goods and therefore cheated their shipmates out of a portion of the profits. Privateering agreements invariably stipulated sanctions against those guilty of such behaviour, but they also dealt with such matters as desertion, insubordination and mutiny. In other words, threats to the hierarchical command structure of the crew were deemed to be offences, strictures that had not applied in seventeenth-century buccaneering ventures. Like their counterparts in the merchant shipping industry or the Royal Navy of the mid-eighteenth century, privateersmen found guilty of committing such sins were to be punished by imprisonment and flogging as well as by loss of entitlement to earnings.

Changing Predatory Prospects

Borrowing the language of the Caribbean, many of the scrupulously legal commerce-raiding ventures of the 1744–1762 period were organised on a 'no purchase, no pay' premise. If there was purchase – in the form of a prize taken and condemned – the proceeds were assembled into a 'common stock', the 'common account' or the 'general fund', evocative terms that had been used to describe the produce of buccaneering and piratical raids. This situation began to change in line with the evolution of the prize war. Suffering heavy losses to large-scale British private ships-of-war and naval ships as the 1744–48 conflict progressed, the French permitted their colonial trade to be carried in neutral vessels during the early stages of the Seven Years War. This shift from armed defence to protection by neutral flag rendered the powerful, heavily manned 'privateer of force' virtually redundant, for neutral carriers were invariably smaller and much less valuable than the great West Indiamen and register ships of the 1740s. Faced with a less attractive and more evasive target, British privateer owners sought to reduce their risks by engaging comparatively small, wage-earning crews, some of which were employed to load and convey cargoes if the prospects of prize taking dimmed.[49] Such arrangements are evident in the thirty privateering articles of agreement relating to the post-1777 period.[50] In most of those signed during the American Revolutionary War, and all of those drawn up after 1793, the seafarers agreed to work for regular wages and a share in just 25 per cent of any prize fund that might be generated. Prize-taking incentives were thereby reduced as predatory prospects altered and the payment of wages according to contract increasingly superseded customary prize-sharing rights in the privateering business.

[49] See D. J. Starkey, 'A Restless Spirit: British Privateering Enterprise, 1739–1815', in D. J. Starkey, E. S. van Eyck van Heslinga and J. A. de Moor (eds), *Pirates and Privateers: New Perspectives on the War on Trade in the Eighteenth and Nineteenth Centuries* (Exeter, 1997), pp. 126–40.
[50] TNA, HCA 30/210.

THE EVOLUTION OF MANAGEMENT TRAINING

IN THE ROYAL NAVY, 1800–1950

8

New Kinds of Discipline: The Royal Navy in the Second Half of the Nineteenth Century

Oliver Walton

Since Andrew Gordon's influential examination of command in the Royal Navy of the nineteenth and early twentieth centuries,[1] there has been little attempt to extend this analysis beyond the operation of fleets to look at the level of the ship, where command shades into management. Following Churchill's famous list of the traditions of the Royal Navy as being rum, sodomy and the lash, the widespread view of naval discipline in the nineteenth century has continued to be centred on corporal punishment. In fairness, corporal punishment was a key topic of debate for contemporaries in the second half of the nineteenth century, as reformers endeavoured to push through the abolition, or at least moderation, of such physical penalties. Yet the lash itself was of much diminished importance, for it was in this period that the Admiralty, under Parliamentary pressure, first limited, and ultimately ended the imposition of flogging as a disciplinary sanction; in 1871 it was effectively suspended for peace time, and more generally in 1879.[2] Historians, too, have been attracted to the story of the end of corporal punishment, and it forms a prominent element in the little research there has been on discipline in this period.[3]

---

[1] A. Gordon, *The Rules of the Game. Jutland and British Naval Command* (London, 2000), ch. 9–19.

[2] E. Rasor, *Reform in the Royal Navy. A Social History of the Lower Deck, 1850–1880* (Hamden CT, 1976), pp. 51–5.

[3] See the relevant sections of the only two academic social histories of the Royal Navy in this period: Rasor, *Reform in the Royal Navy*, pp. 39–61; and O. Walton, 'Social History of the Royal Navy 1856–1900' (unpublished Ph.D. thesis, University of Exeter, 2003), pp. 294–339. Other works touch upon naval discipline more briefly: C. Lloyd, *The British Seaman 1200–1860* (London, 1968), p. 273; P. Kemp, *The British Sailor. A Social History*

Three observations can be made about this focus upon flogging. Firstly, corporal punishment was only one of various penalties that could be imposed upon wrongdoers; the imposition of unpleasant cleaning tasks, loss of free time or restrictions upon the rum ration, for instance, were less contentious and brutal but could be effective disciplinary tools. Secondly, punishment itself represents a particularly narrow view of discipline, for the punishment of the disobedient constitutes only one aspect of maintaining discipline, which is itself best understood as the establishment of efficiency and obedience within a crew.[4] Indeed, throughout this chapter, 'discipline' is used in this broader meaning. Other factors include the more general managerial and leadership skills of the superiors, and various aspects of the terms and conditions of life and work. Thirdly, the attention devoted to corporal punishment assumes that it was central to the relationships between officers and men; it thus leaves unasked, let alone unanswered, the question of how discipline was constructed and maintained when this particular sanction had been first severely curtailed and then removed from the options available to officers. The very fact that discipline in the Royal Navy could be maintained even after the suspension of corporal punishment signals a transformation both in the relationships between officers and men, and the ways in which those relationships were regulated. This paper will explore some of the contours of these new social relations and will suggest that the new kinds of discipline do not fit neatly into a 'Whiggish' narrative of progress, but created a number of further challenges for the management of crew.

Of course, the idea that there might have been 'new' kinds of discipline presupposes there having been 'old kinds', and it is worth briefly considering naval discipline in the sailing navy. There were many factors which influenced crew members in being obedient and improving their efficiency. The basic desire to survive at sea was itself a significant incentive.[5] The sea was a dangerous place and the safe passage of the ship depended upon its efficient operation by officers and crew. Insubordination in the course of work duties

---

of the Lower Deck (London, 1970), pp. 205, 208; H. Baynham, *Before the Mast Naval Ratings of the 19th Century* (London, 1972), pp.19, 30, 33, 141, 143, 154, 156, 163, 165, 179–80, 197–8, 229; J. Winton, *Hurrah for the Life of a Sailor. Life on the Lower Deck of the Victorian Navy* (London, 1977), pp. 14, 68, 70, 174, 176–8; P. Padfield, *Rule Britannia. The Victorian and Edwardian Navy* (London, 1981), pp. 41–3, 51, 183; I. Hamilton, *Anglo-French Naval Rivalry 1840–1870* (Oxford, 1993), pp. 161, 169–70; J. Wells, *The Royal Navy: An Illustrated Social History, 1870–1982* (Stroud, 1994), pp. 11–13, 28.

4 For discussion of definitions of 'discipline', see D. Moreby, *The Human Element in Shipping* (Colchester, 1975), p. 49; N. A. M. Rodger, *Wooden World: An Anatomy of the Georgian Navy* (London, 1986), pp. 205–7; and C. McKee, *Sober Men and True: Sailor Lives in the Royal Navy 1900–1945* (London and Cambridge MA, 2002), pp. 34–5.

5 Rodger, *Wooden World*, pp. 207–8.

might lead to sails not being set correctly, jeopardising the safety of other crew members. Loose ropes or blocks, flying in the wind, could cause serious injury or damage to rig, sails or men. When manoeuvring under pressure in a tight harbour entrance or strong wind, even small scale insubordination might endanger the ship.

The social hierarchy was also a factor which contributed powerfully to discipline and obedience. Ancien régime Britain was characterised by small social units bound by vertical connections of deference and dependence, where social roles were understood and which conferred stability.[6] This is not to idealise this society, which was also characterised by a 'rough' culture, in which there were riots, carnivals and other opportunities for unrest and protest.[7] Sailors, too, were known to have protested in vigorous fashion against mistreatment by officers, some officers receiving beatings from former crew whilst ashore. Such instances were, however, seen as protests against individual treatment, rather than against the hierarchy of society or naval command.[8]

Indeed, society both outside and within the Royal Navy was bound together with links of mutual dependence. Crew depended upon their officers for the disciplinary regime in a naval vessel, but also for the provisioning of food, free time, and rewards for the good performance of tasks. Officers were also dependent upon their crews. This was not simply a matter of the crew providing the means for the captain to fulfil his mission, though that functional dimension was of course significant. Rather, it was both more subtle and more important, for officers built up their reputations over time, and by results. They required an efficient and obedient crew to get those results, and over time could build a career upon those achievements. Furthermore, through much of the 'age of sail', the officers, and especially the captain, were themselves a key factor in recruitment. Those with good reputations for the treatment of their crews or for the capturing of enemy prizes – success in combat being something of a indicator of efficient discipline – were able to fill their complements with crew more easily, and obtain better crew, than those without such good reputations.[9]

---

[6] See, for example, Thomas Chalmers, *The Christian and Civic Economy of Large Towns* (Glasgow, 1821), pp. 2, 5–9; William Cobbett, *Rural Rides* (London, 1853). See also E. Royle, *Modern Britain. A Social History 1750–1985* (London and New York, 1987), pp. 80–2; D. Cannadine, *Class in Britain* (London, 1988, 2000), pp. 24–56.

[7] J. M. Golby and A. W. Purdue, *The Civilisation of the Crowd: Popular Culture in England 1750–1900* (Stroud, 1999), pp. 22–3; J. Black, *Eighteenth-Century Britain, 1688–1783* (Basingstoke, 2008), pp.111–12.

[8] Rodger, *Wooden World*, pp. 206, 208–9.

[9] N. A. M. Rodger, '"A Little Navy of your own Making": Admiral Boscawen and the Cornish Connection in the Royal Navy', in M. Duffy (ed.), *Parameters of British Naval Power 1650–1850* (Exeter, 1992), pp.82–92; N. A. M. Rodger, 'Shipboard Life in the

Insight can also be gained from considering some of the factors which contributed to indiscipline. Officers who were not fair or consistent, or failed to take adequate care for their crew, brought down resentment upon themselves. Such problems might arise in a huge variety of contexts and over many matters, large and small. There were, however, a number of issues which persistently appeared as points of tension, above all pay, food and shore leave.[10] Lack of fresh food or consistent purchase of cheap and substandard victuals was an obvious sign that a captain, or the purser, was inconsiderate towards the crew. The frequency with which pay was distributed or with which shore leave was granted were key indicators of the extent to which the captain trusted his crew. These dynamics were still important even in the early years of our period, the second half of the nineteenth century: the mutiny on HMS *Hero* in July 1859 was easily explained by the fact that general leave had not been given to the crew since March.[11]

Punishment was, then, one facet of the disciplinary system. It was only implemented when good discipline broke down. There was a range of punishments available to officers, both summary and judicial. Many summary punishments took a corporal form, often with a number of lashes being ordered. Courts martial could impose more severe sentences of hundreds of lashes. Yet the brutality of corporal punishment is not the only aspect which should be considered. One of the important features of flogging was its theatricality: the crew was assembled to witness punishment.[12] The punishment of the individual was thus intended as a deterrent to future insubordination by the other members of the ship's community. It also said something about masculinity in the navy, for it should be 'taken like a man'.[13]

Georgian Navy, 1750–1800: The Decline of the Old Order?' in L. R. Fischer *et al.* (eds), *The North Sea. Twelve Essays on Social History of Maritime Labour* (Stavanger, 1992), p. 34; N. A. M. Rodger, *Command of the Ocean. A Naval History of Britain, 1649–1815* (London, 2004), pp. 496–7. For the period between 1815 and the Crimean War, see O. Walton, "A Great Improvement in the Sailor's Feeling towards the Naval Service": Recruiting Seamen for the Royal Navy, 1815–1853', *Journal for Maritime Research* (2010), 27–57.

[10] J. H. Owen, CB 3027. 'Mutiny in the Royal Navy vol. 1, 1691–1919' (Training and Staff Duties Division, Naval Staff, Admiralty, July 1933) p. 149; Rodger, *Wooden World*, pp. 239–41.

[11] National Maritime Museum (NMM), JOD/28, Journal Kept by Walter Bruce Allnutt, Assistant Clerk, HMS *Hero*. The mutiny took place on 18 July 1859; cf. Owen, 'CB 3027', p. 170.

[12] G. Dening, *Mr. Bligh's Bad Language. Passion, Power and Theatre on the Bounty* (Cambridge, New York, and Oakleigh, Victoria, 1992), pp. 115–16; J. Byrn, *Crime and Punishment in the Royal Navy. Discipline on the Leeward Island Station 1784–1812* (Aldershot and Brookfield VT, 1989), pp. 65–6, 71.

[13] Winton, *Hurrah for the Life*, p. 70.

By the middle of the nineteenth century a number of profound changes had occurred which altered the dynamics of discipline in the Royal Navy. Developments in naval architecture played a part. Firstly, improvements in the construction of ships made them safer, reducing the sense of vulnerability to the sea.[14] Secondly, the introduction of steam power also contributed to safety at sea, but arguably had a further influence. With increasing reliance upon steam power, the proportion of the crew whose work was directly involved with the safe propulsion and passage of the ship diminished; this was perhaps a reason why officers continued to place emphasis on sail drills until late in the century.[15] Most men did not work in the stokehold or engine room.[16] For those who did, improvements in the quality of the construction of boilers and engines improved the resilience of the machinery to survive occasional carelessness. For stokers this meant that indiscipline would be more likely to lead to a loss of engine power than an accident, unless the ship were struggling in a strong current.[17] The capacity to cause significant damage to the ship's propulsion system was restricted to the small number of well-paid and highly trained engineer officers and engine room artificers. Thirdly, the expectations of social relationships changed too. The hierarchy, which had been taken for granted for many centuries, was subject to increasing challenge from the late eighteenth century. The French Revolution was the extreme demonstration of this, but even in the Royal Navy the mutiny of the ships at the Nore in 1797 prompted fears that the officers could no longer rely upon the deference of those under their command.[18] By the mid nineteenth century class tensions were central to much political discourse and the growing confidence of the working classes was shown in the nascent trade union movement and in the more vocal demands of Chartism, with its monster demonstrations and huge parliamentary petitions.[19] Some naval officers were clearly unsettled, for

---

[14] The best general accounts of developments in naval architecture are: D. K. Brown, *Before the Ironclad. Development of Ship Design, Propulsion and Armament in the Royal Navy 1815–60* (London, 1990); D. K. Brown, *Warrior to Dreadnought. Warship Development 1860–1905* (London, 1997); R. Gardiner and A. Lambert (eds), *Steam, Steel and Shellfire. The Steam Warship 1815–1905* (London, 1992).

[15] Cf. G. A. H. Gordon quoting Capt. William Dyke Acland in, *The Rules of the Game. Jutland and British Naval Command* (London, 1996), pp. 167, 173–4.

[16] O. Walton, 'Social history', pp. 103-– and appendices B1 and C.

[17] The National Archives (TNA) ADM 156/157 Mutiny correspondence, HMS *Porpoise*, Cdr. Sturdee to R-Adm. Pearson, 16 May 1898.

[18] Rasor, *Reform in the Royal Navy*, pp. 62–4; Rodger, 'Shipboard life', p. 32; Byrn, *Crime and Punishment*, pp. 186–7.

[19] On the rhetoric of class in political debate see, for example, D. Cannadine, *Class in Britain* (London, 1998, 2000), pp. 57–104. Simon Dentith offers an insightful account of the challenges to the older hierarchy in *Society and Cultural Forms in Nineteenth Century*

Captain Sartorius commented in 1848 in the *United Services Journal* upon 'the present altered political and moral state of society', and the same publication saw a vigorous debate about naval discipline, with the pseudonymous 'Medical Staff Officer' 'contemplat[ing] the present very unsettled state of Europe, racked as it is by political convulsions and revolutions' and seeing the Chartist mobs as evidence of the bankruptcy of humanitarian penal reform.[20]

Fourthly, the bonds of patronage also became looser. Of course, officers continued to have a duty of care for the men on their ship, but the extent of mutual dependence was much diminished. Central to this process was the establishment of the Continuous Service system. Where previously men had entered to serve under particular officers on particular ships, from 1853 men entered for ten years of general service in the Royal Navy.[21] Their relationship was thus not primarily with their commanding officers, but with the navy and its administration generally. The implications were outlined by Admiral Phipps Hornby:

> We then gave up the strength of the connexion which each seaman formed with his captain and officers by volunteering to serve with them for three years; and we accepted the difficulties of dealing with men who were drafted here and there without consulting their wishes, and of whom the large majority must necessarily be very young and undisciplined.[22]

This was not the only sphere in which the growing bureaucracy of the Admiralty drew to itself greater control over life in the navy at the expense of the officer corps.[23] In doing so, it created new bases for discipline. The Admiralty's regulation also transformed some of the old sources of indiscipline into quite the opposite. From 1843, it was decreed that pay should be issued monthly, removing at a stroke one historical source of grievance. The pay system was overhauled to provide a system of incentives for advancement

---

England (Basingstoke, 1998), pp. 52–75. On trade unionism, see for example W. Hamish Fraser, *A History of British Trade Unionism, 1700–1998* (Basingstoke and London, 1999), pp. 1–127. An excellent and concise overview of Chartism and its recent historiography is provided in Boyd Hilton, *A Mad, Bad and Dangerous People? England 1783–1846* (Oxford, 2006), pp. 612–21.

[20] Capt. Sir George Rose Sartorius, 'On the State of the Navy', *United Services Journal* (1848) part 2 p. 167; A Medical Staff Officer, 'Corporal punishments', *United Services Journal* (1848) part 2, pp. 580–1.

[21] R. Taylor, 'Manning the Royal Navy: The Reform of the Recruiting System, 1852–62', *Mariner's Mirror* 44 (1958), 302–313; Walton, '"A great improvement"'.

[22] Admiral Phipps Hornby to the Admiralty, quoted in Owen, 'CB 3027', p. 127.

[23] G. A. H Gordon, *The Rules of the Game: Jutland and British Naval Command* (London, 1996), pp. 170–3; R. Morriss, *Naval Power and British Culture, 1760–1850: Public Trust and Government Ideology* (Aldershot, 2003).

and the acquisition of skills; loyalty to the navy was to be rewarded with a pension.[24] The introduction of the naval uniform in 1856 created something in which personnel could take a pride, and on which they could display the badges which denoted the gradations of their status.[25] Food supplies were improved, with new victuals such as sugar, tea and cocoa, while the second half the century saw more professional training for ship's cooks.[26] Shore leave was increasingly regulated by Admiralty rules. Furthermore, those rules not only obliged officers to give men more regular leave; they also gave the sailor 'a great inducement to him to retrieve his character',[27] in other words, it incentivised good discipline. These measures took a typically enlightenment approach, using classification extensively. Thus entitlements to 'general', 'privilege' or 'special' leave conferred progressively more frequent opportunity to go ashore.[28] Captains could make use of this system in the way that they managed their crew. For example, on HMS *Racoon* in 1868, 'anyone whose leave was good had permission to attend a supper at the Recreation Rooms' in Simon's Town, in the Cape Colony.[29]

With these changes, society in the navy was profoundly altered, with new factors underlying discipline. Nor was the place of punishment untouched by the shift. From outside the navy there were calls from both humanitarian Christians and from critics of the ancien régime state for a moderation of the navy's punishments and for officers' treatment of their men to be subjected to parliamentary scrutiny. However, such views also had support within the Royal Navy and notably at the Admiralty, and between 1860 and 1866 a series of Naval Discipline Acts were passed by Parliament with cross-party support. The original impulse may have been one of moderation, but the Admiralty could not resist the temptation to set about codifying naval discipline.[30] After all, hitherto, the legal basis for naval discipline and punishment had been the Articles of War, last amended by Admiral Lord Anson in 1749.

---

[24] Walton, '"A great improvement"'.
[25] TNA, ADM 116/320 Report of the Committee on Uniform Clothing, minutes of evidence; Rasor, *Reform in the Royal Navy*, pp. 101, 165; Walton, 'Social History', pp. 300–1; Michael Lewis, *Navy in Transition 1814–1864. A Social History* (London, 1965), pp. 255–6.
[26] TNA, ADM 7/893 circular 64, 27 September 1873; ADM 7/893 Circular no.16, 20 February 1874.
[27] TNA, ADM 121/68, Capt. G. Wodehouse, HMS *Meeanee* to V-Adm. Smart, 3 January 1866, f. 209.
[28] Rasor, *Reform in the Royal Navy*, p. 156, n.26.
[29] Diary of William Scantlebury, HMS *Racoon*, 1 October 1868 (private collection).
[30] Cf. Similar moderation and consolidation of domestic criminal law from the 1827 to 1861: Boyd Hilton, *A Mad, Bad and Dangerous People*, pp. 318–21, 523, 606; A. Briggs, *Age of Improvement* (London, 1959), p. 436.

The Articles of War were a 'haphazard collection of regulations and admonishments', largely concerned with serious court martial offences committed by officers, and which had little of practical relevance to day-to-day management of a ship's crew.[31] Lord Clarence Paget put the case to the House of Commons in 1860 that

> it is high time that Her Majesty's Government should consider whether this old Act may not be remodelled, whether something like a more merciful view may not be taken in many cases, and whether it is not desirable, in fact, to enter upon complete revision of the naval code.[32]

This was not only a matter of intellectual and juristic tidiness, but was also a response to the new Continuous Service navy, providing for a more moderate system of punishment for the new generation of long-service ratings, and greater consistency between ships in the application of that system. The new system included several checks against harsh treatment by officers. Firstly, and most obviously, the new legislation limited officers' options for summary punishment to a prescribed tariff of penalties.[33] Secondly, their disciplinary regime was subject to extensive scrutiny, as the Admiralty required regular punishment returns to be submitted. As Eugene Rasor found, 'the accumulation of data about punishment provided the material for maintaining bureaucratic supervision over subordinates ... commanders were intimidated, upbraided and in other ways forced to rigidly adhere to the regulations'.[34] Thirdly, more severe punishments could only be imposed by courts martial, which were made much easier to convene. Where previously all the senior officers on the station had to be assembled, after the reforms a quorum of only five officers from at least three different ships was required, and while the president had to hold at least the rank of captain, now up to two lieutenants were eligible to stand as court members.[35] Furthermore, the new disciplinary code allowed courts martial more discretion than had been possible under the Articles of War. They were now empowered to find a defendant guilty of a lesser offence, rather than simply choosing between guilt and innocence of a more severe offence,[36] and had significantly more flexibility in the sentences imposed. Even the offence of mutiny accompanied by violence carried the

---

[31] Rodger, *Wooden World*, p. 218.
[32] *Hansard*, 21 August 1860.
[33] *Queen's Regulations and Admiralty Instructions* (1861) ch. xii, para. 50.
[34] Rasor, *Reform in the Royal Navy*, p. 43.
[35] Naval Discipline Act (1866) para. 58.
[36] Naval Discipline Act (1866) para. 47, 48.

penalty of 'Death, or such other Punishment as is herein-after mentioned', effectively leaving the court an open choice to suit the case.[37]

Underlying all these changes was new thinking about punishment. Where the Articles of War had provided for draconian punishments to be carried out in a theatrical context as a deterrent to similar offences by others, the new system dispensed with that more public deterrent in favour of proportionality, humanity and the hope of improving the miscreant's moral character; an intriguing blend of Benthamite utilitarianism and evangelical Christian humanitarianism.[38] As a guard against injustice, the death penalty could only be carried out after the case had been reviewed by the Admiralty (or commander in chief on a foreign station), and at least a two-thirds majority of the court members was required.[39] Commanding officers could not, except in the case of mutiny, award corporal punishment summarily without a review of the case by another officer.[40] There were also various statutory limitations upon the severity of punishments. No more than forty-eight lashes could be awarded as corporal punishment by either a commanding officer or a court martial.[41] Any capital offence, and all offences by officers, had to be tried by court martial, but commanding officers could deal with anything lesser. However, their powers to impose imprisonment upon an offender were limited to sentences up to six weeks, or three months for deserters.[42] There were also tight restrictions upon the length of time a prisoner could be subjected to solitary confinement.[43] Punishments themselves were intended not to inflict harm upon the wrongdoer or impress the rest with an intimidating show, but to improve the morals of the miscreant through denial of privileges.[44] Thus loss of liberty through penal servitude or imprisonment was at the more severe end of the spectrum, with most naval convicts kept at the navy's own prison at Lewes.[45] Courts martial could also penalise an individual's career with demotion or loss of

---

[37] Naval Discipline Act (1866) para.10. The wording of the 1860 Act (para.x) was only marginally more prescriptive: 'death, penal servitude or imprisonment'.

[38] Rasor, *Reform in the Royal Navy*, pp. 42–4, 51–9 (though he misunderstands the nature of Benthamite thinking about moral regeneration), cf. Boyd Hilton, *A Mad, Bad and Dangerous People*.

[39] Naval Discipline Act (1866) para. 53, clauses 2–3,

[40] *Ibid.*, para. 56, clause 3.

[41] *Ibid.*, para. 53, clause 11.

[42] *Ibid.*, para. 56, clause 2.

[43] *Ibid.*, para. 53 clause 8, para. 56 clause 2

[44] TNA, ADM 121/68, Capt. J. G. Goodenough, HMS *Victoria*, to V-Adm. Smart, 3 January 1866, f. 278; ADM 121/68 f. 507, Cdr. C. M. Luckraft, Governor of Lewes Naval Prison, to the Admiralty, 15 February 1864. Cf. Hilton, *Mad, Bad and Dangerous People*, p. 329.

[45] Naval Discipline Act (1866) part v.

seniority, reprimand, or even ejection from the navy. Commanding officers had a number of 'minor punishments' open to them, which ranged from up to seven days' solitary confinement (though this was heavily regulated), to watered-down rum, loss of free time, cleaning the heads (ship's toilets), and removal from the mess during dinner times. Some punishments were for specific offences: rum could only be denied as a penalty for drunkenness, for instance, while pay could only be deducted for absence without leave.[46]

The initial impact of the reforms might have been interpreted as disastrous, for a wave of mutinies swept across the fleet between 1859 and 1866. These took the form of naval strikes, mainly over the issue of leave. They also represented something of a culture clash, with rising numbers of new men committed to a naval career under Continuous Service entering a navy more used to sailors with only limited corporate loyalty. The mutinies were generally short, and involved little violence.[47] They should perhaps be seen as men testing out the new rules, while their commanding officers were uncertain themselves as to how they should be applied.

However the reforms were met with a favourable reception by most within the navy. According to Captain Coote, 'the uniform practice now known to both officers and men is far better than trusting to the various ideas, and even caprice, which to a great extent existed in dealing with offenders formerly'.[48] The regime certainly became less violent, for the number of instances of corporal punishment with the cat o' nine-tails fell from 577 in 1859 to only 57 ten years later.[49] The use of summary punishment increased somewhat at first, from 961 per 1000 men in 1859, to 1476 per 1000 men in 1865, thereafter the numbers fell steadily to reach a low of just 669 per 1000 men in 1893.[50]

Nevertheless, the reforms raised some new problems for crew management. The growth of Admiralty control over naval discipline, with central management of some aspects, regulation of much of what was left to commanding officers and increased bureaucratic surveillance of officers' disciplinary regime, implied a certain distrust of the officer corps. This was necessary to iron out what Captain Coote had called 'caprice', but it was felt acutely by some officers, whose protests to the Admiralty suggest a feeling of emasculation. They called

---

[46] *Queen's Regulations and Admiralty Instructions* (1861) ch.12, para. 50.

[47] Owen, 'CB 3027', pp. 104–21; Hamilton, *Anglo-French Naval Rivalry*, pp. 169–70, 196; Rasor, *Reform in the Royal Navy*, pp. 62–70.

[48] TNA, ADM 121/68, Capt. R. Coote, HMS *Gibraltar* to V-Adm. Smart, 6 December 1865, f. 185; ADM 121/68, R-Adm. Yelverton to V-Adm. Smart, 13 December 1865, f. 171.

[49] *House of Commons Sessional Papers* (1881) lx, 483–5.

[50] Ibid. *House of Commons Sessional Papers* (1894) liv, pp. 553ff.

for the Admiralty to 'place confidence in the officers', and complained that 'it is unnecessary to subject the punishment returns to their Lordships' scrutiny.'[51] Andrew Gordon has argued that the extension of central authority, increase in accountability and growth of procedure produced an authoritarian command culture in the officer corps in which initiative was stifled;[52] comparable implications can be observed for naval discipline and crew management. The increasingly procedural nature of much of disciplinary management could create uncertainty. Even senior officers were in the 1860s unsure how they were supposed to demote or promote men from one class for leave or conduct to another.[53] Commander Young of HMS *Gibraltar* sought certainty in overzealous application of the regulations, awarding 4741 punishments in three months in 1864.[54] Procedure could also be perverse. The Royal Marine Artilleryman John Wilkinson did not put his leggings on because he had sore shins, and was put on report for wearing incomplete uniform. The next day, 'I let the MD [surgeon] look at my shin this morning he put me in the report and into bed at the same time.'[55]

More significantly, the very procedural system of managing discipline seems to have worked to encourage some abdication of responsibility at a number of levels. A key indicator of this was the dramatic rise in the numbers of courts martial. From only 41 in 1859, the number had doubled by 1865 and reached a peak of 266 in 1881; and that was at a time when the number of naval personnel was falling fairly steadily.[56] As the Secretary to the Admiralty expressed it,

[Their Lordships] fear the greater facility of holding Courts Martial has in some degree tended to induce Captains and Commanding Officers to relieve

---

[51] W. Hickman, (ed.), *Reports and Opinions of Officers on the Acts of Parliament and Admiralty Regulations for Maintaining Discipline and Good Order in the Fleet Passed and Issued since the Year 1860* (London, 1867), pp. 62–3; Rasor, *Reform in the Royal Navy*, pp. 47–8.

[52] A. Gordon, *The Rules of the Game. Jutland and British Naval Command* (London, 2000) ch. 9–19.

[53] TNA, ADM 121/68, Capt. James G. Goodenough, HMS *Victoria*, to V-Adm. Smatt, asking for clarification of procedure for restoring men from second to first class for conduct. Smart passed the letter to Admiralty. W. G. Romaine replied to Smart on 1 February 1865.

[54] TNA, ADM 121/68, W.G. Romaine to V-Adm. Smart, 10 March 1865; ff.35–42, 27 June 1865, report of Court of Enquiry by Captains Goodenough, Dickson and Campbell to V-Adm. Smart.

[55] NMM, JOD/188 Diary of HMS *Alexandra* by 15th Co[mpany] G[unne]r J. Wilkinson, RMA, f. 58, 26 September 1884.

[56] *House of Commons Sessional Papers* (1881) lx, 483–5; *House of Commons Sessional Papers*, (1883) vol. xli, pp. 447–52.

themselves of responsibility, and has weakened the bands of discipline, which must depend on the due but discreet exercise of absolute authority.[57]

Most of the time problems were handled successfully, but where they were not there is a striking consistency of pattern, where the officer dealing with the situation failed to act decisively, but felt the miscreant's behaviour a serious affront to naval discipline. Once this was reported to the officer of the watch, the case often seems to have gone unquestioned until the court martial or even afterwards, if at all. John Sweeney, a Royal Marine on HMS *Hecla* in 1883, hesitated momentarily in responding to an order from Lance-Sergeant Norris that he should clean the capstan. Norris deemed this disobedience, and thus a serious offence. The officer of the watch, the captain and a court martial all upheld this view, and Sweeney was sentenced to eighteen months in prison with hard labour, and to be dismissed as objectionable. Only during the Admiralty review of the case was it observed that 'a little tact on the part of Lance-Sergeant Norris would have rendered this court martial unnecessary'.[58] In the same year, George Quinn, a stoker on HMS *Iris*, had a short temper and a grudge against the engineer. He refused to wear a clean work rig and then refused to fetch alternative attire, claiming that he should only muster his kit for his divisional officer, not the engineer. The officer of the watch referred the matter to the first lieutenant and sent Quinn back to work, where a few minutes later his temper boiled over and he assaulted Mr Moore, the engineer. Seemingly no one, not even during the Admiralty review of the resulting court martial, questioned why neither the engineer nor the officer of the watch had dealt with Quinn firmly; the first decisive figure of authority Quinn encountered was the court martial.[59] In these cases the problems grew out of all proportion because the officers involved trusted the authority of the system in preference to their own.

Such examples demonstrate that the introduction of a new kind of disciplinary system, which was more procedural, was a less clear-cut benefit to naval society than the established narratives of progress and the end of flogging might suggest. Undoubtedly, the reforms in the early 1860s made the shipboard regime less violent and more consistent from ship to ship and officer

---

[57] TNA, ADM 121/68, confidential letter from W. G Romaine to V-Adm. Lord Clarence Paget, f. 667–8.

[58] TNA, ADM 1/6696 Minutes of Court Martial on John Sweeney, RMLI Pt, HMS *Hecla*, memo by R-Adm F.W. Richards dated 13 July 1883. Sweeney was originally sentenced to 18 months in prison with hard labour and to be discharged as objectionable. The Admiralty review cut this to only six months, and rescinded the dismissal.

[59] TNA, ADM 1/6696 Minutes of Court Martial on George Quinn, Stoker, HMS *Iris*, 25 June 1883. The Admiralty review cut the length of the original sentence of five years' penal servitude.

to officer. Society seems to have become more stable, if the declining incidence of recorded punishment can be taken as a guide. It also became more ordered, making use of procedural mechanisms to regulate leave, promotions and punishments. Disciplinary sanctions were revised to fit the crimes better and were targeted at the improving the morals of the individual wrongdoer, rather than providing a brutal deterrent to others. The Admiralty assumed responsibility for reforming several historical sources of seamen's grievances, such as pay, leave and victualling. These benefits were certainly substantial, yet they did not come only at the cost of taxpayers' contributions or political concessions. There were underlying and significant costs. Some of the old mutual dependence of officers and men was weakened. More significantly, the procedural character of the new systems could be blind and blunt, and could encourage reliance upon the system itself rather than upon the judicious exercise of responsibility by those charged with command. The reforms had successfully created a new kind of discipline in the Royal Navy, which was both more humane and more regulated, but this also sowed the seeds of a new set of disciplinary challenges for officers in the management of their crews.

9

Towards a Hierarchy of Management: The Victorian and Edwardian Navy, 1860–1918

Mary Jones

The years from 1860 to 1918 saw the Royal Navy move from marked decline to rapid expansion; from 834 lieutenants in 1883 to 2,227 in 1914. It was a navy which had come from the Old Navy of *ad hoc*, dispersed sailing ships to the battlefleet New Navy, ready (and enthusiastic)[1] to take on any nation that threatened its hegemony. Lord Chatfield declared, 'It was a transformation, not only of material development of the Service, but of the mentality of the whole personnel'.[2] It is this transitional change, involving as it did an incremental change in management that is the subject of this chapter. The sailing navy became the transitional steam/sail navy and the transitional navy became the steam turbine new navy. For convenience, the term Old Navy is used for the years from about 1860 to 1885, Transitional Navy from about 1885 to 1895 and New Navy from about 1895 to 1914. This study is an analysis of the evidence of serving officers, their memoirs, biographies and autobiographies, and the secondary literature that has accompanied it.[3]

---

[1] Rear Admiral W. S. Chalmers, *The Life and Letters of David Beatty* (London, 1951), p. 99, letter dated 17 July 1909, and pp. 132–3, letter dated 2 August 1914.
[2] Admiral of the Fleet, Lord Chatfield, *The Navy and Defence* (London 1942), Preface.
[3] There is a great amount of primary literature, listed in M. Jones, 'The Victorian and Edwardian Naval Officer-corps' (unpublished Ph.D. thesis, University of Exeter, 2000). Secondary literature includes biographies of all the notable naval figures, Beresford, Fisher, Jellicoe etc., and commentaries – usefully, D. M. Schurman, *The Education of a Navy* (London, 1965); G. R. Searle, *The Quest for National Efficiency* (London, 1917); F. M. L. Thompson, *The Rise of Respectable Society 1893–1900* , N. A. M. Rodger *The Admiralty* (London, 1979). Many books dissect Jutland, including, Commander Carlyon Bellairs, *The Battle of Jutland* (London 1919); Admiral Sir Reginald Bacon, *The Jutland Scandal* (London, 1925) and notably, Admiral Viscount Jellicoe of Scapa, *The Grand Fleet 1914–1916, its Creation, Development and Work* (London, 1951).

Three brief case studies, using narratives over three generations in different periods are used to give a taste of contemporary shipboard life and throw new light upon the changes in leadership and management. By virtue of what the writers chose to record of their priorities, values, beliefs etc., they are illustrative of the changes. It is not intended to prove how, why or when the changes took place. Private journals are reliable because the writer has no axe to grind other than the cathartic expression of his own experience. Letters are less helpful because writers may be adapting their information to the letter's recipient. Individual case studies allow us to interpret history from first hand, personal experience, and provide evidential support for the historian's interpretative theories. As Richard Harding comments in the Introduction to this book, they are part of that 'symbiotic relationship of theory and empirical research ... that provides each generation with its new questions and tentative answers'.

It is said that all good management starts at the top. There was little top management of officers in the diverse Old Navy of the 1860s and 1870s. The traditional mode of command since the 1670s when the Royal Navy first started to operate at a distance from England meant that communication with far flung ships was difficult. Admirals and captains were mostly left to their own devices. Some were impressive examples of officers who managed their ships and men with skill and judgement. Others were not. The Old Navy was a mixture of individual officers and crews. As Beresford said, they made for ships of happy memory and ships of unhappy memory. I start with the memory of a sub-lieutenant's experience in two Old Navy ships.

John Locke Marx did not come from a naval family. His father, Francis, led the life of a leisured country gentleman at the family house in Arlebury, Hampshire. He was a notable leader in the local gentry of the neighbourhood; his mother was Anna Maria Selina Locke, daughter of wealthy Devizes banker and M.P. Wadham Locke.[4] Marx joined the Training Ship *Britannia* in 1866 under the severe regime of Captain Randolph. He had taken a third class sub-lieutenant's certificate in seamanship and gunnery, and a second in navigation. We meet him as a sub-lieutenant in 1874, sailing to Malta with Captain Codrington in the *Lord Warden*, the iron-clad flagship of Vice Admiral Sir Hastings Yelverton. There were five lieutenants and eight sub-lieutenants. Research shows that the ships to which officers were sent at this time did not necessarily reflect their showing at *Britannia* or in sub-lieutenant exams. Marx was made flag mate. He kept up a private journal. 'The work is very hard ... I have been copying signals on board the Narcissus ... difficult to keep up'. The commission started well. The Mediterranean cruise provided

---

[4] For life of John Locke Marx, see M. Jones (ed.), *A Naval Life* (Dulverton, 2007).

leisure as well as work – a canoe trip, sightseeing, digging for treasure around Troy. Yelverton was replaced by Vice Admiral Drummond who came on board with Lady Drummond, their three daughters, two maids and a governess. Marx objected at first but then thought having his ladies on board did a lot to improve the admiral's temper which previously had a tendency to 'blow up like blazes on the quarter deck', much to Marx's disapproval. There was an opportunity for Marx to demonstrate his mettle as a junior officer when he volunteered to take charge of a landing party fighting a fire in the local city square. They pulled down the houses and blew them up: 'two or three bluejackets got drunk which was not to be wondered at as the houses were full of wine'. Life was good, 'The Admiral has been pretty civil lately and the Captain is a brick …'.

Things deteriorated though and there was a row with the captain over the signal log: 'I intend not to write up the signal log any more'. Codrington was no longer 'a brick':

> He may put it down to principle but I hardly think it proceeds so much from that as from an innate pleasure in feeling that he has the power of making other and not inferior animals to himself miserable. He bullies everyone. Coffin [a lieutenant] tried to imitate him but I ran him in.

Marx took solace in sex. He had been introduced to 'that damn brothel' and its results as a midshipman: 'Conybeare has gone sick … Babington, Duncombe, Dunbar, Sherrard have been let in at Strada Versevo. Poor Batten has also got an awfully bad dose from the same place.' He made great resolutions to give it up but they did not last. There was pimping aboard ship, 'nice gentlemanly, well dressed people came aboard …'. Marx became ill again. Venereal disease was a problem for captains as well as the sufferers, since much manpower was lost to the navy through venereal disease as a ship in trouble or a heavy gale needed all its personnel. Marx got so bad, he 'could only crawl'. Figures are hard to come by but George King Hall, a sub on *Lord Warden* later, spoke of the 'enormous number of men in the flat laid up with it, not to take into account those that don't come forward'. Captains dealt with this trouble in various ways. When Marx was a midshipman his captain, Cochrane, had simply put his head round the gunroom door and told Marx to 'go to school in future'. Captain Codrington made nothing of it but at Vigo Captain Brandreth moved his ship to the other side, 'there being such a fearful amount of venereal disease knocking about'.

The *Lord Warden* continued its Mediterranean cruise but Marx in his disgruntled and ill state complained about everything:

> The Admiral clearly shows that he is an Old fool, on deck he blows me up like blazes and I do not like him…. The mess has been going to blazes. Mr Soper,

> Messman, is the slipperiest, blackguard on earth … Brown was bowld [?] out drunk much to my disgust as I knew I should get a wigging.

In fact he did not. Marx acknowledged that 'the Captain let me off and behaved like a gentleman' but relations with other senior officers soured, 'it is an utter waste of life being humbugged about by the present set of men. I like Codrington but hate the others very much.' Soper the messman, after many rows with the wardroom officers, gave notice. The officers had to take charge of the mess which Marx thought 'a damnable nuisance'. Things went from bad to worse, 'More rows and horizon looking black … Determined to go at any price to get out of the ship … Very miserable indeed … Very miserable … I would as lief jump overboard'.

It was a time of great frustration for Marx. He was tired of the boring routine of evolutions, target practice and drills and he longed for 'action of some sort'. Sub-lieutenants in the Old Navy could find themselves in positions of command; leading a dhow raiding party, dealing with a local chief as captain's representative, or taking command of an African fort. No such excitement for Marx in the Mediterranean Fleet; it boasted one flag officer and there was no talk of war. The only contemporary action was against the Ashantees on the west coast of Africa.

Marx decided to pull himself together and 'have a yarn with the Skipper … He was alright and … he is in favour of my staying so I will, but I must admit his manner on deck is not always as gracious as it might be …'. However, things still did not improve:

> The Admiral is an old fool. I daresay a good man in his day but past his work and is particularly jealous of his authority while the Captain takes almost entire charge and the Admiral has to lean upon him but occasionally he takes it into his head to act on his own judgement which is usually wrong, and makes a mess of what he undertakes, which enrages the Captain. The Flag Lieutenant is jealous of the Captain and thinks he ought to have all to do with the concern and the Secretary thinks much the same, so between the lot there is anything but harmony … most of their follies and mistakes are visited on my luckless pate.

Allowing for Marx's jaundiced view, management on board the *Lord Warden* seems to have had its problems. There was no easily accepted hierarchy of authority. Admiral and captain had embarrassing rows on deck, jealous and discordant officers vied with each other, and a young sub treated his captain almost as an equal. There was no senior officer or divisional lieutenant to keep an eye out for an unhappy junior. Instead Marx accidentally overheard the first lieutenant's bad opinion of him. 'I had not strength of mind to send down but could not help listening and the consequence was I heard no good of myself and have hated the man heartily ever since'. However, there would appear to have been, in this aspect of the Old Navy, an almost democratic element in officer relationships. Marx was able to 'row' with Codrington and then later 'have a yarn with him' without retribution. Codrington may have appeared to vacillate between strength and weakness, now 'bully' now 'a gentleman', but there was a strength of flexibility which mended relationships and produced a peaceful result. When Marx badly bruised himself falling through the ship, Codrington 'evinced much more feeling than I gave him credit for'. Marx makes no mention of difficulty with the men and when later he earned a bronze medal from the Humane Society for a heroic attempt to rescue a bluejacket, it was in company with another brave bluejacket. He hoped it might help his chances of early promotion, 'but much fear there is no chance, too many do braver actions than I can and do not get it. I have no interest to back it.'

However, he decided he did not 'lead so much of a pig's life' as previously, and was pleased when the admiral him offered him the post of acting lieutenant in HMS *Invincible*:

> I quite like this ship but it is the rummiest ship I have ever been in. Old Tomms and Buckle, the doctor, do not speak and fight on every occasion. Glasspole, Chief Engineer, and Hembridge, are atheist ... and try to ram it down our throats ... Commander Polly is a good sort, a tea totaller but smokes a good deal and is a gentleman ... Old Turner has a swollen testacle and secondaries and has gone to hospital. Williams has a bad throat and will not speak and thinks he is dying ... Barker presents a drunken sort of person a very good fellow and gentleman when not in liquor which he generally is ...

But times got better. The French squadron was in and there was entertainment, dining and dancing and French was spoken – 'with much fluency after dinner'.

Then, on 3 January 1875, Marx got his commission as lieutenant: 'my joy was great ... little did I expect it, had dim visions of waiting two years more..., stood the required champagne and felt a great swell ...'. Perhaps Marx had more 'interest' than he thought. Admiral Drummond seems to have liked him and wanted him to stay in *Lord Warden*. The influential Phipps Hornby had nominated him. But even so, it was a surprisingly early commission. Promotion was slow in the stagnation of the seventies and Marx had not got impressive certificates or reports. The average wait at the time was four years, but Marx had done it in two. It seems to have been an Old Navy promotion of patronage and opportune circumstance. Phipps Hornby was a friend of the family, and Marx had been fortunate to have the opportunity to demonstrate initiative and heroism.

We leave the Old Navy and take up our next case study in the Transitional Navy in 1884, with the experience of Francis Starkie Clayton, captain of *Diamond*, on the Australia Station from 1884 to 1888. *Diamond* was a transitional 'up funnel, down screw' man-of-war frigate with outrigger torpedoes. It was part of the growing small boat navy, facilitating the *Pax Britannica* in a scattered fleet of men of war, corvettes and gun boats.

Captain Clayton wrote to his wife every day. He had joined the navy as a boy in 1852 and been at the battle of Sebastopol. Now he was the typical Victorian captain of his time – the ideal 'father of the ship', with a ship's company of twenty-two officers, thirty-five petty officers, seventy-two seamen, twenty-nine boys, thirty-four marines, an engine room establishment of twenty-three and twelve domestics: '... a great responsibility ...'. Clayton was delighted to find at the outset of the commission, that all his officers, 'whatever else they are, are certainly gentlemen. ... I had Mosse [paymaster] in to smoke a cigar ... he seems a nice gentlemanly fellow ...'. Reflecting the social prejudices of the time, he was

> [a] little doubtful about the chief engineer ... I am particularly fortunate in the two Accountant Officers, both are very nice, gentlemanly men which is not always the case ... Shakespear [first lieutenant] is certainly a capital fellow, full of energy but does everything so quietly ... I should not have cared for a blustering, bullying man however good an officer.

Clayton was delighted to note 'the backbone of breeding' at a local ball. 'Seamen will always pay a more ready and cheerful obedience to officers who are gentlemen.'[5] The concern for gentility was increasing in contemporary Victorian social life where, as Trollope said, 'no-one could be altogether successful unless he be esteemed a gentleman'[6]. To the Admiralty a gentleman by definition, would not only share an attribute of God – 'that Gentleman of the most sacred and strictest honour' [7]– but he would also promise 'the fine and governing qualities'[8] of his class. The Admiralty did not have to worry about training for leadership when it was implied ready-made in the idea of the gentleman. The patronage books of the day show the increasing importance of gentle or aristocratic birth in the applications for nomination of naval cadets.[9]

---

5   G. Dening, *Mr Bligh's Bad Language* (Cambridge, 1992), p. 124.
6   A. Trollope, *The Prime Minister* (London 1876), p. 2.
7   I. Schapera (ed.), *Livingstone's African Journal, 1853–1856* (London, 1963), Vol. 2, p. 374.
8   Matthew Arnold, quoted in H. Perkin, *The Rise of Professional Society* (London, 1989), p. 119.
9   These Patronage Books are held at Britannia Royal Naval College Dartmouth. They are unreferenced but titled by names of respective First Lords, e.g. Duke of Somerset, Right Hon Henry L. Corry, Right Hon. J. Goschen, Right Hon. G. W. Hunt, Right Hon W. H. Smith.

To return to Clayton, his first meeting with his men went well: 'I don't think I have got a single black sheep. I do hope … we shall have a happy commission. I hate having to worry people but if necessary the quarter deck face appears. Indeed, I always have it on when work is going on.' Later he wrote: 'My men have so far been behaving like angels with very few exceptions who I have come down upon very hard to stop the rest and show I am not to be trifled with'. As the commission went on, some of the men tried their luck: 'The first two (Wardroom) stewards have been before me for stealing, … Some of the gentlemen thought because I had been kind and rather indulgent, they could do what they liked with me and I have had to show them they are mistaken'. Despite the quarterdeck face, the men continued to be troublesome in the earlier part of the commission:

There are some dozen on board who are always giving trouble, owing to the war summons one can't get rid of them as you might other times and there is no means of imprisoning them here, however, I will make their lives a burden to them somehow and show them who is master.

The trouble with his men came at the beginning of the commission, before the ship's company had time to really shake down, before they knew their captain and before they had time to bond as a ship's company, sharing the dangers and successes of the sailing together. The source of Clayton's discipline was in the integrity and communicative skills of his gentlemanly personality and his recognised ability as a very fine seaman. Young midshipmen spoke of the confidence his voice gave them above the 'roaring of the wind and flapping of the sails'.[10] He was the unchallenged, but approachable captain. His officers liked him and the men appreciated his care for them, especially when they were sick. When the commission ended and the men were discharged, it was an emotional moment: 'I said goodbye to them and very nearly broke down in doing so, did not think I was so foolish, but most of the men had been with me the whole commission and I felt very sorry at parting with them'. A three-year commission as a captain policing the *Pax Britannica* required all the best leadership skills, not least in sailing, where bravery and skill went hand in hand:

We have been having a rough time of it in the way of weather since leaving Sydney. I have not had my clothes off for the last two nights. I did not know the capabilities of the lieutenants and had to be about all night.… My cabin leaks lamentably so does the old ship herself.

The poor state of many ships in the Transitional period exacerbated the dangers and hazards of sailing in rough waters and bad weather. Although

---

[10] P. Thompson (ed.), *Close to the Wind: Early Memoirs (1866–79) of Admiral Sir William Creswell* (London, 1965), p. 27.

steam was available, coal was only to be used where necessary and in bad weather a ship could run out very quickly. There were several hazardous occasions, but Clayton found that he had got some very good officers: 'the two young lieutenants are A1. I shall be able to go to sleep in peace. Bremer too, knows his work, but he is a fussy old fellow and stammers so the work does not go on quite so well.' This is an aspect of the Transitional Navy. The young lieutenants had taken sub-lieutenant's exams in seamanship, gunnery and navigation started in 1868, and after 1876, in torpedo and pilotage. The older lieutenants were the product of *Britannia* and training at sea. They could be a disappointment: 'I might have got rid of the tiresome old fellow [Bremer] for a time but of course he is out of the way out shooting for the day and I am obliged to send Stoddart who is worth a dozen of him.'

Clayton also suffered from the contemporary lack of lieutenants as they were increasingly required to man the ships of the *Pax Britannica*: 'very tiresome ... they have reduced executive officers by a sub lieut and a gunner so we are very short now. The midshipmen have to be at school and under instructions all day so they are not much available.' Added to which, as a good senior captain he had been sent a troublesome 'middy' from the flagship to sort out. Even so, when it came to fleet sailing, which significantly Clayton had not done for seventeen years, *Diamond* did well and led the flagship.

Apart from his relationship with his officers and his men, Clayton's relationship with his admiral was crucial. In the Transitional period of 1884, the threat of a Russian invasion of India and other predatory foreign interests in the area had forced the Admiralty to take a greater interest in the Australia station and, with the laying of the telegraph cable in 1884 and the arrival of Vice Admiral Tryon, the station was upgraded to flagship status. One of Clayton's first tasks was to visit the new admiral. He was glad to find him prompt in his decisions on some little things. Decisiveness was admired by officers: 'What a real seaman cannot understand is hesitation,' declared Admiral Dundas.[11]

It took time for Clayton to get the measure of Tryon and he got an early flea in his ear when he offered suggestions as to how to guard the coaling station at Albany. When he tried to get the admiral's help in getting the Admiralty to return some money he thought 'Their Lordships' owed him, Tryon would not send on his letter: 'that is the worst of having a man who has been secretary of the Admiralty, he looks at everything from their point of view, ... never to pay a halfpenny that can be avoided'.

However, in terms of the work of the station, Clayton found Tryon very supportive. Clayton's task was to patrol the islands and keep the peace among

---

[11] Admiral Sir Charles Dundas, *An Admiral's Yarns* (London, 1922), p. 154.

the natives. It was not easy and he had to tread a wary path between action and diplomacy: 'the Admiral is averse to the indiscriminate shooting down natives as a punishment which I am glad of but on the other hand when they have to be punished what else can you do?' Public opinion did not agree, it was becoming more humane and questions were being asked in the House about the activities of *Diamond*. Clayton was anxious: 'I do want to hear from the Admiral, if he approves the rest may all go to pot, Admiralty and all …'. Admiral Tryon declared that although there were some small things he might not have approved of he would back him up in everything.

Although continually respectful and tactful, Clayton's relationship with Tryon was not subservient. 'The Admiral … delights in airing some fad. Yesterday it was a question of men wearing blue jerseys as we have had nothing but cold weather for the last month, I think they were doing good and we had a sharp contention about it.' On another occasion, Clayton had to go to the admiral to peruse his covering letter to the Admiralty with the yearly reports: 'I read it over and suggested one or two alterations which as usual he poop-pooped but I shall probably find he has adopted them'. There was a degree of Old Navy democratic equality and freedom in this relationship. When it was time for Tryon to leave, Clayton was sorry to lose him, 'with all his worry. I like him extremely … Then comes a new man with new ideas and probably an entirely new way of working … then if he is not a lover of Tryon he will be down on me as one of his men'.

The new Admiral Fairfax was quite different from Tryon: 'He seems to take the world very easy and is inclined to enjoy himself and not worry us too much'. He was sorry to hear the admiral had decided to take a cruise in Diamond. He would have less freedom and it left him uncertain about his movements because 'the Admiral has not yet got the requisite permission [by] telegram. Really, it is too bad that an Admiral can't move about his own station without permission from home – centralisation with a vengeance'.

Clayton found Fairfax a quiet, easy companion but an alert admiral:

> I can see he keeps his eye lifting as we say when a man is on the lookout [but] there is no doubt our present Chief is not such a good Commander in Chief as Tryon tho' privately I like him well enough and the best of the two. It is a great drawback that you can't get an answer out of him … I find with a little gentle pressure and leading the way you want him, you can generally get what you require but you have to be very careful, as if he thinks for the moment that you want to run counter to his wishes, you are done as he can be obstinate as a pig.

The transition period was a time of advancement in executive management. The Admiralty (or at least the First Lord, the Earl of Northbrook) became seriously concerned about which officers were worthy of promotion. Perhaps the social status of 'gentleman' was not enough and the confidential report system was started. In 1880 it applied to all officers, but there was such an outcry in support of an unwritten acceptance of an officer's character because he was, by definition 'a gentleman', that in 1882 it was reduced to a written report for lieutenants only. In 1885 the Luard Inquiry into the Education of Executive Officers was held because the Admiralty was worried about the poor quality of sub-lieutenants' exams, especially the consistently poor quality of the Navigation exam. In 1886, a 'ferociously competitive'[12] exam for *Britannia* entry was introduced and as a result there was a notable correlation between a good pass at *Britannia* and a first class certificate in the Seamanship exam. Officers themselves were realising that good examination performance was becoming tied to career progress and complained that a third for seamanship ruined any prospects of later promotion.

The change to a more proactively managed New Navy reached Australia:

> That tiresome fellow Hammill had just come off and began night signals, he is one of those tiresome Mediterranean new brooms whose brain is full of drills and exercises and it is rather a nuisance just at the end of the commission.... Our new brooms are very smart at present, fresh from England with lots of energy.

Naval officers were also making their presence felt in England with their support of the *Pall Mall Gazette*'s campaign to advance the navy in 1884, which helped to produce the Navy Defence Act of 1889. The Admiralty was becoming more significant: 'more naval men are getting a foothold which I trust we shall stick to. I would not mind getting employment there but I don't think it is at all likely as I am not one of the scientific people.' It was left to his son, our last case study, to be one of the scientific people.

With the turn of the century, and Britain's stumbling involvement in the South African war, there was a sense that Britain and its navy were falling behind and an outcry for national efficiency was heard everywhere.[13] Questions were asked about the 'war readiness of the fleet'.[14] The word 'efficient' appeared in Admiralty confidential reports of senior officers. The scientific New Navy, with its electricity, telegraphic signals, torpedoes, dreadnoughts and battle cruisers, now demanded officers with accredited, specialised, professional expertise. This intensified, centralised, hierarchical structure of officer management was designed to produce an 'efficient' navy, e.g., fit for purpose – victory at sea. Toward this end the Admiralty attached increasing importance to examination performance and grades of certificates. Advantages of

---

[12] Commander E. P. Statham, *The Story of the Britannia* (London 1904).
[13] Searle, *The Quest for National Efficiency*, chapter 3; *Naval Review* 1 February (1913), Introduction.
[14] A. S. Hurd, *Naval Efficiency: The War Readiness of the Fleet* (London, 1902).

ship postings and seniority accrued to officers who did well in examinations and gained high quality certificates. Advanced courses had been started at Greenwich in 1873 to promote the 'scientific' navy but they were not popular at first. 'No officer who is worth anything will go to Greenwich after his practical course unless he is obliged to do so', said Chatfield in 1904,[15] but by the turn of the century it was becoming evident that lieutenants needed to pass an advanced course at Greenwich if they were to make progress and get 'on the scale'. The 'long course' in gunnery or torpedo was a necessary adjunct to promotion. However, an officer needed to be recommended for these and it became harder to qualify for the courses. Officers needed 'three and possibly four or five firsts as sub-lieutenant'[16] to be accepted on the long gunnery course. War courses were started in 1905. Judgements appear to have been accurate and perceptive – Beatty was 'smart and able but inclined to be rash in conclusion', while Wemyss 'had a strong personality and a good grasp of strategical situations'.[17] Those officers pronounced successful in the war courses generally did well in the promotion stakes. Prowess rather than personalities could overtake the 'Buggins turn' or sideline patronage. K. G. Dewar, the Gunnery specialist said, 'I had to work hard to obtain five firsts ... a system which made me a lieutenant at twenty over the heads of about 130 of my contemporaries'.[18] However, the aristocratic network retained its patronage ramifications in ship, squadron, courts martial and sexual liaison.[19]

Into this New Navy system came Lieutenant-Commander Ralph Clayton, the son of Captain Francis Clayton. He joined *Britannia* in 1900 and wrote regularly to his mother. He, like Dewar, also gained five first class certificates as sub-lieutenant, but promotion came less quickly as more officers were getting first class certificates and there was less need for lieutenants in 1904. After serving as torpedo officer on the cruiser *Blenheim* and the battleship *Edward V11*, he joined the prestigious battle cruiser *Queen Mary* in 1913. The dispersed fleets of the Imperial Navy had been brought home by the First Sea Lord, Admiral Sir John Fisher, and amalgamated into the Atlantic Home Fleet. It had not been universally welcomed. Its outcome was a centralised navy devoted to 'grid iron' tactics and the tactics of a big steam battlefleet. There was no room for individual action. The traumatic collision of *Victoria* with *Camperdown* in 1893 had sealed the abandonment of TA (movement

---

[15] Chatfield, *Navy and Defence*, p. 184.
[16] Ibid.; The National Archives (TNA), ADM 203/99 Reports on Officers attending the War Course, 1905–1914.
[17] Ibid.
[18] Dewar, *Navy Within*, p.46.
[19] Beatty's mistress, Eugenie Fawcett, was the sister of fellow officer, Godfrey Fawcett.

with or without signals[20]) in favour of fleets controlled by signals from central command[21] and captains who simply, as Beatty complained, had to do as they were told.

> There was a young man who said, 'D - n!
> I suddenly see that I am
> Only able to move in a predestined groove;
> I'm not ev'n a 'bus – I'm a tram'.[22]

Compared with a torpedo lieutenant in the Old or Transitional Navy, Ralph Clayton was now just a cog in a battleship: 'Electric wires, lighting and motors, is what we talk about all day now'.

The 1st Battle Cruiser Squadron was the government's ambassador. It visited Germany and Russia 'cementing the peace of Europe with roast beef and caviar'. There was much mutual entertaining and Ralph met the Czar and his family; 'we all put our names in the visitors book and coming generations will find mine on the page opposite the Emperor's'.

Returning to England, life became a routine matter of drills and torpedo trials. Ralph made a mistake in his calculations and his mines sank to his great consternation, but divers managed to trace the bubbles and rescue them so 'no unpleasant Court of Inquiry'. He kept out of the way of the gunnery experiments under Sir Robert Arbuthnot as he had not had his hair cut for two months, 'and he has strict ideas on the question of length'. He worked hard on the important torpedo practice of the year: 'the only time torpedoes get the attention they merit. As we're not used to so much, it is somewhat embarrassing; especially as one's achievement is minutely analysed'. He resented the fact that gunnery officers' practices were given so much more attention.

In August of 1914 war was declared. It seems to have come as a surprise to Ralph: 'But that is chiefly because one cannot possible imagine our being involved in war over a question on which 99% of us haven't the least interest ...'. There was initial excitement, then everything settled down: 'The war is rather boring ... our standard of excitement goes up, and there are not enough events to keep things interesting. Every afternoon we sleep after lunch till teatime, and there isn't much to do in the morning or after tea.'

To Ralph's disappointment, the popular Captain Reginald Hall was suddenly replaced by temporary Captain Bentink: 'He talks easily but not so much as Captain Hall and is much quieter and less highly strung than the latter. Altogether we approve of him and should like him to stay.' Bentink did not stay, despite Admiral Beatty arguing for him to do so. Ralph was sorry; 'I

---

[20] See A. Gordon, *Rules of the Game* (London, 1996), p. 97.
[21] Ibid., pp. 300–1.
[22] Lady Poore, *Recollections of an Admiral's Wife* (London, 1916), p. 289.

am afraid we are unlucky in our present man, and that he will be very difficult to get on with.' The present man was Captain Cecil Prowse. Hall went to Intelligence, and Bentink went on to become Chief of Staff.

There was also a change at the Admiralty. In October 1914 Fisher was back as First Sea Lord.

> The change at the Admiralty meets with plenty of approval, though naturally, it is not quite general ... I think his appointment was the best that could be made in the circumstances; I am not sure that there is anyone to equal him. If only he and Churchill agree, we are sure to have a strong policy, and at the same time, a sensible one.

Confined mostly to the ship, Ralph missed his Edwardian social and cultural life, in which he had participated in aristocratic country house weekends, – 'a delightful three days with Lady Howick' – and sporting outings with fellow officers. Throughout Ralph's career he always seemed more concerned with his social and cultural life than his work. Victorian and Edwardian social life was a life of increasing civility. Osborne cadets became increasingly sensitive as to the use of bad language and the desirable Captain Bentink talked easily and quietly. Polite conversation and refined behaviour was expected in the officer class. New Navy officers were welcome in the country houses of the aristocracy.

However, Clayton continued to bemoan the absence of the noisier, excitable Captain Hall: 'no luck comes our way now. Capt. Hall took it all away to Admiralty.' Even Christmas was depressing:

> The mess deck was decorated as usual and all the officers went round headed by the band, but ... the Captain had no idea of talking to the men and the whole affair only took ten minutes instead of an hour ... Capt. Hall would have made it a very different show, and there would have been some enthusiasm.

The civility which officers showed to each other is reflected in the respect and concern which Ralph showed to his men over charitable gifts:

> The men don't like the idea of Charity and wouldn't come for them. Then I sent everything forward to them, without asking who took them, and assured them they were made by people I knew and specially for them. Remember, they are picked men, with no mean idea of themselves.

He thought lack of education was 'the chief obstacle in the way of the lower classes improving much. We notice it tremendously on board . No amount of driving will make the vast majority exhibit any exertion ...'. Perhaps coaling provided the bonding which sailing had hitherto done: 'Had to coal again on Thursday ... all night – a desperate business which only ended in daylight. Between twelve and four there wasn't much life left amongst the men. I put in an hour's digging and haven't got over the effects yet.'

In March of 1916 Commander James was replaced by Sir Charles Blane. Ralph thought Blane would get on better with the captain than James and that 'may be an advantage to us all'. But the new navigating commander named Pennell was 'our own Captain's selection, which is not in his favour....'. Ralph felt it was time for his promotion to commander and he started negotiating for a change. He wanted 'a more lively job'. The commanders of the Old and Transitional Navy benefited from opportunities of promotional advancement presented by the expanding navy at the end of the century, but the 1900 entry like Ralph suffered from the post-war contraction of the navy.

There was 'less and less to do aboard' and frustratingly the officers heard very little about what was going on in the war. Apart from the odd game of golf or a walk, diversion was provided largely by the discussion of what was going on at the Admiralty:

> Admiral De Robeck is much younger and has most people's confidence ... wish McKenna was got rid of ... the description of him as the ministerial mule browsing around Downing st. has taken our fancy immensely ... there is great dissatisfaction with Winston Churchill's propensity for giving orders apparently emanating from the Admiralty, which the rest of the Board do not approve, he had better be replaced altogether by Lord Fisher.... probably the combination of Jackson, Jellicoe and Balfour is as strong as we could get.

Promotions were by strict seniority or the patronage of senior officers, unless officers had been involved in the war. When promotions went to *Inflexible* and *Invincible* for the Falkland battle, Ralph bemoaned that, 'The lowest on this list ... goes over my head, though he is much older than I am, and he wasn't even in the Britannia at the same time'. Later, 'I've had a great disappointment over the departure of the Lieut.-Comdr. He was a little senior to me and I had a right to expect his relief would be junior to me; unfortunately the new fellow is my senior by a month'. He saw Captain Bentink, who said he would have to get Captain Prowse's approval or there would be difficulty in his leaving. Ralph did not find it easy to raise the subject with the captain, 'as he never gives any opportunity for such conversation. However, I did see him on Monday night . He didn't definitely object, ... so on Tuesday I wrote to Capt. Hall and also to the Captain of Vernon. I hope to hear from them'. But the captain of *Vernon* already had three torpedo lieutenants waiting for new appointments. With the ending of the *Pax Britannica* navy, promotional opportunities for lieutenants decreased. Torpedo lieutenants were not as highly regarded as gunnery lieutenants, being thought too independent of mind: 'good, but lacking in tact and judgement, difficult to employ with others.'[23] was the sort of confidential

---

[23] TNA, ADM 203/99 Report on T. W. Kemp at War Course.

report that appeared for torpedo officers. They were less likely to reach the heights of the Admiralty.

Ralph made as many approaches as he could to senior officers but he had not sufficient 'interest' to be successful, and there was no chance for him to demonstrate initiative or heroism to bring himself to notice. Still looking for a transfer, on 7 May, Ralph wrote his last letter home: 'As long as the war lasts it will be quite impossible for a Torpedo Lieutenant to get out of an important ship like this'. Then came the call for action he had been so long looking forward to: '... I saw the Old Navy making ready to lead out the New Navy under a grey sky and a falling glass'.[24]

At 4.26 on the afternoon of 31 May *Queen Mary* blew up and sank at the battle of Jutland. She took 57 officers and 1,208 men of the Old and New Navy with her. She also took the supremacy of the Admiralty. Their Lordships never regained their hierarchical domination. Thereafter there was an anguished split between the supporters of Jellicoe and those of Beatty, as Jellicoe was blamed for losing the battle and Beatty was regarded as prevented from winning it. It resulted in an acerbic and bitter quarrel, as supporting admirals joined in on one side or another. The loss of the undisputed leadership of the First Lord led to the fragmentation of Admiralty and the subsequent 'multitude of counsellors' and eventual joint services headquarters[25] which has continued to be more descriptive of the conduct of the Admiralty than 'Their Lordships'.

To conclude, in the period covered by these case studies, the navy moved from an old hierarchical system of leadership based on dispersed squadrons with officers of independent initiative, empiricism, and experience of fighting, as evidenced by Marx and F. Clayton, to a new hierarchical system of management based on a peaceful battlefleet navy of officers with professional, technological, and social expertise operating within a narrow, restricting hierarchy of prescribed captains, commanders and admirals, culminating in the authority of the First Sea Lord, as evidenced by Ralph Clayton. This New Navy was not suited to making war. As Andrew Gordon has shown, Jellicoe clearly fought Jutland consistent with the New Navy's 'action-principles with which he had imbued his forces'.[26] It had deleterious results.

These New Navy 'action principles' had been imbued into a body of officers who shared a corporate identity based largely on training, education, and similar social life, 'probably at no other time in history has the Royal Navy's officer corps been so uniformly moulded in its cultural self image as in 1914'.

---

[24] R. Kipling, *The Fringes of the Fleet* (London, 1916).
[25] Rodger, *Admiralty*, pp. 145–58.
[26] Gordon, *Rules*, p. 565. For a masterly exposition of the role of Old and New Navy during this period, see the whole book.

Corporate identity, an important factor early identified by Mahan in his Naval Types, has been taken up by Hogg as the current social identification theory to show amongst other things that officers from the same corporate identity are more likely to accept each other's leadership.[27] Corporate identity was less evident in the Old Navy where the group of officers were much more dispersed from the centre of training and education and often lived with a small, disparate company of fellows on a foreign station for three years or more. Marx's 'rum' ship held a distinctly disparate corporate identity. In the Transitional Navy, moving from individual to corporate, Francis Clayton noted ruefully, that he was not 'one of the new men'. Ralph Clayton exemplified the corporate life of officers in the peaceful New Navy. At its best it provided for competent ship management and the peaceful if not boring life he found on *Queen Mary* before the war. But when it came to the Admiralty and a power regime that culminated in the domination of the First Sea Lord, there was little corporate identity amongst 'Their Lordships' to curtail the system of nepotism and personal following which had always existed in the Old and New Navy, and was at its most questionable when a First Sea Lord had at his command Britain's entire front-line strength.[28]

These problems were exacerbated by the Battle of Jutland and its aftermath. The apparently impregnable monolith of the New Navy was shown to have feet of clay. Its corporate identity concealed deficiencies in leadership. Its authoritarian management obscured the danger of arbitrary personal power that was ultimately detrimental to victory.

---

[27] A. T. Mahan, *Types of Naval Officers* (London, 1901); Michael A. Hogg, 'A Social Identity Theory of Leadership', *Personality and Social Psychology Review* 5:3 (2001),p. 184.
[28] Gordon, *Rules*, p. 565.

10

Leadership Training for Midshipmen, 1919–1939

Elinor Romans

The principal aim of the inter-war Royal Navy's officer training systems was to imbue young officers with 'Officer-Like Qualities'; an undefined although well understood set of values which can be divided into three broad areas; seamanship, leadership and gentlemanliness. Officer-like qualities thus encompassed all the characteristics required in a good naval officer; including courage, determination, honour, social graces and technical knowledge.

The Royal Navy employed a wide variety of officers who entered and were trained in varying ways. Medical officers and chaplains entered the navy as qualified professionals and went through a short course designed to teach them to behave like naval officers. The bulk of naval officers entered the service as executive, engineering or paymaster branch cadets, their training was partly along common lines. A number of men were promoted from the ranks and their training was entirely separate from that of those entering as cadets. In this essay I will concentrate on the training of executive officers entered as cadets.

Young executive officers progressed through several training stages. For most, the first stage was a four-year period at Dartmouth Naval College, entering at the age of thirteen and concentrating on academic knowledge and absorbing naval culture. For the remainder, who entered at seventeen, it was a year aboard a training ship designed to introduce them to naval life and reinforce their academic knowledge. All then went to sea as cadets for eight months, this spell being designed to introduce them to the realities of life at sea and to the men of the fleet. The following period, lasting two years and four months, was spent serving in the fleet as a midshipman and was particularly important in developing officer-like qualities. After passing examinations, officers became sub-lieutenants and concentrated upon enhancing their professional knowledge and gaining practical experience.

The training of inter-war Royal Navy officers has generally escaped the attention of naval and educational historians both professional and amateur. This omission is rather surprising given the wealth of source material available and the importance of the subject – the success of the Royal Navy rested on its officers and, by extension, on their training.

The literature generally fits into two categories – that contained within general histories of the inter-war Royal Navy, and that in histories of the officer training colleges. Despite having been published several decades ago, and the bias of its ex-naval officer author, Stephen Roskill's two-part *Naval Policy between the Wars* provides a useful introduction to the concerns of the naval authorities in this period and therefore to the factors which governed officer training.[1] There are also two useful books written by former naval officers which, although lacking Roskill's scholarly touch, are packed with anecdotal detail and so provide a good introduction to life in the fleet in this period. They are John Wells' *The Royal Navy – An Illustrated Social History 1870–1982*, and Charles Owen's *Plain Yarns from the Fleet*. Both authors include substantial and thoughtful accounts of their own training.[2]

Recently, Brian Lavery has produced three books concerned in varying degree with officer training in the Second World War. These books (*Churchill's Navy*, *Hostilities Only* and *In Which They Served*)[3] are largely based on the same source material and, because they are concerned with wartime experiences, are not particularly useful to those studying the inter-war Royal Navy. However, Lavery's work does offer a useful insight into the problems and dilemmas the Royal Navy faced in training officers in peacetime.

The reader interested in the training of midshipmen might also wish to consult Charles Walker's study, *Young Gentlemen*. The bulk of the book is a not entirely reliable guide to the history of the midshipman; although the chapters on the life of modern (1938) midshipmen are invaluable.[4] A

---

[1] S. Roskill, *Naval Policy between the Wars, Volume I: The Period of Anglo-American Antagonism 1919–29* (London, 1968); S. Roskill, *Naval Policy between the Wars, Volume II: The Period of Reluctant Rearmament 1930–39* (London, 1976).
[2] J. Wells, *The Royal Navy: An Illustrated Social History 1870–1982* (Stroud, 1994); C. Owen, *Plain Yarns from the Fleet: The Spirit of the Royal Navy during its Twentieth-Century Heyday* (Stroud, 1999).
[3] B. Lavery, *Churchill's Navy: The Ships, Men and Organisation, 1939–1945* (London, 2006); B. Lavery, *Hostilities Only: Training the Wartime Royal Navy* (London, 2004); B. Lavery, *In Which They Served: The Royal Navy Officer Experience in the Second World War* (London, 2008).
[4] C. Walker, *Young Gentlemen: The Story of Midshipmen from the XVIIth Century to the Present Day* (London, [1938]).

more scholarly approach was adopted by Geoffrey Penn and Michael Lewis.[5] However none of these three studies discusses in detail the methods by which midshipmen were trained.

The bulk of the existing writing on inter-war officer training is concerned with the Royal Naval College Dartmouth. A number of books have been produced, all following more or less the same pattern – they tell the story of the college buildings and their inhabitants with less regard to what they were taught or why; they also tend to use many of the same sources. All the authors had strong links to the college, being serving or former staff members.[6] Some attention has also been paid to the Royal Naval College Osborne which closed in 1921.[7]

Historians have also neglected the changes to naval officer training brought about by the 1931 Invergordon mutiny. This is despite the emphasis placed by most historians of the mutiny on the relationships between officers and men and a general feeling that the breakdown of this relationship was a key factor in the mutiny.

From the foregoing it can be seen that nobody has yet produced a full history of Royal Navy officer training in this period, let alone its place in the wider history of the service. The period before 1914 has attracted the interest of authors such as Andrew Gordon, Donald Schurman and Nicholas Lambert, anxious to explore how naval training and tactics responded to technological innovation.[8] Harry Dickinson produced a detailed account of the development of officer training policy, highlighting the navy's emphasis on character development rather than academic study.[9]

Numerous Royal Navy officers have produced autobiographies and many of these discuss their training in detail. Amongst the autobiography writers who discuss their inter-war training in general, and boat work in particular, are Charles Anderson and Edward Ashmore.[10]

There is a good variety of primary source material concerned with inter-

---

[5] G. Penn, *Snotty: The Story of the Midshipman* (London, 1957); M. Lewis, *England's Sea Officers* (London, 1939).

[6] E. Davies and E. Grove, *Dartmouth: Seventy-Five Years in Pictures* (Portsmouth, 1980); J. Harrold and R. Porter, *Britannia Royal Naval College 1905–2005: A Century of Officer Training at Dartmouth* (Dartmouth, 2005); E. Hughes, *The Royal Naval College Dartmouth* (London, 1950); S. Pack, *Britannia at Dartmouth* (London, 1966).

[7] M. Partridge, *The Royal Naval College Osborne: A History 1903–1921* (Stroud, 1999).

[8] A. Gordon, *The Rules of the Game: Jutland and British Naval Command* (London, 2000); D. Schurman, *The Education of a Navy* (London, 1965); N. Lambert, *Sir John Fisher's Naval Revolution* (Columbia SC, 1999).

[9] H. Dickinson, *Educating the Royal Navy: Eighteenth and Nineteenth Century Education for Officers* (Abingdon, 2007).

[10] C. Anderson, *Seagulls in My Belfry: The Very Personal Story of a Naval Career* (Bishop

war Royal Navy officer training. Official documents reveal attitudes amongst senior naval officers and show how policy developed in response to the concerns of officers, both junior and senior, serving in the fleet. That officers of all ranks were concerned about naval training is illustrated by The *Naval Review*, a journal produced by and for naval officers, which contained a great number of articles concerned with the subject during this period. *Naval Review* authors remained anonymous, ensuring that they could express their views with reasonable freedom and honesty.[11]

The best insight into the daily lives of midshipmen, although not much use in discerning their inner thoughts and feelings, is the journals they were obliged to produce. Journals were intended to encourage observation, develop writing skills and enforce attention to detail. Midshipmen were required to record the activities of their ship, as well as their own doings, and to describe the people and places they encountered.[12] Journals were regularly inspected which ensured that the work in them was of a high standard but tended to stifle the creativity of midshipmen (as well as making them reluctant to express their opinions).

Officer Cadet Training

The methods the Royal Navy chose for training its officers were, in part, dictated by the raw material – the boys who entered as cadets. It is therefore necessary to examine the two systems of officer entry. The majority of executive officers entered the Royal Navy at the age of thirteen under the Fisher-Selborne scheme. Introduced in 1903 this scheme aimed to officer the fleet with men who were both seamen and scientists – equally capable of watch keeping on the bridge or in the engine room. This required a highly specialised secondary schooling concentrating on mathematics and engineering. No school in the country offered this education and so the navy was obliged to provide it. A young age of entry was also attractive because the navy believed that several years of seagoing experience were needed before an officer could

---

Auckland, 1997); Edward Ashmore, *The Battle and the Breeze: The Naval Reminiscences of Admiral of the Fleet Sir Edward Ashmore*, ed. E. Grove (Stroud, 1997).

[11] J. Goldrick, 'The Irresistible Force and the Immovable Object: The Naval Review, the Young Turks and the Royal Navy, 1911–1931' in *Mahan is Not Enough: The Proceedings of a Conference on the Works of Sir Julian Corbett and Admiral Sir Herbert Richmond*, ed. James Goldrick and John Hattendorf (Newport RI, 1993), pp. 83–102.

[12] Taken from the instructions to midshipmen printed in the front of each journal issued.

be commissioned. Finally, it was believed that the best boys were mostly likely to be attracted to the navy at this age.[13]

The vast majority of candidates for the thirteen year old entry were drawn from prep schools. This was largely dictated by practical concerns as the Royal Navy needed boys who already had a good knowledge of mathematics and science and the state system could not provide them. Furthermore, the navy was looking for embryonic gentlemen and prep schools could be expected to have provided the necessary background. The prep schools themselves were suited by the thirteen-year-old entry; naval cadetships carried considerable prestige and so sending a stream of boys to Dartmouth helped a school attract more pupils. Parents might be concerned about launching their son into a career at the age of thirteen, but the Royal Navy was seen to offer a sound education, steady long-term employment prospects, and high social status.[14]

By 1913 it had become apparent that the Fisher-Selborne scheme could not meet the rising demand for officers in the fast expanding fleet. The solution was the Special Entry which recruited seventeen year olds from public schools and put them through a year long course on the cruiser HMS *Highflyer*.[15] In 1919 it was decided that the Special Entry was the best means of opening the officer entry to lower middle and working class boys, recruited from the increasingly impressive grammar schools.[16]

Would-be cadets faced three tests; apart from medical tests there were interviews and academic examinations. Dartmouth candidates took the interview first and those who did best took part in the qualifying examination. Conversely, Special Entry candidates faced competitive examinations followed by a qualifying interview. This variation reflected the Admiralty's desire to avoid the cramming of thirteen year olds and the large number of weak candidates for the Special Entry. The Special Entry examinations were administered by the Civil Service Commission and candidates could take one set of papers to qualify for all three of the armed services. The army and the RAF followed similar recruiting procedures to those for the Special Entry and recruited from a similar pool of candidates. The army struggled to attract

---

[13] The advantages of the thirteen-year-old entry were laid before the Board of Admiralty in a minute by Fisher dated 21 November 1902 and contained in National Archives (TNA) file ADM 7/941. Entering officers at this age was widely opposed, and opposition continued until the Fisher-Selborne scheme was finally discarded in 1948.

[14] The adequate supply of cadets was of constant concern to the Navy, and a factor in many discussions about the cadet entry for example the Custance and Bennett committees (TNA, ADM 116/1288 and ADM 116/2791 respectively).

[15] For the origins and development of the scheme see TNA, ADM 116/1213.

[16] See TNA, ADM 1/8551/41 and ADM 1/8567/249.

sufficient high quality candidates but it was trying to recruit several hundred boys per year whereas the navy was normally looking for around forty.[17]

Naval interviewers were looking for the same qualities in Dartmouth and Special Entry candidates alike although they expected them to be more developed in the older boys. These qualities included a genuine interest in, and desire to serve in, the Royal Navy, self-confidence, determination, and intelligence. Candidates were asked general knowledge questions which focussed on geography and naval history and might also be asked about their hobbies.[18] Candidates' headmasters were required to report on their pupils – what influence they had on others, whether they were honest, reliable, and morally sound.[19] Membership of sports teams was highly desirable and Special Entry candidates were expected to have been team captains or prefects. The aim was to identify boys who were keen and intelligent enough to absorb naval training and who showed leadership ability. There were no practical tasks and no notice was taken of how candidates interacted with each other.

Both groups were examined in English, history, mathematics and science subjects. These subjects reflected those to be studied in the Navy, and a high standard was sought – the Dartmouth examinations were thought to be harder than the common entrance. Foreign languages were also involved; Special Entry candidates could choose between Latin, Greek, French or German, and Dartmouth candidates took French and Latin. Latin was not on the naval curriculum but was included because of its importance in the curricula of most prep and public schools.

Once they arrived at Dartmouth cadets found themselves studying an academic curriculum heavily biased towards mathematics and science. There was also a substantial amount of practical engineering – the legacy of the Fisher-Selborne scheme. The course was designed to produce officers with a wide range of technical skills and knowledge.[20] Cadets would not find Dart-

---

[17] The navy conducted a comparative study in 1931 as part of the Bennett Committee investigation into the entry and training of naval officers. See TNA, ADM 116 /2791 Bennett Committee Report, in particular Appendix D part B, which provides a table showing the number of applicants for each service.

[18] Partridge provides a range of accounts (pp. 45–50). Interviewers were provided with very limited guidance as to how the interviews should be conducted, examples can be found in TNA, ADM 116/6354.

[19] The value and content of the Headmaster's report was discussed at length by the Custance Committee in 1912, see TNA, ADM 116/1288 Third Report of the Custance Committee enclosures 6 and 6a, pp. 64–5.

[20] The naval and educational authorities governing the college never entirely agreed as to what should be included in the curriculum or how it should be taught. Fisher's plans for the college are laid out in Admiralty Board Minute of 21 November 1902, contained in TNA, ADM7/941. The development of the curriculum can be traced through the

mouth's engineering lessons particularly useful in the future, but they would benefit from learning handicraft skills and patience, and developing a general understanding of all things mechanical.

Surprisingly little time was devoted to the specialist skills and knowledge cadets would need in their future careers. Dartmouth emphasised academic subjects, with naval subjects taking a back seat. However cadets were still being developed into officers through means subtle and unsubtle. The whole atmosphere of the college was calculated to inspire cadets and immerse them in the customs, traditions, and atmosphere of the service. Naval uniform was worn, naval slang was used, and naval routine was observed – the academic staff of the college was firmly subservient to the naval. Moreover ship models, paintings, and naval relics were scattered throughout the college.[21]

On entering the college each term took the name of a famous British admiral – the clearest signal of how the college taught leadership. Dartmouth did not provide formal leadership lessons or give cadets much responsibility. Instead, leadership was learnt by a form of osmosis with cadets being provided with examples to aspire to. History lessons focussed on naval history and the key text was Geoffrey Callender's *Sea Kings of Britain*.[22] Callender's work verged on hagiography – by detailing the lives of Britain's great admirals he aimed to inspire their successors. He was not entirely successful. One former cadet described Drake as the 'patron saint' of his term[23] but attitudes tended to be more cynical. A cadet was heard to exclaim 'oh no, not another picture of the death of the immortal Nelson'[24] and Charles Owen derided *Sea Kings of Britain* as 'sycophantic'.[25]

On a day to day basis cadets were provided with a real life naval officer to model themselves on – their term officer. His job was enormously important – a combination of teacher, surrogate parent, and drill sergeant. He was responsible for the discipline, motivation, and moral tone of his cadets and his future career rested on their success. In 1928, the captain of the college remarked that 'to enumerate the duties of a term officer is practically impossible'.[26]

---

writings of the college headmasters Cyril Ashford and Charles Godfrey, the Director of Naval Education's Annual Reports for 1903–1913 (TNA, ADM 268/39) and the reports of inspections made of the college by the Board of Education (TNA, ED 109/821–824).
[21] Detailed research into the role of the college environment in shaping cadets has been conducted by Quintin Colville.
[22] G. Callender, *Sea Kings of Britain*, 3 vols. (London, 1907–1911).
[23] G. Hackforth-Jones, *The Greatest Fool* (London, 1948), p. 31. Although a novel, the book was closely based on Hackforth-Jones's own experiences as a cadet.
[24] P. Seymour, *Where the Hell is Africa?* (Bishop Auckland, 1995), p. 3.
[25] Owen, *Plain Yarns from the Fleet*, p. 18.
[26] TNA, ADM 116/2362 Letter from Captain M. E. Dunbar-Nasmith to Commander in Chief Plymouth, 23 August 1928.

In truth cadets were supervised to an excessive degree; in 1936 the captain of the college wrote that 'The cadets are under more or less continual supervision and do not have to think for themselves'.[27] Until November 1932 all games fixtures were arranged and refereed by officers.[28] More seriously the term system strictly segregated cadets by age meaning that only those selected as cadet captains had any opportunity to practice leadership. In 1938 a public school style house system was adopted, ensuring that cadets of different ages mixed together and that the older cadets could develop leadership skills through overseeing their younger colleagues.[29]

Special Entry cadets concentrated on professional subjects, albeit alongside lessons in mathematics and science. Their curriculum focussed on seamanship and navigation with frequent instructional cruises. Until the summer of 1939 they were always housed in a ship, it being felt necessary to compensate for their short training period by accustoming them to life afloat as soon as possible. However they were isolated from the rest of the fleet, their ship pursuing a separate programme of cruises. Between 1926 and 1932 training took place aboard HMS *Erebus* at Devonport, with cadets making short cruises aboard HMS *Carstairs*. The naval authorities were so determined to isolate the cadets that *Erebus* was kept at an isolated anchorage with gunnery training parties required to travel to her by boat on a daily basis.[30]

This dual use of *Erebus* was the result of severe cuts to the strength of the fleet which forced the Admiralty to abandon dedicated sea training ships for cadets. In 1924 the Admiralty abolished the Dartmouth training cruiser, aboard which in peace time cadets had previously spent eight months. The training cruiser had a separate programme to the rest of the fleet, circumnavigating the British Isles or visiting the Baltic, Mediterranean or West Indies.[31] She had a small complement of ratings and cadets were employed in tasks such as cleaning and sweeping.[32] Her purpose was to accustom cadets to life

---

[27] TNA, ADM 1/8832 Letter from Captain F. Dalrymple-Hamilton to Second Sea Lord, 3 October 1936.
[28] See TNA, ADM 1/8767/98 Memorandum by Director of Training and Staff Duties, 14 November 1932, in response to School's Inspectorate 1932 report on Dartmouth (see TNA, ED 109/823).
[29] TNA, ADM 1/8832.
[30] TNA, ADM1/8695/34 is concerned with the selection and employment of *Erebus* as combined cadet and gunnery training ship.
[31] The programmes of the cruisers can be reconstructed through reference to their logs, or the reports their captains submitted to the Admiralty, these can be found in the National Archives.
[32] TNA, ADM 1/8568/264 details the reductions made to the complement of HMS *Temeraire* when she became a training ship in 1919, similar adjustments were made to other ships converted to the role.

LEADERSHIP TRAINING FOR MIDSHIPMEN

at sea, and to introduce them to naval ratings. Experienced men, known as 'sea daddies', took cadets under their wing teaching them advanced seamanship and explaining the realities of life on the lower deck. The knowledge of ratings gained in the training cruiser was vital in developing cadets as leaders and could not have been gained elsewhere because relationships between ratings and young officers were far more formal.

Following the abolition of the training cruiser, Dartmouth cadets joined fleet ships straight after leaving the college and served aboard for eight months as cadets before promotion to midshipmen. This system proved unsatisfactory – cadets struggled to settle down, lacked practical skills and suffered from a dearth of self-confidence.[33] In 1932 the navy reintroduced the training cruiser, having decided that the gains outweighed the disadvantages of cost and the loss of a cruiser to the active fleet.[34] In a change of policy Dartmouth graduates were placed in a cruiser alongside newly joined Special Entries. This proved successful with the Dartmouth cadets sharing their naval knowledge and the Special Entry bringing enthusiasm and variety.

Training of Midshipmen

Only when they became midshipmen were young officers expected to act as leaders. But even then they were firmly subordinated and continued to gain much of their leadership training through observation. Midshipmen lived in the gunroom, separated from officers and ratings alike. They slept in hammocks like ratings but were provided with servants like officers. Like boy seamen they spent much of their time under instruction and could be punished by caning. Life in the gunroom could be extremely unpleasant especially for junior midshipmen. The gunroom was ruled by the sub-lieutenant, a young officer placed in a genuine leadership position for the first time in his career.

This was arguably the most serious flaw in the Royal Navy's officer training system. Sub-lieutenants received little assistance in governing boys little younger than themselves and of the same social class. Lacking experience they frequently resorted to asserting themselves through harsh discipline or allowed the senior midshipmen to bully the junior. Consequently in many gunrooms the sub-lieutenant was a figure of hate rather than help or inspiration.[35]

---

[33] In 1932 the Captain of the College (Captain N. A. Wodehouse) collected reports on its products from the fleet. These letters are held in the College archive.
[34] See TNA, ADM 116/2806A.
[35] Information about gunroom bullying can be found in a variety of sources. For sample

Midshipmen had relatively little contact with commissioned officers. One officer, normally the navigator, acted as 'Snottie's Nurse' and was responsible for ensuring that the midshipmen made progress in their studies. He was normally a distant figure, leaving the day to day management of his midshipmen to others. Midshipmen attached to a particular department had considerable contact with the officer who ran it but these officers were required to teach only their own specialist work. Contact with senior officers, in particular admirals and ship's captains, was rare. It normally consisted of being invited to dinner or breakfast, an ordeal rather than a pleasure.

The curriculum for midshipmen was varied and included classroom work, frequent navigation practice, time attached to the engineering department, short courses in aviation and signalling, three months in a destroyer and as much time as possible doing the work of the ship including acting as assistant officer of the watch.

There was also a full social programme including dances, picnics, balls, sporting events and sight-seeing trips. This system was designed to educate the young officer in all aspects of his profession, developing his practical skills, technical knowledge and social graces. The daily lives of midshipmen changed little through the period. They might be assigned to a specific duty, such as assisting the navigation officer or being in charge of a boat, if not they would keep watches. All midshipmen were required to write up their journals, practice navigation, and spend at least a few hours a week in the classroom in addition to studying in their free time.

As at Dartmouth, and in the training cruisers, there were no classes in leadership – it continued to be learnt through observation and experience and the time spent as a midshipman was particularly important for developing it. The education of midshipmen was steadily reformed throughout the inter-war period with an increasing emphasis being placed on practical learning of all types. The academic syllabus was dramatically reduced and orders were issued stating that midshipmen were to do as much practical work as possible and be given responsible jobs rather than be put to typing, cleaning, or watching men undertake some highly technical task. The expansion of the Royal Navy in the later part of the period was also beneficial – fewer midshipmen were carried by each ship and, given the shortage of senior ratings and junior officers, they were far more likely to be given responsible roles.

official responses to incidents, see TNA, ADM 156/156 and ADM 156/2. An interesting account is found in Churchill College, Cambridge, MISC 27, 'J. C. H. Nelson, Memoirs of a Life in the Royal Navy 1918–1950', p. 2.

Leadership Training

The syllabus changes were largely prompted by the experience of the First World War which had suggested that the Royal Navy was placing too much emphasis on officers' scientific and technical knowledge whilst neglecting strategy, tactics, seamanship and leadership.[36] Even before that war it had become apparent that the syllabus of instruction for midshipmen was over-complicated and could not be fitted into the available time. In January 1912 it had been reported that midshipmen in the Channel Fleet spent at least an hour and a half in the classroom each day and were tested weekly. This, combined with the need to study for examinations, ensured that most midshipmen neglected their practical studies.[37]

Later that year, the Admiralty had set up a committee to recommend changes to make the Fisher-Selborne system more effective. The committee, headed by Admiral Reginald Custance, prioritised reforming the training of midshipmen. It recommended a reduced academic syllabus and more emphasis on practical training. The Committee's proposals were adopted which eased the academic burden on midshipmen but, unfortunately, effectively removed strategy and tactics from the curriculum.[38]

Inter-war changes to the education of midshipmen emphasised the development of officer-like qualities. It was gradually accepted that studying large amounts of theory whilst serving in the fleet was neither practical nor appropriate. This changed attitude was summed up by Admiralty Fleet Order (AFO) 442/23 published in 1923 stating that: 'The primary object of midshipmen serving at sea is to enable them to obtain experience in their duties as officers'.[39]

In preparing this AFO the Director of Training and Staff Duties, Captain Vernon Haggard, sought the advice of officers serving in the fleet. He was told that midshipmen were tired, lethargic, and lacking in officer-like qualities.[40] The actual impact of the AFO was limited because midshipmen were

---

[36] Particular pressure came from Herbert Richmond who served as Director of Training and Staff Duties in 1918 and later pursued a campaign for reform through the *Naval Review* and the national press. Wartime discussions about training can be found in TNA, ADM 116/1707 and ADM 116/1478.
[37] TNA, ADM 116/1288 Letter from Vice-Admiral commanding the Second Division of the Home Fleets (Vice-Admiral J.R. Jellicoe) to Secretary of the Admiralty 27 January 1912.
[38] TNA, ADM 116/1288. The first volume contains the relevant reports, and the third a record of the action taken.
[39] TNA, ADM 1/8688/183 contains AFO 442/23 dated 23 February 1929.
[40] TNA, ADM 1/8688/183.

still required to attend classes almost every day. However, the simplification of the syllabus and a reduction in the number of examinations ensured that midshipmen were able to devote more time to practical work.

In 1929 Fredrick Field, Commander in Chief Mediterranean Fleet, wrote a letter to Their Lordships which laid down the many deficiencies of the existing system in considerable detail. He considered the academic syllabus for midshipmen to be excessive – noting that if carried out it must 'practically defeat the primary object' of midshipmen being at sea – to learn seamanship and leadership.[41] Aside from a reduction in academic studies, Field called for midshipmen to devote more time to navigation and boat work and for a certificate of boat handling proficiency to be introduced. It is evident that he regarded boat work as the most effective available means of developing officer-like qualities.

Field's proposed reforms appeared all the more urgent in the aftermath of the Invergordon mutiny of September 1931, in which the authority of the Atlantic Fleet's officers was effectively usurped by their crews who staged a peaceful strike lasting several days. Invergordon forced the Royal Navy to re-examine the most important aspect of officer-like qualities – leadership. Admiral Kelly's report on the mutiny found that although the junior officers serving in the Atlantic Fleet had done nothing to cause the mutiny they had also done very little to prevent it. Whilst their men respected and trusted them they did not believe they had any influence over Admiralty policy. The mutiny might have been prevented had the officers been warned of the proposed strike action but their men were unwilling to confide in them. More seriously the senior officers of the fleet had failed to take decisive action to end the mutiny and their response to it had generally been timid. Kelly concluded that the mutiny had demonstrated an increasing gulf between the lower deck and the wardroom and unmasked the deficiencies of naval leadership at all levels.[42]

As First Sea Lord, Field oversaw the four-month long discussions that precipitated the publication of AFO 2313/32 on 30 September 1932 which gave each stage in the training of the junior officer a clear purpose. Cadets were to be educated, provided with a theoretical basis upon which professional knowledge could be built. Dartmouth should provide both general and professional education; Special Entry cadets required only professional education. Midshipmen were to acquire officer-like qualities including leadership and seamanship. Their education was to be primarily practical – precluding any extensive academic syllabus. A new syllabus was introduced which was

---

[41] TNA, ADM 116/1208A Letter of 27 December 1929.
[42] TNA, ADM 178/111 Kelly's report submitted 9 November 1931.

far smaller and required midshipmen to spend only two hours a week in the classroom.[43]

Field's reforms were of vital importance in remedying the deficiencies of the existing officer training system. The Fisher-Selborne scheme had relied on a flawed policy of extensive classroom education for midshipmen which had proved disastrous; theory needed to be learnt ashore and sea time was precious and had to be used for teaching professional skills. Field remedied this and also gave each stage of officer education the clear purpose which had previously been lacking.

How far these reforms were prompted by Invergordon is unclear. Field had been advocating reform for several years beforehand and his concerns were shared by many other officers. He might therefore have made educational reform a priority of his term as First Sea Lord even without the prompting of the mutiny. However the mutiny forced the navy to acknowledge many of its failings and forced the issue to the top of the agenda. Further, it must be acknowledged that in the aftermath of the mutiny the Royal Navy was in something of a crisis; evidenced not only by Kelly's report but also by the enthusiasm for the revival of sail training (which had been abolished in 1899).

The major attraction of sail training was that sail training vessels were not bound by treaty limits and could be constructed in unlimited numbers whereas re-introducing the training cruiser meant the loss of a ship to the fleet. However it also offered a formative experience that could be shared by young officers and ratings alike; reinforcing a shared sense of identity in addition to encouraging the development of officer-like qualities in cadets and qualities of obedience and loyalty in boy seamen.[44] These proposals were ultimately rejected by Field's successor, Ernle Chatfield, on the basis that the navy had better and more important things to spend money on.[45]

Field's reforms provided the foundation for all further inter-war policy on officer education. In 1938 the Watson Committee recommended that schoolwork for midshipmen should be entirely abolished except for that needed to teach navigation. This suggestion was rejected – those consulted feeling that a mechanical age required mechanically minded officers and that therefore it was necessary for midshipmen to study science and engineering. Although a suggestion that midshipmen should spend eight months in destroyers to

---

[43] TNA, ADM 116/2806A Contains the discussions leading to, and a copy of, AFO 2315/32.
[44] See TNA, ADM 116/2283; ADM 116/2806A; ADM 1/9086 and ADM 1/8756/150.
[45] TNA, ADM 1/9086 Memorandum by Chatfield for the Board of Admiralty 30 January 1933.

benefit their seamanship and officer-like qualities was viewed positively, it was rejected as impractical.[46]

One area remained completely neglected in the midshipman's education – tactics and strategy. Originally the naval history section of the syllabus had covered this area, albeit not in great detail. Naval history had been removed from the curriculum in 1912 and nothing had taken its place. Midshipmen might have been taught tactics and strategy by officers or gained understanding from being on the bridge or in the plotting room during exercises. Instead, at action stations midshipmen were employed as messengers or in gunnery roles where they did vital work but learnt little.

The facilities and materials needed to teach strategy and tactics to midshipmen certainly existed. War games could be played out on plotting tables either aboard ship or in special facilities ashore. These facilities were normally used to plan exercises and develop new tactics – activities from which midshipmen were excluded. Only occasionally were they used by junior officers.[47]

The question of tactical and strategic training for junior officers was not addressed until 1935 when a committee headed by Vice-Admiral William James was appointed to consider it. This committee recommended a three-month course in strategy, tactics, and staff work to be taken by all executive lieutenants, but their plan was rejected in favour of a month-long course for sub-lieutenants.[48]

Boat work and Leadership Training

As indicated above, the main purpose of midshipman's time was to learn leadership, and the navy's chosen means of doing this was through boat work. Boat work offered young officers a chance to develop seamanship skills as well as judgement, patience, foresight, sharp reactions and the ability to respond quickly to a crisis. It also allowed them to take charge of a small group of men and emphasised the importance of welding these men into an effective team. Finally, it was cheap – rowing and sailing did not burn fuel, use ammunition,

---

[46] TNA, ADM 116/3709 Summary of Watson Committee findings circulated by Second Sea Lord 16 July 1938. Commented on by the Director of the Education Department, Instructor Captain A. E. Hall; the Deputy Chief of the Naval Staff, Rear-Admiral A. B. Cunningham; the Second Sea Lord, Vice-Admiral M. E. Dunbar-Nasmith; the Director of Training and Staff Duties, Captain W. L. Jackson.

[47] These exercises are occasionally described in midshipmen's journals, by far the most extensive series of exercises described is that in Midshipman MacKeown's journal: Royal Naval Museum 1987.13.

[48] TNA, ADM 1/9041 and ADM 1/9591.

or require any great investment beyond the initial purchase of the required craft.

Boat work was an important part of the curriculum at Dartmouth and in the training cruiser. The theoretical side was covered by the two-volume *Manual of Seamanship*; it occupied 85 of the 437 pages of the 1937 edition of *Volume One* – the most of any subject. There was a further chapter in *Volume Two*. Subjects included the construction and anatomy of boats, different sailing rigs, pulling technique, hoisting and lowering, handling boats in various conditions, maintenance procedures and how to rig the boat for diving, troop carrying, and other purposes, as well as the all important etiquette. If all else failed officers could turn to *Volume Two* for advice on salvaging sunken boats.[49]

Boat work was arguably the most important naval subject on the Dartmouth curriculum. Cadets devoted many afternoons to sailing and pulling (the naval term for rowing), undertaking a variety of practical evolutions and racing against each other. The boats in use at Dartmouth were mostly of service type although some civilian-style craft were available. Service boats tended to be heavy, stoutly constructed, and rather difficult for boys to handle, some were also easy to capsize or sink. Powered boats were little used at Dartmouth, but cadets did gain some experience in handling them and some knowledge of their engines. In the absence of the training cruiser the college enjoyed the services of the minesweeper HMS *Forres* which took senior cadets on short cruises along the south-west coast. The practical experience provided by *Forres* was invaluable; the presence of the ship also served to reinforce the naval emphasis of the college, reminding cadets that they were embryonic naval officers rather than mere schoolboys.

There was considerable enthusiasm for sail because it was seen as particularly good for gaining understanding of the sea and of weather conditions. Pulling was praised because it developed teamwork and physical strength and stamina. Powered craft were seen as useful in developing ship handling skills and fast reactions; one officer writing that he and his fellows, 'acquired any ability we may possess to think quickly and keep calm in an emergency from the handling of power boats and cars or motorcycles'.[50]

Officer training requirements were not the only factor in the choice of a boat for a particular task, many officers felt it was unfair to force men to sail or pull when powered craft were quicker, more convenient and required less physical effort on the part of their crews. Powered craft had risen to the fore

---

[49] Admiralty *Manual of Seamanship* Volume 1 (London, 1937); Admiralty *Manual of Seamanship* Volume 2 (London, 1932).
[50] Anonymous, 'This Boat Question', *The Naval Review* 23 (1935), 346–7 (p. 346).

during the First World War and the post-war Royal Navy lacked men with sufficient experience to handle a heavily laden craft under sail in poor weather.

All ships continued to be equipped with sailing and pulling boats but they were increasingly confined to recreational use although pulling was still favoured for lifesaving work – engines being sometimes slow to start and never entirely reliable. Pulling was also an excellent means of maintaining fitness levels especially as there was the added inducement of fleet regattas, which were amongst the social highlights of the year and invariably contested with fanatical zeal. Some officers also argued that sailing and pulling improved morale and strengthened their men's sense of naval identity.[51]

By the time they became midshipmen and joined their first fleet ships young Royal Navy officers could expect to have gained a good deal of experience under sail and oar and a limited amount of experience in powered craft. However, the majority of this experience would have been gained under favourable conditions and not in poor weather or in heavily laden craft.

The midshipman in charge of a boat would typically have twenty-four hours on duty followed by twenty-four off. Whilst on duty he would, at least in theory, be entirely responsible for the safety and appearance of the boat in his charge which would carry out a variety of tasks. Most commonly transporting stores and carrying personnel to and from the ship. In addition all midshipmen were required to devote a proportion of their recreational time to boat work, particular emphasis being placed on preparation for regattas, sailing races, and other competitions in which they might enhance the reputation of their ship. Boats might also be used for picnics or other shore side recreation.

From the foregoing it may be appreciated that the time midshipmen actually spent doing practical work in boats was rather limited. In 1923 it was calculated that midshipmen in HMS *Queen Elizabeth* spent an average of 790 days serving in the fleet of which 220 were weekends, 123 devoted to fleet exercises, gunnery and divisional drills, 122 spent under formal instruction, 91 spent on leave, 49 devoted to general drills, 39 to reviews, regattas and sporting contests, and a mere 36 devoted to boat work. The 130 days that are unaccounted for were presumably spent aboard destroyers or in the engineering department.[52]

The thirty-six days the average *Queen Elizabeth* midshipman devoted to boat work in a little over two years was unlikely to produce the required

---

[51] The place of sailing and pulling in the modern Royal Navy was the subject of sustained debate in *The Naval Review* between November 1919 and February 1921 and arose again in February and May 1935.
[52] TNA, ADM 1/8688/183 Submission by Commander in Chief Atlantic (Admiral J. M. De Robeck), 4 June 1923.

officer-like qualities. It must also be born in mind that this figure is an average; *Queen Elizabeth*, like all major warships, had more midshipmen than boats and so some midshipmen inevitably lost out. Furthermore the midshipmen whose chances of spending significant time working in boats was most limited were those most in need of such experience. This was because boats were amongst the most visible faces of a warship and poor seamanship on the part of the midshipman in charge of a boat would bring discredit upon the entire ship – therefore only the more competent midshipmen were trusted to take charge of a boat.

A midshipman was not merely responsible for the safety of a boat and its cargo; he was also responsible for its appearance and for making sure that its duties were carried out not merely efficiently but with panache and a touch of showmanship. The diligent midshipman bought extra cleaning supplies for his boat and supervised the crew whilst they shined the bright work and pipe-clayed the canvas cushions. The boat was expected to be neat and tidy with spare gear stowed away and ropes neatly coiled down. The crew were also expected to be smartly turned out and well behaved with lounging around, spitting and – on occasion – smoking being considered taboo. In most ships neglect of any of these details would result in the punishment of the midshipman – most commonly by having his leave stopped but on occasion by caning.

The risk (or in some cases likelihood) of punishment was the aspect of boat work most resented by midshipmen.[53] Fear proved an effective teacher and was generally sufficient to ensure attention to details that might otherwise have been overlooked. It also encouraged good seamanship; showing off or taking unwise risks was less likely when the price for doing so was high. Learning these lessons as midshipmen meant that naval officers were less likely to be found wanting later in their careers when handed the key responsibility of being the captain or first lieutenant of a ship.

Although resentful in the short term, most midshipmen subsequently accepted the treatment they had received. They realised that the prospect of punishment had ensured their effective development and in many cases adopted boat work as a means of ensuring discipline and high performance in their own subordinates. For example Edward Ashmore, who ended his career as the First Sea Lord, thought that boat work was of little practical wartime value but an ideal means of instilling smartness and discipline in the peacetime navy.[54]

The other advantage of the naval tendency to punish midshipmen, and in

---

[53] Anderson, *Seagulls in my Belfry*, p. 34; Owen, *Plain Yarns from the Fleet*, p. 43.
[54] Ashmore, *The Battle and the Breeze*, p. 23.

particular to cane them, was that it ensured they had the sympathy of the lower deck. Ratings had many reasons to dislike and disrespect cadets and midshipmen – who when they joined the fleet were naïve, to some degree incompetent, and had little understanding of the lower deck. However, the knowledge that the midshipman would be punished for any mistake was generally enough to ensure that a boats crew maintained the highest possible standards of cleanliness and seamanship. Midshipmen were well aware of this and most developed strong relationships with their crews, in particular their coxswains.

By doing so they became familiar with the attitudes and concerns of the lower deck; knowledge essential later in their careers. Although this aspect of boat work received little official attention it was greatly appreciated by midshipmen – many who wrote autobiographies paid tribute to their boats' crews. Charles Anderson noted that 'over and over again they saved me from my own incompetence'.[55] Charles Owen found there was 'no prouder participant or onlooker than his own crew when a midshipman pulled off a really smart manoeuvre'.[56]

Boat coxswains were, almost without exception, experienced and highly trained ratings of proven good character – men who fully justified the considerable responsibility placed on their shoulders. Despite this, boats crews were subject to a great deal of supervision from senior officers. Any unusual or potentially dangerous operation was almost certain to be supervised by a commissioned officer. There were a number of reasons for this, some of them reasonable, others less so. The supervision of dangerous or unusual activities was entirely justifiable given that many midshipmen lacked practical experience and could not be relied upon to quickly give clear and appropriate orders in an emergency.

Supervision frequently extended to an officer taking charge of the situation and sidelining the midshipman altogether, a development which benefited neither the education nor the self-confidence of the midshipman. In some ships midshipmen were supervised even when the work of their boat was routine and posed little risk. This was because of the over-officering of the inter-war fleet. The executive officer complement of ships was dictated by the number of officers needed in combat; consequently in peacetime many executive officers had little work to do and no outlet for their skills and talents. This situation did not arise in the engineering or paymaster branches where complements were dictated largely by the number of men needed to keep the ship operational on a day to day basis. Under-employed executive officers

---

[55] Anderson, *Seagulls in my Belfry*, p. 33.
[56] Owen, *Plain Yarns from the Fleet*, p. 118.

were naturally keen to take advantage of any available opportunity to exercise their talents, a problem exacerbated by poor promotion prospects. Only a quarter of executive officers were promoted to the rank of commander and this meant that officers needed to take advantage of any opportunity to distinguish themselves or display superior officer-like qualities.

Such tendencies might have been checked by senior officers, but this was unlikely to happen as competition for promotion to the highest ranks of the service was also extremely fierce. By allowing a lieutenant or lieutenant-commander to bypass a midshipman and take charge of a situation a senior officer minimised the chance of any accident or display of poor seamanship, and therefore the chance of any blot on the reputation of the ship or, by extension, himself.

Whilst it is easy to criticise this failure to allow midshipmen to exercise their talents it should not be forgotten that boat work did pose real risks including the potential for serious loss of life. All forms of work at sea pose some element of danger and small boats are particularly vulnerable to the weather, hazards posed by other ships, and to catastrophic handling errors (if only by virtue of their crews frequently being inexperienced or over-confident).

In theory boat work offered an ideal means of training midshipmen as both seamen and leaders. It was cheap, and needed only a limited number of men, yet offered purposeful and practical education. It developed a variety of skills, including initiative, decisiveness and good seamanship, and provided one of the best opportunities for young officers to work closely with ratings. However, the lack of time devoted by most midshipmen to boat work, and the degree of supervision to which they were subject, negated the educational value of the subject.

This limitation was particularly problematic because the other training midshipmen received suffered from the same flaws. These flaws were inevitable so long as the Royal Navy persisted in its chosen system of teaching leadership. This system had much to recommend it; allowing officers to develop at their own pace, adopt a leadership style that suited them, and learn from a variety of exemplars of all ranks. However it was seriously undermined by the lack of actual leadership opportunities for young officers.

Nonetheless, the leadership training that the inter-war Royal Navy provided for its young officers can only be considered successful. Serious indiscipline was rare in the fleet and the majority of ratings were both loyal and obedient. The vast majority of Royal Navy officers met the required standards and provided capable leadership in war or peace; the leadership ability of regular officers was a critical factor in ensuring victory in the Second World War. The war demonstrated the ability of the officers trained by the peacetime navy to harness men of widely varying background and naval experience, to utilise new technology and to withstand all hazards posed by nature or the enemy.

Select Bibliography

Abrahamson, E., 'The Emergence and Prevalence of Employee Management Rhetorics: The Effects of Long Waves, Labor Unions and Turnover, 1875 to 1992', *Academy of Management Journal* 40 (1997), 491–533

Anderson, C., *Seagulls in My Belfry: The Very Personal Story of a Naval Career* (Bishop Auckland, 1997)

Andrews, K. R., *Elizabethan Privateering: English Privateering during the Spanish War, 1585–1603* (Cambridge, 1964)

Bacon, Admiral Sir R., *The Jutland Scandal* (London, 1925)

Bailey, J. B. A., 'Military History and the Pathology of Lessons Learned: The Russo-Japanese War, A Case Study', in W. Murray and R. H. Sinnreich (eds), *The Past as Prologue: The Importance of History to the Military Profession* (Cambridge, 2006), pp. 170–94

Balderston, M., and D. Syrett (eds), *The Lost War: Letters from British Officers during the American Revolution* (New York, 1975)

Barnes, G. R., and J. H. Owen (eds), *The Sandwich Papers, Vol. I*, Navy Record Society 69, (London, 1932)

Baugh, D., *British Naval Administration in the Age of Walpole* (Princeton NJ, 1965)

Baynham, H., *Before the Mast: Naval Ratings of the 19th Century* (London, 1972)

Bellairs, C., *The Battle of Jutland* (London 1919)

Benjamin, D. K., and C. F. Thornberg, 'Organization and Incentives in the Age of Sail', *Explorations in Economic History* 44 (2007), 317–41

Benjamin, D. K., and C. F. Thornberg, 'Comment: Rules, Monitoring, and Incentives in the Age of Sail', *Explorations in Economic History* 40 (2003), 195

Black, J., *Eighteenth-Century Britain, 1688–1783* (Basingstoke, 2008)

Bonner Smith, D. (ed.), *The Letters of Lord St. Vincent, Vol. II*, Navy Records Society 61 (London, 1926)

Bowen, H. V., and A. González Enciso (eds), *Mobilising Resources for War: Britain and Spain at Work during the Early Modern Period* (Barañáin, 2006)

Briggs, A., *Age of Improvement* (London, 1959)

Bromley, J. S., 'Outlaws at Sea, 1660–1720: Liberty, Equality and Fraternity among the Caribbean Freebooters', in J. S. Bromley (ed.), *Corsairs and Navies* (London, 1987), pp. 1–20

Bromley, J. S., 'The French Privateering War, 1702–13', in J. S. Bromley (ed.), *Corsairs and Navies* (London, 1987), pp. 213–42

Brown, D. K., *Before the Ironclad. Development of Ship Design, Propulsion and Armament in the Royal Navy 1815–60* (London, 1990)

Brown, D. K., *Warrior to Dreadnought. Warship Development 1860–1905* (London, 1997)
Bruce, A., *The Purchase System in the British Army, 1660–1871*, Royal Historical Society Studies in History, No. 20 (London, 1980)
Byrn, J., *Crime and Punishment in the Royal Navy: Discipline on the Leeward Island Station 1784–1812* (Aldershot and Brookfield VT, 1989)
Cannadine, D., *Class in Britain* (London, 1988, 2000)
Cannadine, D. (ed.), *Admiral Lord Nelson: Context and Legacy* (London, 2005)
Chalmers, T., *The Christian and Civic Economy of Large Towns* (Glasgow, 1821)
Chalmers, W. S., *The Life and Letters of David Beatty* (London, 1951)
Chatfield, Admiral of the Fleet Lord, *The Navy and Defence* (London, 1942)
Chatfield, Admiral of the Fleet Lord, *The Navy and Defence. Volume 2. It Might Happen Again* (London, 1947)
Chemers, M. M., 'Leadership Effectiveness: Functional, Constructivist and Empirical Perspectives', in D. van Knippenberg and M. A. Hogg (eds), *Leadership and Power : Identity Processes in Groups and Organizations* (London, 2003), pp. 5–17
Chesterton, G. K., *All Things Considered* (London, 1919)
Clark, J. C. D., 'Providence, Predestination and Progress; or Did the Enlightenment Fail?', in D. Donald and F. O'Gorman (eds), *Ordering the World in the Eighteenth Century* (Basingstoke, 2006), pp. 27–62
Coats, A., 'Efficiency in Dockyard Administration 1660–1800 : A Reassessment', in N. Tracy (ed.), *The Age of Sail*, vol. 1 (London, 2003), pp. 116–32
Cobbett, W., *Rural Rides* (London, 1853)
Cohen, E., 'Military Misfortunes', *Military History Quarterly* (1990), 106–12
Cole, G., 'Royal Navy Gunners in the French Revolutionary and Napoleonic Wars', *Mariner's Mirror* 95:3 (2009), 284–95
Conway, S., *The British Isles and the War of American Independence* (Oxford, 2000)
Conway, S., 'The Mobilization of Manpower for Britain's Mid-Eighteenth-Century Wars', *Historical Research* 77 (2004)
Conway, S., *War, State, and Society in Mid-Eighteenth-Century Britain and Ireland* (Oxford, 2006)
Davies, E., and E. Grove, *Dartmouth: Seventy-Five Years in Pictures* (Portsmouth, 1980)
Davis, R., *The Rise of the English Shipping Industry in the Seventeenth and Eighteenth Centuries* (Newton Abbot, 1962)
Demers, C., *Organizational Change Theories: A Synthesis* (London, 2007)
Dening, G., *Mr. Bligh's Bad Language. Passion, Power and Theatre on the* Bounty (Cambridge, New York and Oakleigh, Victoria, 1992)
Dentith, S., *Society and Cultural Forms in Nineteenth-Century England* (Basingstoke, 1998)
Dickinson, H., *Educating the Royal Navy: Eighteenth and Nineteenth Century Education for Officers* (Abingdon, 2007)
Divine, D., *Mutiny at Invergordon* (London, 1970)

Donald, A. J., and J. D. Ladd (eds), *G. H. Blumberg, Royal Marine Records: Part II, 1793–1836*, Royal Marines Historical Society Publication No. 4 (Eastney, 1982)

Duffy, M., *Soldiers, Sugar and Seapower: The British Expeditions to the West Indies and the War Against Revolutionary France* (Oxford, 1987)

Duffy, M. (ed.), *Parameters of British Naval Power 1650–1850* (Exeter, 1992)

Duffy, M., *The Younger Pitt*, Profiles in Power (London, 2000)

Duffy, M., '"... All was Hushed Up?" The Hidden Trafalgar', *Mariner's Mirror* 91 (2005), 216–40

Duffy, M., S. Fisher, B. Greenhill, D. Starkey and J. Youings (eds), *A New Maritime History of Devon, Vol. I: From Early Times to the Late Eighteenth Century* (London, 1992)

Duffy, M., S. Fisher, B. Greenhill, D. Starkey and J. Youings (eds), *A New Maritime History of Devon, Vol. II: From the Late Eighteenth Century to the Present Day* (London, 1994)

Duffy, M., and R. Morriss (eds), *The Glorious First of June: A Naval Battle and its Aftermath* (Exeter, 2001)

Dundas, Admiral Sir C., *An Admiral's Yarns* (London, 1922)

Edwards, P., *The Story of the Voyage: Sea-Narratives in Eighteenth Century England* (Cambridge, 1994)

Farquharson-Roberts, M. A., 'The *Lucia* Mutiny: A Failure of the Royal Navy's Internal Communications', *RUSI Journal* 154:2 (2009), 104–7

French, A., 'The British Expedition to Concord, Massachusetts, in 1775', *Journal of the American Military History Foundation* 1:1 (1937)

Gardiner, R., and A. Lambert (eds), *Steam, Steel and Shellfire: The Steam Warship 1815–1905* (London, 1992)

Gardner, N., *Trial by Fire: Command and the British Expeditionary Force in 1914* (Westport CT, 2003)

Garitee, J. R., *The Republic's Private Navy: The American Privateering Business as Practiced by Baltimore during the War of 1812* (Middletown CT, 1977)

Gaskill, M., 'The Displacement of Providence: Policing and Prosecution in the Seventeenth and Eighteenth Centuries', *Continuity and Change* 11 (1996), 341–74

Gibbs, P., *Across the Frontiers* (London, 1938)

Gifford Jr., A., 'The Economic Organization of 17th- through mid 19th-Century Whaling and Shipping', *Journal of Economic Behavior and Organization* 20 (1993), 137–50

Glenton, R., *The Royal Oak Affair: The Saga of Admiral Collard and Bandmaster Barnacle* (London, 1991)

Golby, J. M., and A. W. Purdue, *The Civilisation of the Crowd: Popular Culture in England 1750–1900* (Stroud, 1999)

Goldrick, J., 'The Irresistible Force and the Immovable Object: The Naval Review, the Young Turks and the Royal Navy, 1911–1931' in J. Goldrick and J. Hattendorf (eds), *Mahan is Not Enough: The Proceedings of a Conference on the Works of Sir Julian Corbett and Admiral Sir Herbert Richmond* (Newport RI, 1993), pp. 83–102

Goodman, D., *Spanish Naval Power, 1569–1665: Reconstruction and Defeat* (Cambridge, 1997)

Gordon, G. A. H., *The Rules of the Game. Jutland and British Naval Command* (London, 1996)

Grint, K., *Leadership, Management and Command: Rethinking D-Day* (London, 2008)

Grove, E., ed., *The Battle and the Breeze: The Naval Reminiscences of Admiral of the Fleet Sir Edward Ashmore* (Stroud, 1997)

Guimera, A., 'Gravina and the Naval Leadership of His Day', *Journal for Maritime Research* 7:1 (2005), 44–69

Haas, J. M., *A Management Odyssey: The Royal Dockyards, 1714–1914* (New York, 1994)

Hamilton, C. I., *The Making of the Modern Admiralty: British Naval Policy-Making, 1805–1927* (Cambridge, 2011)

Hamilton, I., *Anglo-French Naval Rivalry 1840–1870* (Oxford, 1993)

Hamish Fraser, W., *A History of British Trade Unionism, 1700–1998* (Basingstoke and London, 1999)

Harding, R., *Seapower and Naval Warfare, 1650–1830* (London, 1999)

Harrold, J. and R. Porter, *Britannia Royal Naval College 1905–2005: A Century of Officer Training at Dartmouth* (Dartmouth, 2005)

Hart, R. A., 'Feeding Mars: Logistics and the German Defeat in Normandy', *War and History* 4 (1996), 418–35

Hayes, G., 'Science and the Magic Eye: Innovation in the Selection of Canadian Army Officers, 1939–1945', *Armed Forces and Society* 22 (1995/6), 275–95

Hayward, J., *For God and Glory: Lord Nelson and His Way of War* (Annapolis MD, 2003)

Hayward, S. F., *Churchill on Leadership: Executive Success in the Face of Adversity* (New York, 1997)

Hebbert, F. J., 'The Belle-Ile Expedition of 1761', *Journal of the Society of Army Historical Research* 64 (1986), 81–93

Hennessy, G. H., and A. J. Donald (eds), *General H. E. Blumberg, Royal Marine Records from 1755 to 1914*, Royal Marines Historical Society Publication No. 2, (Eastney, 1979)

Herzberg, F., *One More Time, How Do You Motivate Employees?* (Boston MA, 2003)

Hill, C., 'Radical Pirates?', *The Collected Essays of Christopher Hill, III, People and Ideas in Seventeenth Century England* (Brighton, 1986), pp. 161–87

Hilton, B., *A Mad, Bad and Dangerous People? England 1783–1846* (Oxford, 2006)

Hogg, M. A., 'A Social Identity Theory of Leadership', *Personality and Social Psychology Review* 5:3 (2001)

Horsfield, J., *The Art of Leadership in War: The Royal Navy from the Age of Nelson to the End of World War II* (Westport CT, 1980)

SELECT BIBLIOGRAPHY

Houlding, J. A., *Fit for Service: The Training of the British Army, 1715–1795* (Oxford, 1981)

Hughes, E., *The Royal Naval College Dartmouth* (London, 1950)

Hurd, A. S., *Naval Efficiency: The War Readiness of the Fleet* (London, 1902)

James, B. G., *Business Wargames* (Tunbridge Wells, 1984)

Jellicoe, Admiral Viscount, *The Grand Fleet 1914–1916: Its Creation, Development and Work* (London, 1951)

Jones, M. (ed.), *A Naval Life* (Dulverton, Somerset, 2007)

Jones, S., and J. Gosling, *Nelson's Way: Leadership Lessons from the Great Commander* (London, 2005)

Kemp, P., *The British Sailor. A Social History of the Lower Deck* (London, 1970)

Kert, F. M., *Prize and Prejudice: Privateering and Naval Prize in Atlantic Canada in the War of 1812* (St John's NL, 1997)

Kipling, R., *The Fringes of the Fleet* (London,1916)

Knight, R. and M. Wilcox, *Sustaining the Fleet 1793–1815: War, the British Navy and the Contractor State* (Woodbridge, 2010)

Lambert, A., *Admirals: The Naval Commanders Who Made Britain Great* (London, 2008)

Lambert, N., *Sir John Fisher's Naval Revolution* (Columbia SC, 1999)

Lavery, B. (ed.), *Shipboard Life and Organisation, 1731–1815* (Aldershot, 1998)

Lavery, B., *Hostilities Only: Training the Wartime Royal Navy* (London, 2004)

Lavery, B., *Churchill's Navy: The Ships, Men and Organisation, 1939–1945* (London, 2006)

Lavery, B., *In Which They Served: The Royal Navy Officer Experience in the Second World War* (London, 2008)

Le Fevre, P.,'Sir John Borlase Warren, 1753–1822' , in P. Le Fevre and R.Harding (eds), *British Admirals of the Napoleonic Wars : The Contemporaries of Nelson* (London, 2005), pp. 219–44

Lee, C. D., 'Alexander Selkirk and the Last Voyage of the *Cinque Ports Gally*', Mariner's Mirror 73 (1987), 385-99

Lewis, M.. *England's Sea Officers* (London, 1939)

Lewis, M., *Navy in Transition 1814-1864. A Social History* (London, 1965)

Lloyd ,C. (ed.) *The Keith Papers: Selected from the Papers of Admiral Viscount Keith. Vol. III*, Navy Records Society (London, 1955)

Lloyd, C., *The British Seaman 1200–1860* (London, 1968)

Mackay, R., and M. Duffy, *Hawke, Nelson and British Naval Leadership, 1747–1805* (Woodbridge, 2009)

Mahan, A. T., *Types of Naval Officers* (London, 1901)

Marder, A. J., *From the Dardanelles to Oran: Studies of the Royal Navy in War and Peace, 1915–1940* (Oxford, 1974)

Mathias, P., 'Risk, Credit and Kinship in Early Modern Enterprise', in J. J. McCusker and K. Morgan (eds), *The Early Modern Atlantic Economy* (Cambridge, 2001), pp. 15–35

McKee, C., *Sober Men and True: Sailor Lives in the Royal Navy 1900–1945* (London and Cambridge MA, 2002)

Miller, D., *Commanding Officers* (London, 2001)
Moreby, D., *The Human Element in Shipping* (Colchester, 1975)
Morriss, R., *Naval Power and British Culture, 1760–1850: Public Trust and Government Ideology* (Aldershot, 2003)
Morriss, R., *The Royal Dockyards during the Revolutionary and Napoleonic Wars* (Leicester, 1983)
Morriss, R., *Naval Power and British Culture: Public Trust and Government Ideology* (Aldershot, 2004)
Morriss, R., *The Foundations of British Maritime Ascendancy: Resources, Logistics and the State, 1755–1815* (Cambridge, 2011)
Murdoch, S., *The Terror of the Seas: Scottish Maritime Warfare, 1513–1713* (Leiden, 2010)
Naish, G. P. B. (ed.), *Nelson's Letters to His Wife and Other Documents, 1785–1831*, Navy Record Society 100 (London, 1958)
Northouse, P. G., *Leadership: Theory and Practice*, 3rd edn (London, 2010)
Owen, C., *Plain Yarns from the Fleet: The Spirit of the Royal Navy during its Twentieth-Century Heyday* (Stroud, 1999)
Pack, S., *Britannia at Dartmouth* (London, 1966)
Padfield, P., *Rule Britannia. The Victorian and Edwardian Navy* (London, 1981)
Palmer, M. A. *Command at Sea: Naval Command and Control since the Sixteenth Century* (Cambridge MA, 2005)
Pares, R., 'The Manning of the Navy in the West Indies, 1702–1763', *Transactions of the Royal Historical Society* 19 (1937), 31–60
Partridge, M., *The Royal Naval College Osborne: A History 1903–1921* (Stroud, 1999)
Penn, G., *Snotty: The Story of the Midshipman* (London, 1957)
Perkin, H., *The Rise of Professional Society* (London, 1989)
Perrin, G. (ed.), *The Keith Papers*, Vol. I, Navy Record Society 62 (London, 1927)
Petrides, A., and J. Downs (eds), *Sea Soldier: An Officer of Marines with Duncan, Nelson, Collingwood and Cockburn* (Tunbridge Wells, 2000)
Philips, C. H. (ed.), *The Correspondence of David Scott relating to Indian Affairs, 1787–1805*, Vol.1 (London, 1951)
Pollard, S., *The Genesis of Modern Management: A Study of the Industrial Revolution in Great Britain* (London, 1965)
Poore, Lady, *Recollections of an Admiral's Wife* (London 1916)
Prida, G. B., L. C. Delgardo, V. M. N. Garcia and J. S. Fernández (eds), *Trafalgar: Historia y Memoria de un Mito* (Cadiz, 2008)
Prior, R., and T. Wilson, *Command on the Western Front: The Military Career of Sir Henry Rawlinson, 1914–1918* (Oxford, 1992)
Rankin, N., *Churchill's Wizards: The British Genius for Deception 1914–1945* (London, 2008)
Rasor, E., *Reform in the Royal Navy. A Social History of the Lower Deck, 1850–1880* (Hamden CT, 1976)

Richardson, A., and A. Hurd (eds), *Brassey's Naval and Shipping Annual 1925* (London, 1925)
Richmond, H. W., *The Navy in the War of 1739–48* (Cambridge, 1920)
Roberts, A., *Churchill and Hitler: Secrets of Leadership* (London, 2003)
Rodger, N. A. M., *The Admiralty* (London, 1979)
Rodger, N. A. M., *The Wooden World: An Anatomy of the Georgian Navy* (London, 1986)
Rodger, N. A. M., '"A Little Navy of your own Making": Admiral Boscawen and the Cornish Connection in the Royal Navy', in M. Duffy (ed.), *Parameters of British Naval Power 1650-1850* (Exeter, 1992), pp. 82–92
Rodger, N. A. M., 'Shipboard Life in the Georgian Navy, 1750–1800: The Decline of the Old Order?' in L. R. Fischer, H. Hamre, P. Holm and J.R. Bruijn (eds.), *The North Sea. Twelve Essays on Social History of Maritime Labour* (Stavanger, 1992)
Rodger, N. A. M., *The Insatiable Earl: A Life of John Montagu, 4th Earl of Sandwich* (London, 1994)
Rodger, N. A. M., *Command of the Ocean. A Naval History of Britain, 1649–1815* (London, 2004)
Rogers, B. M. H., 'Dampier's Voyage of 1703', *Mariner's Mirror* 10 (1924), 367–81
Rogers, B. M. H., 'Woodes Rogers's Privateering Voyage', *Mariner's Mirror* 19 (1933), 196–211
Rogers, D. J., *Waging Business Warfare* (New York, 1987)
Roskill, S., *Hankey: Man of Secrets, Volume ii, 1919–1931* (London, 1972)
Roskill, S., *Naval Policy between the Wars, Volume I: The Period of Anglo-American Antagonism 1919–29* (London, 1968)
Roskill, S., *Naval Policy between the Wars, Volume II: The Period of Reluctant Rearmament 1930–39* (London, 1976)
Royle, E., *Modern Britain. A Social History 1750–1985* (London and New York, 1987)
Sánchez, R. T. (ed.), *War, State and Development. Fiscal-Military States in the Eighteenth Century* (Barañáin, 2007)
Schapera, I. (ed.), *Livingstone's African Journal, 1853–1856* (London 1963)
Schurman, D. M., *The Education of a Navy* (London, 1965)
Searle, G. R., *The Quest for National Efficiency* (London, 1917)
Sechrest, L. J., 'Public Goods and Private Solutions in Maritime History', *Quarterly Journal of Austrian Economics* 7 (2004), 3–27
Seymour, P., *Where the Hell is Africa?* (Bishop Auckland, 1995)
Sheffield, G. and D. Todman (eds), *Command and Control on the Western Front: The British Army's Experience, 1914–18* (Staplehurst, 2004)
Simpson, A., *The Evolution of Victory: British Battles on the Western Front, 1914–1918* (London, 1995)
Simpson, A., *Directing Operations: British Corps Command on the Western Front, 1914–1918* (Staplehurst, 2006)
Starkey, D. J., *British Privateering Enterprise in the Eighteenth Century* (Exeter, 1990)

Starkey, D. J., 'War and the Market for Seafarers, 1736–1792', in L. R. Fischer and H. Nordvik (eds), *Shipping and Trade: Essays in International Maritime Economic History* (Pontefract, 1990), pp. 25–42

Starkey, D. J., 'A Restless Spirit: British Privateering Enterprise, 1739–1815', in D. J. Starkey, E. S. van Eyck van Heslinga and J. A. de Moor (eds), *Pirates and Privateers: New Perspectives on the War on Trade in the Eighteenth and Nineteenth Centuries* (Exeter, 1997), pp. 126–40

Statham, Commander E. P., *The Story of the* Britannia (London 1904)

Storr, C. (ed.), *The Fiscal-Military State in Eighteenth Century Europe* (Farnham, 2008)

Stradling, R. A., *The Armada of Flanders: Spanish Maritime Policy and European War, 1568–1668* (Cambridge, 1992)

Sugden, J., *Nelson: A Dream of Glory* (London, 2005)

Swanson, C. E., 'American Privateering and Imperial Warfare, 1739–1748', *William and Mary Quarterly* 42 (1985), 357–82

Swanson, C. E., *Predators and Prizes: American Privateering and Imperial Warfare, 1739–1748* (Columbia SC, 1991)

Sweetman, J. (ed.), *The Great Admirals: Command at Sea, 1587–1945* (Annapolis MD, 1997)

Syrett, D., *Shipping and the American War 1775–83: A Study of British Transport Organization* (London, 1970)

Syrett, D., 'The Victualling Board Charters Shipping 1775–82', *Historical Research* 68, Issue 166 (1995), 212–24

Syrett, D., 'Towards Dettingen: The Conveyancing of the British Army to Flanders in 1742', *Journal of the Society for Army Historical Research* 84 (2006), 316–26.

Syrett, D., *Shipping and Military Power in the Seven Years War: The Sails of Victory* (Exeter, 2008)

Syrett, D., and R. L. DiNado (eds), *The Commissioned Sea Officers of the Royal Navy 1660–1815*, Navy Records Society (London, 1994)

Taylor, R., 'Manning the Royal Navy: The Reform of the Recruiting System, 1852–62', *Mariner's Mirror* 44 (1958), no. 4, 302–13

Thomas, J. H., *The East India Company and the Provinces in the Eighteenth Century. Vol. I Portsmouth and the East India Company 1700–1815* (Lampeter, 1999)

Thompson, F. M. L., *The Rise of Respectable Society 1893–1900: A Social History of Victorian Britain 1830–1900* (London, 1988)

Thompson, P., ed., *Close to the Wind: Early Memoirs (1866–79) of Admiral Sir William Creswell* (London, 1965)

Thomson, J. E., *Mercenaries, Pirates and Sovereigns: State-Building and Extraterritorial Violence in Early Modern Europe* (Princeton NJ, 1994)

Toms, D., and R. Barrons, *The Business General: Transform Your Business Using the Seven Secrets of Military Success* (London, 2006)

Travers, T., 'Command and Leadership Styles in the British Army: The Gallipoli Model', *Journal of Contemporary History* 29 (1994), 403–42

Van Knippenberg, D., and M. A. Hogg (eds), *Leadership and Power: Identity Processes in Groups and Organizations* (London, 2003)

Walker, C., *Young Gentlemen: The Story of Midshipmen from the XVIIth Century to the Present Day* (London, 1938)

Walton, O., '"A Great Improvement in the Sailor's Feeling towards the Naval Service": Recruiting Seamen for the Royal Navy, 1815–1853', *Journal for Maritime Research* 12 (2010), 27–57

Wells, J., *The Royal Navy: An Illustrated Social History, 1870–1982* (Stroud, 1994)

Wheeler, T., *Take Command! Leadership Lessons from the Civil War* (New York, 2000)

Whinney, B., *The U-Boat Peril: A Fight for Survival* (London, 1986)

White, C., ed., *Nelson: The New Letters* (Woodbridge, 2005)

Winfield, R., *British Warships in the Age of Sail, 1793–1817* (London, 2005)

Winton, J., *Hurrah for the Life of a Sailor: Life on the Lower Deck of the Victorian Navy* (London, 1977)

Index

Abercrombie, Major General Sir Ralph 96–9
Admiralty Board, 48
Admiralty Fleet Orders 109
Anson, Admiral George 19, 48, 55, 56, 79, 149
Articles of Agreement 132
Articles of War 20, 149–51
Austrian Succession, War of, 48, 79, 95

Barham, Lord *see* Middleton, Sir Charles
Batavia 32, 40
Battle of Trafalgar 11, 17–19, 43–7
Beatty, Admiral 111, 167
Bentinck, Lord, President of Madras 39
Bomb vessels 64–76
Bombay 40–2
Bombay marine 31–2, 41
Bombay Presidency 31–2
Bombay shipbuilding 31, 37, 42
Brest squadron 50–2
Bristol 138

Cadiz 50–1
Campbell Hardy, Lieutenant 119
Canton 30
Cape of Good Hope 30
Carteret, Earl 48–52, 55
Channel Islands and privateering 127, 137
Channel Islands 102
Chartism, influence 148
Chatfield, Admiral Lord 111, 114, 157, 167, 185
Christian, Rear Admiral Hugh Cloberry 96–9
Clayton, Francis Starkie, 161–7
Clayton, Ralph, 167–71
Cochrane, Hon Basil 34, 37–9

Cocks, William 70–2
Collingwood, 82–3
Commerce raiding, *see* privateering
Competition between naval boards 95
Continuous service, 148, 150, 152
Corporal punishment, *see* flogging
Country Trade (East India) 31, 39
Courts martial 36, 53–4, 146, 150–1, 153, 167
Crew Robert, Sec to Board of Ordnance 65, 66, 69, 72, 73

Dampier, William 127
Dartmouth, Royal Naval College 114, 173, 175, 177–84, 187
Curriculum 178–80
Discipline 143–55, 163
Dutch East Indies 30, 39

East India Command structure, 31–2
East India Company 29, 35–7, 42, 128
East India ships 30, 32, 41, 100, 125
East Indies Station, extent of 30
Elkins, Lieutenant 118
Elphinstone, Sir George 33
Examinations 167, 173, 177–8, 183–4

Field, Admiral Sir Frederick 110–1, 184–5
Flogging 139, 143–5, 154
Franco Spanish combined fleet 17, 48, 51

Geddes axe, *see* redundancies
George V 115
Gravina, Admiral Frederick 19

Haddock, Admiral 50–1
Haggard, Captain Vernon 183
Hanoverian troops 98

INDEX

Hertzberg analysis 120–1
High Court of Admiralty 125, 129, 131
Hornby, Admiral Phipps 148, 161
Horses, transportation of 96, 100
Hudson's Bay Company 128
Hughes, Vice Admiral 32

Invergorden mutiny 118, 175, 184
    Hertzberg analysis of 120–1

Jardine Matheson 39
Jutland, Battle of 171–2

Keith, Admiral Lord 38, 67
Kelly, Admiral 118

Lestock, Rear Admiral Richard 51–5
Letter of Marque 128

Madras hospital 34
Manila galleon 127
Marham, John 70
Marine/Navy relations 84–6, 88–91
Marines 53, 62, 68, 74, 77–94, 119, 153–4
Marines at Invergordon 119
Marines officers' social background 80–4
Market for seafarers 133–4
Marx, John Locke 158–161
Mathews, Vice Admiral Thomas 51–5
Mauritius 32
Middleton, Sir Charles (later Lord Barham) 19, 76, 96
Midshipmen 114, 163–4, 173–192
Morale inter war 117

Naval Discipline Acts, 19th century 149
Naval leadership debate 14–16
    leader as hero 43–4
    leader in network 45–7
Naval uniform, 110–11, 120, 149, 165, 179
Navy Board 33–4, 38, 52, 62, 87, 96, 104, 128
Nelson, Horatio, 11, 16, 45–7, 56, 64, 70–2, 81, 91–2, 179
Nepean, Evan 65, 66, 69
Newcastle, Duke of 48–51, 79

Nore mutiny, 85, 119, 147
Norfolk 103
Norris, Admiral Sir John 50–1, 55

Office of Ordnance, *see* Ordnance Board
Officer Cadet Training 176–81
Oldfield, Captain Thomas 91–2
Ordnance Board 34, 61–75, 96, 106

Paget, Lord Clarence 150
Panama, 50–1
Parsee shipbuilders, *see* Bombay shipbuilding
Pay, food and shore leave 146, 149
Pay and allowances, interwar 111–13
Payments to privateersmen 133, 137
Pelham brothers, 19, 55
Pellew, Rear Admiral Edward 40
Philippines 30, 127
Pitt, William 47–8
Portsmouth 95–107
Prisoners of war 102–3
Privateering 123–40
    business 125–31
    incentives 131–6
    organisation 131–6
Prize courts 129, 138
Prize shares 139
Profit sharing 134–5
Promotion opportunities interwar 117–18

Rainier, Admiral Peter,
    advice on successful command 34–5
    and the Navy 33–4
    and the Navy Board 33–4
    communications and intelligence 40–2
    financial management 39–40
    logistics management 36–9
    subordinates 34–6
Red Sea 30, 38, 40–1
Redundancies 113–17
Refitting, cleaning transports 100
Rodgers, Woodes 127
Royal Artillery 61–76
Royal Marine Artillery 62

INDEX

Shelvocke 128
Ships
  Naval
    Acheron 70
    Amazon 53
    Blenheim 167
    Britannia 158, 164–7
    Burford 32
    Camperdown 167
    Captain 52
    Carstairs 180
    Dasher 65
    Diamond 161
    Discovery 68
    Edward VII 167
    Erebus 180
    Etna 70, 74
    Explosion 66, 67, 73, 75
    Forres 187
    Gibralta 153
    Hampton Court 52
    Hecla 67, 75, 154
    Hero 146
    Highflyer 177
    Royal Oak 117
    Inflexible 170
    Invincible 161, 170
    Iris 154
    Jamaica 53
    Lord Warden 158–61
    Lucia 117,
    Nelson 119
    Norfolk 118
    Perseus 68
    Princessa 49
    Queen Elizabeth 188
    Queen Mary 167, 171
    Racoon 149
    Rodney 118
    Sulphur 67
    Tartarus 73
    Thunder 65, 70, 74
    Trident 35
    Vernon 170
    Vesuvius 65
    Victoria 167
    Volcano 67
    Zebra 67

Privateers
  Ann Gally 132
  Boscawen 133
  Chambers 132
  Duke 130, 134
  Dutchess 130
  Hercules 132
  Hudsons Bay Frigat 132
  Lowestoff 138
  Lyon 132
  Mars Privateer 135
  Mentor 134
  Prince Frederick 134
  Royal Family 131
  Snap Dragon 134
  Surprize 138
  Swift 138
  Winchelsea 137
Transports
  Adventure 103
  Betsy 100
  St Mary's Planter 99
Southampton 95–107
Special Entry, recruitment 114, 177–81, 184
St Vincent, First Lord of the Admiralty, 69, 71, 83
Steam, impact of in safety 147
Stuart, Major General 32, 88
Suffren, Admiral 32

Tomlinson, Rear Admiral Wilfrid 119
Toulon 18, 48–53
Training, Midshipmen, 181–2
  boat work 186–90
  leadership training, 13–186
  Officer cadets 176–81
Transport agents 104
Transport Board 61–2, 64, 66, 76, 96–107
  integrity and independence 105–6
  number of ships hired 104–5
  organisation of 96–7
  reorganisation 96
Transport service 128
Transports to Gibraltar, West indies 96–100
Trincomalee 32, 40

INDEX

Tryon, Admiral 163–5
Tyrwhitt, Admiral Sir Reginald 119–20

Venereal disease 159–61
Vernon, Admiral Edward 49–52
Victualling Board 36–8, 61–2, 64, 96, 102, 105–7
Victualling office 128

Wellesley, Richard 31–2, 39
West Indies 48–53, 98–105
Willoughby, Lieutenant Nesbit 35–6
Winchelsea, Earl of 19, 48–52, 55
Woodriff, Captain Daniel 95–107